Wilson's Cavalry Corps

Wilson's Cavalry Corps

*Union Campaigns
in the Western Theatre,
October 1864 through Spring 1865*

by
JERRY KEENAN

McFarland & Company, Inc., Publishers
Jefferson, North Carolina, and London

For Mother,
who was always there;
in loving memory

British Library Cataloguing-in-Publication data are available

Library of Congress Cataloguing-in-Publication Data

Keenan, Jerry.
    Wilson's cavalry corps : Union campaigns in the western theatre,
October 1864 through spring 1865 / by Jerry Keenan.
        p.   cm.
    Includes bibliographical references and index.
    ISBN 0-7864-0528-7 (library binding : 50# alkaline paper) ∞
    1. Wilson's Cavalry Raid, 1865.   2. Wilson, James Harrison,
1837–1925.   3. United States—History—Civil War, 1861–1865—Cavalry
Operations.   4. Tennessee—History—Civil War, 1861–1865—Cavalry
Operations.   5. Alabama—History—Civil War, 1861–1865—Cavalry
Operations.   6. Georgia—History—Civil War, 1861–1865—Cavalry
Operations.   I. Title.
E477.96.K44   1998
973.7'38—dc21   98-22479
                                                               CIP

Manufactured in the United States of America

*McFarland & Company, Inc., Publishers
   Box 611, Jefferson, North Carolina 28640*

Acknowledgments

I t is often said—and rightly—that the author of every work of nonfiction had much help and support along the way. Certainly this has been true for me in the writing of this book. In the more than three decades since I began my study of Wilson's Cavalry, many individuals and institutions generously and graciously answered questions and provided research materials, without which the creation of the present volume would not have been possible.

Institutions that have aided my cause include the Alabama Department of Archives, the State Historical Society of Colorado, the Norlin Library at the University of Colorado, the Georgia Historical Society, the Illinois State Historical Library, the Indiana State Library, the State Historical Society of Iowa, the Michigan Historical Commission, the Milwaukee Public Library, the Ohio Historical Society, the Pennsylvania Historical Commission, the Southern Historical Collection at the University of North Carolina Library, the Tennessee State Library and Archives, the State Historical Society of Wisconsin, and the William Henry Smith Memorial Library in Indianapolis.

Individuals who were especially helpful include Guy and Mary Goddard of Oklahoma City, who kindly furnished me with a typescript copy of *Tom Goddard's War*. The late E. B. "Pete" Long was ever encouraging and directed me to others who had explored the career of James Harrison Wilson. Edward G. Longacre, himself the author of an outstanding biography of Wilson, read and critiqued an early draft of the manuscript. Ed's support and encouragement were more helpful than he realized. Spencer B. King provided me with a copy of the *Georgia Review* containing his article "April in Macon." The late James R. Maxwell of Raleigh, North Carolina, graciously furnished copies of letters from his grandfather James R. Maxwell of the Ninety-eighth Illinois Volunteers. Paul C. Pehrson, who wrote his master's thesis on Wilson, critiqued my bibliography and offered helpful suggestions. John Y. Simon of Southern Illinois University provided a copy of Pehrson's thesis and was most encouraging about the scope of my work.

I would also like to express my appreciation to the long-suffering members of the Colorado Civil War Roundtable who have surely heard more about James H. Wilson's cavalry corps than they ever really wanted to know.

For the many others whose questions, suggestions, and chance remarks helped in some way, but whose names I have failed to properly record, thank you.

Finally, but by no means least importantly, I extend my deepest gratitude to family and friends, especially my wife, Carol, whose support was and is unfailing.

For any errors of either omission or commission in this study, I alone bear full responsibility.

Table of Contents

Preface

This study actually had its genesis during the Civil War centennial. While preparing an article on General James Harrison Wilson's Selma campaign, it gradually became evident to me that there was far more to the story than could adequately be covered in a single article. A book-length study seemed to be in order.

We have histories of the major Civil War field armies. The cavalry operations of Jeb Stuart, Philip Sheridan, Nathan Bedford Forrest, and Joe Wheeler, among others, have also been amply chronicled. There is, in addition, Stephen Starr's outstanding three-volume history of the Union cavalry. Despite this coverage, the full story of Wilson's cavalry remains untold—and this is the niche I hope to fill. To do so, I will pursue the following threefold objective:

- First, I will present a complete history of Wilson's Cavalry Corps from its creation in the autumn of 1864 to its disbandment in June 1865.

- Second, I will offer yet another look at the much-examined Franklin-Nashville campaign, but from the fresh perspective of the Federal horsemen. I will also discuss the Selma campaign that followed, since it could hardly be excluded from any history of the Cavalry Corps. Moreover, when viewed as an integral part of the Corps' total history, the Selma campaign takes on a significance not present when it is treated as a separate entity. The evolution of the Corps from a collection of independent regiments and brigades in the autumn of 1864 to the superb organization that struck south from the Tennessee River in the spring of 1865 can be fully appreciated only when studied as part of the overall history of the Cavalry Corps.

- Finally, I will address the bureaucratic and logistical problems that Wilson had to resolve in creating the infrastructure for his new corps. That he was able to meet these needs while simultaneously trying to cover the Federal flanks during the withdrawal to Franklin and

Nashville has always seemed, to me at least, a rather remarkable achievement.

The Cavalry Corps, Military Division of the Mississippi has long since earned the right to have its story told. I can only hope that I relate this history in a manner worthy of those who created it.

Jerry Keenan
Boulder, Colorado

Introduction

When Major General William T. Sherman launched his now-famous eastward movement from Atlanta on a bright November morning in 1864, he took with him the flower of his command: some 65,000 well-equipped, battle-tested veterans. This army had been stripped to its fighting and marching trim; those who were ill or otherwise unfit to meet the rigors of the forthcoming campaign were left behind. This army brimmed with pride and a belief in itself that bordered on invincibility—a belief that was shared by at least one outside of its own ranks. Erstwhile opponent General Joseph Eggleston Johnston, who had better reason to know than most, once called it the "finest army since Caesar's Legions."[1]

Yet for all its prowess, Sherman's army had always been plagued by the lack of first-rate cavalry support. In large part, this was due to Sherman's own attitude toward cavalry, which did little to encourage the growth and development of his mounted arm. (Fortunately for Sherman, a superiority of men and matériel more than made up for the inadequacy.)

Sherman had long ago concluded that cavalry was of little *real* value. He grudgingly admitted that leaders such as General Benjamin Grierson and Colonel John T. Wilder had enjoyed some successes, but he was equally quick to point out the disasters incurred by generals Samuel Sturgis, Sooy Smith, and George Stoneman. More often than not, Sherman argued, cavalry wasted good horseflesh while accomplishing very little in the process.

One of Sherman's corps commanders during the Atlanta campaign, Major General Jacob Cox, thought the wild-riding cavalry sorties "were never worth the candle,"[2] and Sherman agreed. Yet during the last half of the Atlanta campaign, Sherman sent his troopers out on three such sorties in less than a month, then fumed over their failure to destroy Major General John Bell Hood's lifeline. By the time Atlanta had fallen, Sherman was saying that cavalry simply "could not or would not work hard enough to disable a railroad properly."[3]

Major General William Tecumseh Sherman (National Archives).

Sherman's appraisal of the Confederate cavalry was frequently in the same vein, though he considered Nathan Bedford Forrest and Joe Wheeler far superior to his own mounted commanders. Forrest, in fact, had been the bane of Sherman's existence for so long that Sherman informed Secretary of War Edwin McMasters Stanton that the rebel raider "should be followed to the death if it costs ten thousand lives and breaks the Treasury."[4]

Sherman's disgust with his own horsemen was not entirely without justification, but at the same time, his efforts to remedy the situation left much to be desired. He perceived that cavalry could best be employed as raiders—fast-moving columns that swept in, destroyed a railroad or bridge, then disappeared, emerging later to strike at another objective. Yet each time one of these forays failed to achieve the desired result, Sherman's opinion of his cavalry dropped a notch lower.

The traditional hell-for-leather image of cavalry disgusted Sherman, and he was correct in his belief that such notions had no place in modern warfare. What he failed to perceive was the great tactical potential of mounted infantry. Forrest had demonstrated the value of this concept on numerous occasions and one of Sherman's own commanders, Colonel Wilder, had supplied additional proof at Hoover's Gap, Tennessee, during the Tullahoma campaign.

Somehow, Sherman (and others) failed to profit from these examples. He explained away the ineffectiveness of his horsemen by simply blaming the cavalry in general and his own mounted commanders in particular.

The problem had not escaped the notice of Major General Ulysses S. Grant. When he moved east Grant had taken Philip Sheridan with him and had eventually given the bandy-legged little Irishman command of all cavalry in the Army of the Potomac. Sheridan had reorganized his horsemen and employed them en masse with striking results. Grant thought the same thing could happen in the west, and in a September 1864 dispatch to Sherman, he offered to try and remedy the situation:

> Do you not require a good cavalry leader? It has seemed to me that you have during your campaign suffered for the want of an officer in command of cavalry whose judgment and dash could be relied on. I could send you General Ayres, who I believe would make a capital commander and know him to be one of our best officers in other capacities.[5]

Sherman agreed:

> I do very much want a good cavalry officer to command, and have been maneuvering three months to get Mower here, but Canby has him up White River. My present cavalry needs infantry guards and pickets, and it is hard to get them within ten miles of the front. If you think Ayres will do I would like him. Romeyn B. Ayres is, or was, as bad a growler as Granger. I would prefer Gregg or Wilson, anybody with proper rank will be better than Garrard. Kilpatrick is well enough for small scouts, but I do want a man of sense and courage to manage my cavalry and will take anyone you have tried.[6]

Within 24 hours after receiving Sherman's reply, Grant contacted General George G. Meade, commander of the Army of the Potomac, regarding the availability of General David McMurtrie Gregg.

> Has Gregg returned yet? I will have to send a cavalry commander to Sherman and think of sending Gregg. At present and to this time, there has not been an officer with the cavalry in the west whom it was safe to trust without infantry to guard them from danger. The rebels are equally bad off. With either Gregg, Torbert or Wilson in command of Sherman's cavalry, they could travel over the western country with impunity.[7]

Meade replied that while Gregg was available, he was reluctant to part with him because he and General Henry Eugene Davies were the only ranking cavalry officers attached to the Army of the Potomac. On the other hand, Meade suggested, Sheridan had a number of qualified men—Torbert, Merritt, Custer, Devin, Chapman, and McIntosh.[8]

Whether Wilson's name was excluded from Meade's list by accident or intent made little difference because Grant now directed Sheridan to assign either Alfred T. A. Torbert or Wilson. Torbert had no desire to leave the east, so the job went to Wilson, who was formally assigned through Special Order Number 44, dated September 30, 1864:

> In compliance with instructions from the Lieutenant General commanding, Brig. Gen. J. H. Wilson is hereby relieved from duty with the Third Cavalry Division, and will report without delay to Major-General Sherman, commanding Military Division of the Mississippi as chief of cavalry.[9]

Because Wilson was a junior brigadier and would assume command of officers senior to him, Grant requested that Wilson be brevetted major general of volunteers, effective immediately. The request was approved by Lincoln, and on the morning of October 2, 1864, Wilson departed from Third Cavalry Division headquarters at Harrisonburg, Virginia, for his new assignment in the west.[10]

As the Civil War moved into its fourth and final year, James Harrison Wilson could be numbered among the Federal army's bright new stars, one of a bevy of talented young officers who had risen rapidly in rank and command responsibility. At age 27, Wilson had proven himself to be an extremely capable young officer. He had a penchant for organization and seemed to succeed magnificently at any challenge set before him. His erect carriage made him appear somewhat taller than his actual five feet, ten inches. Of medium build, he was a fine physical example of young manhood.

Major General James Harrison Wilson, 1865 (reproduced from the Collections of the Library of Congress).

A contemporary described him as a "slight person of light complexion and with a rather pinched face."[11]

An intense young man with a full measure of arrogance, Wilson was driven by an almost ruthless ambition to succeed. Outspoken to a fault, he once described an exchange with Grant that has since become a Civil War classic.

> [Grant asked:] Wilson, what is the matter with this army?
> I replied at once: General, there is a great deal the matter with it, but I can tell you much more easily how to cure it.
> Whereupon he asked me: How?
> Send for Parker, the Indian chief and after giving him a tomahawk, a scalping knife, and a gallon of the worst whiskey the Commissary Department can supply, send him out with orders to bring in the scalps of major generals.
> This brought a smile to the General's face, promptly followed by the question: Whose?
> Oh, the first he comes to, and so on in succession til he gets at least a dozen.[12]

Wilson had graduated from West Point in 1860, sixth in a class of 41 and might well have been first had it not been for the demerits acquired with his sharp tongue. Following graduation he was assigned to the army's elite Topographical Engineers, serving briefly in the Pacific Northwest. When war broke out he was transferred to the east, taking part in the Port Royal expedition.

While awaiting a field assignment following Port Royal, he served as General George Brinton McClellan's ADC at South Mountain and Antietam, being promoted to first lieutenant in the interim. Later, he was appointed chief topographical engineer, Army of the Tennessee. In early 1863 he was promoted again, this time to lieutenant-colonel, and assigned as inspector general and assistant engineer on the Vicksburg project. It was during this period that Wilson began a long-term friendship with Grant, one that would, sadly, end with bitterness on the part of both men.[13]

In October 1863, Wilson was brevetted to brigadier general of volunteers. The following February, on Grant's recommendation, he was selected to head up the fledgling Cavalry Bureau in Washington, despite the fact that he completely lacked experience in the mounted service. This fact notwithstanding, in the short space of two months, Wilson did an almost miraculous job of revitalizing the bureau, weeding out much of the graft and seeing to it that many of the regiments were supplied with the new Spencer carbine.[14]

In April 1864, he was recalled to the field at Grant's request and given command of Sheridan's Third Cavalry Division. The appointment was not well received. Wilson was a junior brigadier, which meant that several others who were entitled to the job by virtue of seniority were left to fume. One of Grant's characteristics, however, was his loyalty to those who were loyal to him. It was a trait that would cause Grant considerable distress later during his presidency. His choice to promote Wilson over others would not be without repercussions.[15]

Despite his acknowledged skills, this assignment was Wilson's first independent field command. Though he made some costly mistakes, he learned rapidly. His tenure in the Cavalry Bureau had given him a hands-on feeling for what it took to mount and equip the Union cavalry. As the commander of Sheridan's Third Division he learned about leading a large mounted force in various combat situations. If he lacked extensive field experience in the cavalry, his service during the past year nevertheless enabled him to bring to this new assignment a broader range of experience than most other officers with greater longevity in the mounted branch could have offered.

Just eight months earlier, Wilson had departed from the western theatre totally devoid of experience in the mounted arm. Since then, he had emerged as one of the most promising young cavalry commanders in the Federal ranks.[16] From Grant to Sherman went the following endorsement of Wilson's ability:

> General Wilson has been ordered to report to you and that he may have rank to command your cavalry, I have asked that he be brevetted a major general and assigned with that rank. I believe Wilson will add fifty per cent to the effectiveness of your cavalry.[17]

Wilson would remember this as the "greatest compliment of my life."[18] Ahead lay the greatest challenge of his young military career. With customary aplomb, Wilson eagerly anticipated the new assignment, though in later years he would acknowledge, "Had I known what lay ahead, I might not have gone with heart so buoyant."[19]

The cavalry of Sherman's military department was about to undergo a transformation, one that would eventually produce a mounted arm that was arguably the equal of Sheridan's vaunted brigades. The Cavalry Corps, Military Division of the Mississippi, as it would be designated, was to play a significant role in the western theatre of operations during the final months of the Civil War.

One
The Foal Is Sired

I believe Wilson will add fifty per cent to the effectiveness of your cavalry.—Grant to Sherman, October 4, 1864[1]

The first leg of Wilson's journey, by horseback down the Shenandoah Valley to Martinsburg, West Virginia, proved to be uneventful, despite the ever present danger of John Mosby's guerrillas. From Martinsburg, Wilson traveled by train to Washington, spending the night at the capital with Assistant Secretary of War Charles A. Dana, whom he had known during the Vicksburg days. Joining them was Colonel James P. Martin, an old West Point classmate, who presented Wilson with a fine dapple-gray gelding from the government stables. Wilson promptly dubbed his new mount "Sheridan," owing to the animal's "blazing black eyes and extraordinary spirit."[2]

Sheridan became the second of Wilson's personal mounts, the other being a little bay horse with black markings, dubbed "the Waif" by Grant because Wilson had acquired him as a stray during the Vicksburg campaign. Both animals were immediately shipped on ahead to Nashville, while Wilson remained behind to clear up a few last-minute details.[3]

Though he had been absent from the western theatre for the better part of a year, Wilson was not entirely unfamiliar with the situation in Sherman's department, and in the interim he had developed some rather definite ideas regarding the employment of cavalry. Before leaving Washington, he wrote to his friend General John A. Rawlins, Grant's chief of staff, and, with customary Wilson candor, politely demanded the authority he believed was needed to meet the responsibilities of his new assignment. He wrote,

> Am on my way to command Sherman's cavalry, and as the generals with it are all my seniors, I want ample and complete authority. I think it should be reorganized as a corps, with efficient brigade and division commanders, as in the east. As soon as I get there I'll

make nominations, and with Sherman's approval hope to get the officers I need.[4]

From Washington, Wilson left for the west, traveling through Baltimore, Wilmington, and Philadelphia, where he attended to business and social matters, including a call on Ella Andrews, the young woman who would one day become his wife. Wilson then resumed his journey to Nashville, which he reached in mid-October.[5]

In Nashville, Wilson called on Major General George H. Thomas, who would assume command of Sherman's military division in the latter's absence. While there, Wilson received a detailed analysis of the cavalry situation from Brigadier General Richard W. Johnson, then the nominal chief of cavalry for the department.

From Nashville, Wilson traveled on through Chattanooga, Tennessee, and Dalton, Georgia, to Sherman's field headquarters near Gaylesville, Alabama, some 70 rail miles northwest of Atlanta, arriving on October 22 after three weeks en route.[6]

The first night at Sherman's headquarters proved to be memorable for young Wilson. The autumn air was clean and crisp, the sky was clear, and a blazing campfire in front of Sherman's tent provided additional stimulus for a discussion that lasted well beyond midnight. The two men enjoyed a close friendship dating back to Vicksburg and the events that had transpired in the intervening year and a half supplied ample fuel for review. Sherman expressed himself on a number of topics: the war, Grant's capacity as overall commander, the upcoming presidential election, and the future of his own army. But above all, Wilson noted, he was "full of the March to the Sea," the plan for which was discussed at length. Wilson was not averse to presenting his own views on the subject.[7]

Sherman's proposal to turn his back on Atlanta and strike out across Georgia for the Atlantic seaboard had generated some uneasiness among Lincoln, Stanton, and Grant. Though all three men appreciated the logic underlying Sherman's argument and respected his soldierly skills, they were nevertheless uncomfortable with the general idea. For one thing, Sherman would be existing off the land and out of touch for some time. Even more worrisome was how Sherman's absence was going to affect the responsibilities of his rather substantial Military Division of the Mississippi. Traditionally, operations were conducted within one's sphere of responsibility. Sherman proposed to disregard that rule and march where others had never considered treading. Under other circumstances, this plan might not have seemed quite so troubling, but given the state of affairs at the time, there was some cause to wonder whether matters in his department ought not to be attended to first before sallying out on that kind of expedition.

The nature of this unfinished business centered mainly on the still very much alive and active Confederate Army of Tennessee which would have virtually unrestricted freedom of movement with Sherman out of the picture. The fall of Atlanta had been a signal triumph for a Federal cause that in the past few months had been long on casualty lists, but rather bereft of victories. Atlanta was a symbol; the significance of its fall was not something to be taken lightly in assessing the overall progress of the war. Nevertheless, even though Atlanta had fallen, the army that had defended it was far

General John Bell Hood, CSA (reproduced from the Collections of the Library of Congress).

from vanquished. Then, too, there was always Nathan Bedford Forrest, whose presence could scarcely be ignored.

If the Federal high command was nervous about the prospects of what might happen once Sherman disappeared into the bowels of Georgia, Sherman himself was not at all worried, having reflected on the situation at great length and, he believed, provided plenty of insurance for any development. The way Sherman sorted things out, Forrest was always going to be a threat, and he (Sherman) could do more damage to the Confederacy by marching through Georgia than by chasing after Forrest.

John Bell Hood's Confederate Army of Tennessee, on the other hand, represented a legitimate threat, but Sherman was leaving behind ample resources to deal with that threat, regardless of what Hood might choose to do, which at that moment was anyone's guess. During the two months following the fall of Atlanta, Hood had drawn Sherman out of Atlanta, back along the route of the Yankee advance of the past summer, planning to turn on the pursuing Federals at the right time and place. As it developed, however, Hood couldn't quite seem to find the right set of circumstances, so the

Major General George H. Thomas (reproduced from the Collections of the Library of Congress).

chase continued. It was a case of the hound not quite catching the fox.

By the time Wilson joined him at Gaylesville, Sherman had concluded that the effort wasn't worth the candle. Exactly what Hood might do was not entirely clear (perhaps not even to Hood himself at this juncture). Sherman had concluded that he could best serve the Federal cause by leaving others to tend to Hood, while he marched off to eviscerate the Confederacy. It was entirely possible that once he headed east, the roles of the past month would be reversed and Hood would become the pursuer. If this proved to be the case, so much the better; but if not, Sherman had absolute confidence that the resources he was planning to leave behind would be more than adequate to meet any exigency.[8]

The man to whom Sherman had entrusted the responsibilities of his military department was Major General George H. Thomas, commander of the Department of the Cumberland and arguably the staunchest defensive fighter in the Federal ranks. The "Rock of Chickamauga," as he was known, Thomas had been separated from the command of his beloved Army of the Cumberland, which he had led through the Atlanta campaign, and sent back to Nashville. From there he was directed to oversee the affairs of Sherman's Military Division, including the defense of Middle Tennessee against all comers. "If you can defend the line of the Tennessee in my absence of three months, it is all I ask," Sherman told his deputy in an October 19 communiqué.[9]

Where his cavalry was concerned, Sherman was not reluctant to express his lack of faith to Wilson. With few exceptions, he thought his horsemen had fared badly. Sooy Smith's defeat by Forrest the previous February, followed by Samuel Sturgis's disaster at Brice's Crossroads and George

Stoneman's blunder during the Atlanta campaign, were but three of many instances. As a consequence, he had reservations about what, if anything, might be accomplished with the cavalry.

Despite Grant's sterling recommendation of Wilson's capability and both Thomas's and Grant's suggestion that Wilson be turned loose with the cavalry to accomplish what Sherman himself proposed to do with the main army, Sherman declared that he "had not so much faith in cavalry as he [Grant] had, and preferred to adhere to my original intention of going myself with a competent force."[10] Before Wilson's arrival, Sherman had planned to combine all of his cavalry into three small divisions, and while Wilson was still in Nashville, had wired him to bring along 2,400 fresh troops. They would see the "hardest fighting of the war," Sherman declared, adding that "I am going into the very bowels of the Confederacy, and propose to leave a trail that will be recognized fifty years hence."[11]

However, Wilson's own brief assessment of the situation, coupled with the information provided by General Johnson, prompted him to disagree completely with this plan. He advised Sherman that with proper organization and management there was enough manpower to form six and perhaps even seven large divisions. Moreover, he urged that the cavalry be equipped with breech-loading carbines, brought together in a single, unified corps, and employed en masse, in the style of Sheridan's cavalry. It was a sweeping plan and somewhat at odds with the views he had held as chief of the Cavalry Bureau back in April.[12]

Sherman listened and was impressed, but remained unconvinced. Still, something had to be done with the horsemen and Sherman finally acquiesced, giving Wilson carte blanche to handle the cavalry in his own way. Sherman told Wilson, "Do the best you can with it and if you make any reputation out of it I shall not undertake to divide it with you."[13]

Sherman's acquiescence to Wilson's proposal was probably due as much or more to his own preoccupation with the march to the sea as it was to a belief in his new young cavalry chief's theories on the organization and employment of cavalry. In a sense, Sherman was washing his hands of what, for him, had been a sticky problem. With the exception of one division that would accompany the main army, the cavalry would remain in the west. Sherman's only direct order to Wilson in this regard was to have General Hugh Judson Kilpatrick's division fully mounted and equipped to make the march to the sea. Sherman said, "I know Kilpatrick is a hell of a damned fool, but I want just that sort of man to command my cavalry on this expedition."[14]

In addition, Wilson recalled, Sherman "forcibly" suggested that as soon as Hood had been disposed of and the new cavalry corps had reached a state of readiness, it should be brought east to cooperate with him in the final effort against General Lee's army. Beyond this, though, Wilson would have wide latitude in reorganizing and employing his new command.[15]

Accordingly, on October 24, 1864, through Special Field Order Number 103 from Headquarters of the Military Division of the Mississippi, Major General James H. Wilson was officially named commander of all mounted troops within that jurisdiction, the new organization to be thereafter designated as the Cavalry Corps, Military Division of the Mississippi.[16]

Two
The Reins of Command

[A] task worthy of any young soldier's highest ambition. —Wilson,
Personal Memoirs[1]

In a sense, Wilson's position was not entirely new. There had been chiefs
of cavalry in the past, the most recent being Brigadier General Richard
W. Johnson, who had been appointed to that post by Sherman on
August 19, 1864. Johnson's position, however, had been mainly administrative, with little or no authority regarding the actual field organization and
employment of cavalry. By contrast, Wilson was given discretionary powers rivaling those of a department commander.[2]

Wilson inherited a complex and cumbersome command structure.
Under the old system, each of the four departments making up Sherman's
military division had a chief of cavalry who coordinated the movement of
all mounted units within his jurisdiction, reporting directly to the department commander, or, in special situations, to Sherman himself.

It was a system at cross-purposes with a military machine that had otherwise become very effective and relentless. It was a system that authored
confusion, promoted bickering, and retarded uniformity of operation—and
most important, of spirit—among its regiments and brigades. Under the new
modus operandi instituted by Wilson, all mounted detachments, regiments,
brigades, and divisions would henceforth report directly to Wilson's headquarters.[3]

The paper strength of the new command made it appear far stronger
than it was in reality. The returns reflected an aggregate strength of nearly
50,000, while the number present for duty was less than 23,000 and of this,
only 12,000 were actually in the field with Sherman. Moreover, the returns
were incomplete, remounts were all but unobtainable, and units were scattered from one end of Sherman's division to the other. Wilson wrote,

> Every army commander and nearly every corps commander had a
> cavalry escort of greater or less size, while regiments, brigades, and
> divisions were scattered from east Tennessee to the Missouri River,
> with dismounted men and convalescents at every hospital, depot
> and camp from Chicago and St. Louis on the north, to Vicksburg
> and Atlanta on the south.[4]

To organize all of this into an effective field command and live up to Grant's
prediction was, as Wilson later recalled, "a task worthy of any young soldier's highest ambition."[5]

The Department of the Cumberland, Brigadier General Washington
L. Elliott, chief of cavalry, furnished the bulk of Sherman's horse wing then
in the field. Elliott's cavalry was composed of three divisions, led respectively by brigadier generals Edward Moody McCook, Kenner Garrard, and
H. J. Kilpatrick. A fourth division under Colonel George Spalding had been
detached from the main army since the outset of the Atlanta campaign.
Brigadier General John T. Croxton's brigade of McCook's division was
patrolling a line south from Nashville, through Stevenson, Decatur, and
Florence, Alabama.

Major General George Stoneman, who had led the cavalry belonging
to the Army of the Ohio through the Atlanta campaign, had recently
departed for Knoxville to assume the temporary duties of department commander and had been replaced by Colonel Israel Garrard. Owing mainly to
Stoneman's fiasco in the Atlanta campaign, the Ohio division had incurred
heavy losses and was now detached from the main army. Of its two brigades,
only Colonel Horace Capron's was then in the field, it being on patrol duty
around Pulaski, Tennessee. The division's second brigade was in Louisville,
awaiting remounts.

The chief of cavalry for the Army of the Tennessee was a former
infantry brigade commander Brigadier General Joseph Farmer Knipe.
Appointed to that post by department commander Major General O. O.
Howard in late September, Knipe's duties, like Richard Johnson's for the
entire military division, were mainly administrative. The mounted units of
this department were concentrated in the southwest corner of Tennessee,
where they comprised the Cavalry Corps, District of West Tennessee, commanded by Brigadier General Benjamin H. Grierson.

Grierson, who had led the much-publicized raid from LaGrange,
Tennessee, to Baton Rouge in the spring of 1863, was headquartered at
Memphis. Grierson had a division under Brigadier General Edward Hatch
at Clifton, Tennessee, and another under Colonel Edward F. Winslow operating out in Missouri and Arkansas.

Finally, there were two divisions of Tennessee cavalry, five dismounted

Brigadier General Joseph F. Knipe (reproduced from the Collections of the Library of Congress).

Indiana regiments and the unassigned Fifteenth Pennsylvania Cavalry, distributed among the garrisons at Nashville, Pulaski, Tullahoma, and Wauhatchie, Tennessee, together with a number of smaller detachments scattered throughout Sherman's division, serving as orderlies, escorts, and camp guards.[6]

One of Wilson's first official acts was to initiate some transfers and reassignments. Both Kenner Garrard and Washington Elliott were old-line

Brigadier General Eli Long (State Historical Society of Wisconsin).

regulars and senior to Wilson, though his new brevet, backed by Sherman's authority, gave him undisputed command over both men. Nonetheless, Wilson had no wish to embarrass either officer and wanted to avoid resentment among his subordinates as well. Consequently, he concluded that it might be better if the two were reassigned. Sherman agreed and the necessary orders were issued accordingly, with both Elliott and Garrard receiving infantry commands under Thomas.

Ironically, Wilson had replaced Garrard once before, as head of the Cavalry Bureau the previous February. Wilson had also replaced Kilpatrick when he assumed command of Sheridan's Third Division in April. Technically, Kilpatrick's division was still a part of the new cavalry corps, but since Kilpatrick would shortly be marching off with Sherman, the Third Division did not enter into Wilson's current plans.[7]

While still at Gaylesville, Wilson wrote to Brigadier General John A. Rawlins and Colonel Adam Badeau, his friends on Grant's staff. Certain that both men would share his words with Grant, Wilson set out to build a case for his needs. He described the deplorable condition of the western cavalry, pointing out the deficiency in numbers, the shortage of horses, weapons, and equipment. On top of that, Forrest was threatening the Federal supply lines with a force of 26,000, thus making it imperative that the cavalry be brought up to its full potential as quickly as possible.[8]

Though Sherman had taken only Kilpatrick's division, Wilson nevertheless expressed some fear to Rawlins that in view of the uncertain situation with Hood, Sherman might change his mind and the cavalry might yet wind up being divided between Sherman and Thomas. Forcibly voicing his opposition to such a move, which, in his opinion, could only place the cavalry on the defensive, Wilson told Rawlins that

> cavalry is useless for defense; its only power is in a vigorous offensive; therefore I urge its concentration south of the Tennessee and hurling it into the bowels of the South in masses that the enemy cannot drive back as it did Sooy Smith and Sturgis.[9]

In closing, Wilson reminded Rawlins that he had twice requested that Grant furnish him with several established cavalry officers from the east. The list included Custer, Upton, Mackenzie, Pennington, and Reno. Wilson asked Rawlins to see what could be done to obtain these men. He wrote, "All I wish is to get my tools in an efficient condition. I shall answer for the consequences."[10]

Returning from a combination shakedown-reconnaissance expedition to Blue Mountain, Alabama, on October 29, Wilson rejoined Sherman's headquarters near Rome, Georgia, and finished up with his transfers and reassignments. Garrard was instructed to furnish Kilpatrick with whatever horses and equipment he needed to ready his Third Division for the upcoming march. Garrard was then directed to proceed to Nashville and turn command of his division over to Brigadier General Eli Long, a Kentuckian who had formerly commanded the division's second brigade.

On October 31, Brigadier General McCook was ordered to assemble his division and return to Nashville. Brigadier General Hatch, meanwhile, had been directed to bring his division to Rome as quickly as possible, sending any dismounted men to Nashville. At the same time, Grierson was ordered to collect what he could of Winslow's division and prepare to launch a raid through northern Mississippi and Alabama. However, in view of the increased activity on Hood's part, Wilson telegraphed Thomas on October 31, requesting that Hatch be halted en route and deployed to shadow Hood's movements.[11]

On November 1, Wilson's fear that his new corps might yet be divided was allayed by virtue of Sherman's Special Field Order Number 112, which officially directed Wilson to report to Thomas in Nashville to continue his work of reorganizing the cavalry and assisting Thomas in preparing a defense against Hood.[12]

With Kilpatrick's division set and Garrard and McCook on their way to Nashville, there was nothing further to be done at Sherman's headquarters. Accordingly, on November 2, Wilson left for Nashville, where the threat of a Confederate invasion of Middle Tennessee seemed to loom ever more likely with each passing day.

Three
Prelude

*If you can defend the line of the Tennessee in my absence of three months,
it is all I ask.* —Sherman to Thomas, October 19, 1864[1]

Geooorge Henry Thomas was born in Southampton County, Virginia,
on July 31, 1816. He graduated from West Point in 1840, ranking
twelfth in a class of 42. Unlike Robert E. Lee, with whom he had
served in the old Second Cavalry (along with Albert Sidney Johnston,
William J. Hardee, and John Bell Hood, among others), Thomas put country ahead of state, one of the few Southern-born officers to do so.

A large man, standing six feet and weighing over two hundred pounds,
Thomas was ordinarily quiet and unpretentious, preferring to let his accomplishments speak for themselves. A painstaking dedication to thoroughness and
detail frequently gave the impression that he was cumbersome and slow to
move, a trait that earned him the sobriquet "Old Tom," as a West Point cadet
and later, "Slow Trot" as an instructor at the Academy. But to the men of the
Army of the Cumberland, who loved him, he would always be simply, "Old
Pap." More than anything else his penchant for organization and his determination not to move before he was ready exasperated both Grant and
Sherman. In fact, because of this trait, Grant nearly relieved Thomas of command on the eve of his greatest victory.[2]

Thomas spent the first few months of the war in the east, before being
transferred to Kentucky in August 1861. In the battles of Mill Springs, Shiloh,
Corinth, and Stones River, he established himself as a first-rate fighter. But
during the bloodletting at Chickamauga, at a place named Snodgrass Hill,
Thomas really rose to prominence, steadfastly holding the left flank of
Rosecrans's shattered army against repeated assaults, thereby immortalizing
himself as the "Rock of Chickamauga." Following the disastrous Tullahoma
campaign, he was given command of the Army of the Cumberland, leading
it at Lookout Mountain and throughout the Atlanta campaign.[3]

By late September 1864, the military situation in the west had entered a new phase. With Atlanta safely in Federal hands, Sherman set out to run down Hood's army and eliminate it as a threat. At the same time, Thomas was sent back to Nashville to look after the affairs in Sherman's vast military department, which included, among other matters, dealing with Forrest, whose raiding antics continued to frustrate the Federals. Thomas set a trap for the elusive Confederate cavalryman, but Forrest evaded the net, demonstrating yet again that he could move in and out of Middle Tennessee largely with impunity.[4]

Thomas did not relish the idea of policing Middle Tennessee while Sherman's main army, including his old Fourteenth Corps, remained in the field. Still, the Department of the Cumberland was his responsibility, so the assignment was not entirely inappropriate. Notwithstanding, the mission hardly seemed fitting for an officer of Thomas's stature. In effect, Sherman was asking his senior lieutenant to look after the neighborhood while he marched off to cleave the "terrible swift sword" of the Union through the bowels of Georgia. From Sherman's point of view, the choice made all the sense in the world. Thomas was a little too ponderous for Sherman's taste and was not the kind of subordinate Sherman wanted on his eastward march. On the other hand, Thomas's characteristic attention to detail and organization made him exactly the right man to watch over Sherman's military department. One of the ironies of the Civil War is that Thomas, seemingly snubbed and left behind when Sherman marched off to the sea, wound up with the opportunity to achieve his greatest victory.

By late October, Sherman had become convinced that further pursuit of Hood was futile and had returned to Atlanta to begin preparations for his march across Georgia, which he perceived as holding infinitely more promise than chasing Hood. Such a movement might well induce Hood to turn and follow him, thus reversing their roles of the past few weeks. Of course there was always the possibility that Hood might choose to invade Tennessee instead, but as Sherman saw it, Thomas was well equipped to deal with that eventuality.

To assist Thomas, Sherman sent back to Tennessee, between October 20 and 30, the Fourth and Twenty-third Corps, commanded by major generals David Sloan Stanley and John McAllister Schofield, respectively. In addition, two divisions of the Sixteenth Corps under Major General Andrew Jackson Smith were ordered back to Nashville from Missouri, where they had been involved in repelling Confederate Major General Sterling Price's invasion. Thomas had requested his old Fourteenth Corps, but it was one of the best in Sherman's army and the latter refused to part with it.[5]

In Sherman's absence, Thomas was directed to "exercise command over all troops and garrisons not absolutely in the presence of the general-in-chief."

The directive had an impressive ring to it, but until his reinforcements arrived, Thomas had the unenviable task of protecting the whole of Middle Tennessee with a very fragmented command. Once Stanley, Schofield, and A. J. Smith arrived, Thomas would have a formidable force, but until then he was vulnerable.[6]

The problem was twofold. First, it was a matter of concentration. At the moment, his troops were distributed among various garrisons and a number of strategic points along the Tennessee railroad system. Some of Wilson's horsemen were watching the fords along the Tennessee River and there were a number of incomplete and unassigned regiments in Nashville.

As Hood's movements toward Middle Tennessee grew increasingly more threatening, a rapid concentration of troops became imperative. The question was where to concentrate: Nashville, Chattanooga, or Murfreesboro? Until Hood committed himself, Thomas had to maintain strong garrisons at several strategic points. Time was a critical factor for both invader and defender.

In addition to the need for concentration, Thomas also had to concern himself with welding these various units into an army. Like any organization, an army's success as a fighting force depends, among other things, on its ability to function as team, and teamwork is not a quality one creates overnight. Yet this was the challenge facing Thomas as the autumn of 1864 deepened. Sherman felt comfortable with the numbers that accumulated under the umbrella of Thomas's command. What he failed to appreciate was that these units still needed to be forged into an army, not just a collection of soldiers. Perhaps it is to Sherman's everlasting credit that somehow he knew that George Thomas, the portly Virginian, was equal to the challenge.

In addition to taking Forrest and Hood into account, Thomas also had to be concerned with the threat that Robert E. Lee posed to East Tennessee; although this was a far less pressing worry, it wasn't something that could simply be dismissed out of hand.[7] From his headquarters on High Street in Nashville, Thomas pressed forward with the Herculean task of organizing his scattered command into a unified force. In this final autumn of the war, Nashville was a cauldron of confusion, filled with incoming regiments of raw recruits and furloughed veterans on their way home. The city was also the most important Federal supply point in the west. Men and matériel passed through at a prodigious rate and it required an administrative effort of the first magnitude to maintain a steady, uninterrupted flow. An outer defense line of forts and trenches that had been under construction for two years was now being rushed to completion, adding to the confusion.

To further complicate his life, Thomas also had to deal with Tennessee's rampant guerrilla activity and internal politics, which were particularly difficult and volatile in this border state. As governor, Andrew Johnson, a solid Union man who would shortly become vice president of the United States, exercised personal control over all volunteer regiments from his state, refusing to recognize Thomas's authority where these troops were concerned.[8]

Thomas's assignment was relatively straightforward: If Hood chose to turn and follow Sherman, Thomas was authorized to mount an invasion of Alabama, penetrating as far south as Selma. However, in the event that Hood elected to invade Tennessee, Thomas's job was to repel that invasion. The defense of Middle Tennessee remained his primary responsibility.[9]

For Thomas, the situation grew increasingly unsettled as the autumn weeks passed. The difficulties associated with getting his command assembled and organized were vexing enough, but when Hood's movements were factored into the equation, it was a mess. Lack of information was not the problem. Cavalry patrols, spies, deserters, and prisoners all combined to produce a great deal of intelligence as to Hood's movements, though much of it was unreliable and contradictory.[10]

Although it was by no means certain, there was a growing likelihood that the Confederates would cross the Tennessee River and move north; the question was if they did, what would be their objective? Moreover, would it be a raid, a demonstration, or something more? It was hard to know.

By the end of October, some kind of movement appeared to have become a fait accompli, with reports that Hood had begun crossing the Tennessee River at Florence. The report resulted in Stanley's Fourth Corps, some 12,000 strong, being sent directly from Chattanooga to Pulaski, Tennessee, 75 miles due south of Nashville, which Stanley reached on November 1. "Make preparations at once for a stubborn defense of Pulaski," Thomas advised him. Strategically situated on the north-south axis to Nashville, Pulaski was a logical point to contest any northward movement on Hood's part. From here, one could cover the direct approach to Nashville or shift east or west, depending on Hood's movements.[11]

Schofield, meanwhile, had also been ordered to Pulaski, but was diverted to Johnsonville to deal with Forrest, who was on another raid. Reaching Johnsonville on November 5, Schofield discovered that Forrest had destroyed several Federal gunboats, burned the big supply dump, and completely routed the inexperienced garrison there. After detaching two brigades to guard the depot, Schofield, pursuant to Thomas's instructions, then turned and countermarched to Pulaski, which he reached on November 14, and assumed command of all Federal forces in the immediate area.[12]

Stanley was actually the senior officer, but Schofield was a department commander (Department of the Ohio) and assumed command on that basis. If Hood did move north, Schofield's orders were to slow that movement as much as possible, while retiring toward Nashville. The idea was to buy

Major General John M. Schofield (reproduced from the Collections of the Library of Congress).

time for Thomas to marshall his forces. Mainly, Thomas needed A. J. Smith's two divisions, and he wanted Wilson's horsemen mounted and equipped.[13]

When Wilson arrived in Nashville on November 6, he faced a task of reorganization second only to that of Thomas himself. Fortunately for Wilson, he found Thomas more than willing to cooperate. Thomas had a history of working to improve the efficiency of mounted troops and his determination to fully support Wilson paid off in a large way for the Federal cause, though Thomas suffered much criticism for doing so.[14]

Wilson brought three hand-picked officers with him from the east, men who would contribute much toward bringing order out of all the administrative chaos surrounding the new cavalry corps. Major Eugene Beauharnais Beaumont would become the acting assistant adjutant general; Captain Elias Brown Carling, chief quartermaster; and Captain Henry Erastus Noyes, aide-de-camp. In Nashville, the trio was joined by Lieutenant Colonel Andrew Jonathan Alexander, chief of staff, and Captain Joseph Corson Read, chief of commissary.[15] During the next two weeks, Wilson and his staff worked day and night, perfecting a corps organization, and requisitioning remounts, arms and ammunition, much of which was found to have been on back order since September.[16]

Horses were far and away the biggest concern and ironically enough, this was due in part to Wilson himself. While chief of the Cavalry Bureau, he had laid down stringent rules governing the purchase of horses. The regulations had been needed, of course, but as a result, civilian contractors were finding it all but impossible to meet the current demand.[17] The often exasperating and frustrating job of procuring remounts was handled by two special inspectors of cavalry: Major William P. Chambliss and Captain John Green, both of whom Wilson would later commend as having contributed more than anyone "toward promoting the efficiency of the cavalry in this military division."[18]

By November 9, Wilson's staff had outlined the framework of the new corps organization. There were to be eight divisions of two brigades each, with the brigades composed of five regiments each. Previously, the policy had been to organize a division into three brigades, but Wilson felt this created a tendency to hold back the third brigade as a reserve force, thus depriving a division of a third of its authorized strength.[19]

Wilson's repeated requests to Grant for established cavalry officers had been turned down, and he was forced to choose from the pool of officers immediately available to him. Fortunately, there were some first-rate individuals on hand; of the seven men initially assigned to divisional commands, only two were replaced later. Wilson had requested and been granted the services of Brevet Major General Emory Upton, an aggressive young officer then recovering from a severe wound suffered in the Battle of Opequon. Two years Wilson's junior, Upton had already distinguished himself in both the artillery and infantry branches and by the end of the war would be an accomplished cavalry leader as well.

By November 9, 1864, Wilson and his staff had completely restructured the various mounted brigades and regiments to form a new corps. The First, Second, Third, and Seventh divisions had formerly been attached to the Army of the Cumberland; the Fourth and Fifth were from the Cavalry Corps, District of West Tennessee, while the Sixth was from the Army of the Ohio. The regiments making up the Eighth Division were yet to be assigned. The commanders of the divisions are as follows:

First Division: Brigadier General Edward Moody McCook
Second Division: Brigadier General Eli Long
Third Division: Brigadier General Hugh Judson Kilpatrick
Fourth Division: Brigadier General Benjamin H. Grierson
Fifth Division: Brigadier General Edward Hatch
Sixth Division: Unassigned
Seventh Division: Colonel George Spalding
Eighth Division: Unassigned[20]

Two command changes followed within a week. On November 16 Brigadier General Joseph Farmer Knipe assumed command of the Seventh Division, replacing Colonel George Spalding, who reverted to command of the Twelfth Tennessee Cavalry. Wilson had originally thought to give the Sixth Division (temporarily under Colonel Israel Garrard) to Emory Upton when he arrived, but evidently changed his mind and on November 17 assigned Brigadier General Richard W. Johnson to command of the Sixth Division.[21]

Officially, the corps looked impressive. However, the force that Wilson

Wilson (seated on steps in center, leg outstretched) and staff, Third Cavalry Division, Virginia, 1864 (U.S. Signal Corps photograph no. 111-B-163 [Brady Collection] in the National Archives).

was actually able to put into the field at this juncture was far removed from the organization that existed on paper. Owing to a lack of both men and horses, the Eighth Division was soon dropped from the rolls. General Edward McCook's Second Brigade, First Division, and General Eli Long's entire Second Division were in Louisville being remounted. General Grierson was attempting to bring back Colonel Edward Winslow's Brigade from Missouri, while the divisions of Johnson and Knipe were still in the process of being organized. After these adjustments, General Edward Hatch's Fifth Division and General John Croxton's First Brigade of McCook's First Division were left, both were along the Tennessee River monitoring Hood's movements. Finally, one small brigade under Colonel Horace Capron was on patrol west of Pulaski.[22]

By November 21, with Hood definitely across the Tennessee River and heading north, Wilson, pursuant to Thomas's directive, turned the administrative details over to Major Beaumont and headed south to Pulaski to assume personal command of his troops.[23]

Four
Florence to Columbia

Use every means to delay him [Hood] *as long as you can, and, if possible to prevent, do not permit him to cross the river.* —Thomas to Croxton, October 30, 1864[1]

W hile Thomas prepared to defend Middle Tennessee against what looked increasingly like a major Confederate invasion, a strange sidelight of this war was occurring as one Kentuckian carefully monitored the movements of another about 100 miles south of Nashville.

Along the north bank of the Tennessee River, a Federal brigadier of cavalry, John Thomas Croxton, had positioned his command to cover the various fords between Florence, Alabama, and the mouth of the Elk River. Here, Croxton patiently waited and watched for signs of fellow Kentuckian John Bell Hood to commence a northward movement with his veteran army.

A former lawyer, Yale graduate, and devout abolitionist, Croxton's handsomely bearded features suggested a resemblance to Christ. At 27 he was regarded as one of the finest unit commanders in Wilson's new cavalry corps. Once referred to as the "gallant and dashing Croxton," he had served with distinction in the west, becoming one of Thomas's favorites. At Chickamauga, Croxton had been ordered by Thomas to take his command and clear a certain patch of woods of rebel stragglers. He soon returned, pursued by an entire Confederate division. On reporting to Thomas, Croxton said he would have brought them all in if he had known precisely which ones Thomas wanted.[2] Within a decade, Croxton would die of tuberculosis while serving as United States minister to Bolivia, but in October 1864 he was very much alive and ready to give fair warning the moment Hood committed himself.[3]

Croxton's brigade was composed of the Eighth Iowa, Second Michigan, and First Tennessee cavalries, along with his old regiment, the Fourth Kentucky Mounted Infantry, of which he had been colonel until promoted to brigadier and given the brigade command in July 1864.[4] At the conclusion

29

of the Atlanta Campaign, Croxton's brigade had been sent to Louisville for remounting. Returning to the field, it was then detached from its parent unit, General Edward McCook's First Cavalry Division, Army of the Cumberland, and ordered to report directly to Thomas, who was in need of good cavalrymen to use against Forrest and Wheeler, both of whom had been causing trouble in Middle Tennessee.[5]

The hunt for Forrest revealed only that the Confederate raider had again disappeared south of the Tennessee River and Wheeler had withdrawn to harrass Sherman. Accordingly, Croxton's brigade was now redirected to patrol a segment of the river line where it seemed most likely that Hood would attempt a crossing. The new assignment was not without compensation. Recently on short rations, the brigade found itself in an area where "liberal supplies of chicken, hogs, and cattle," were found.[6]

At any rate, by October 29 Croxton had dispersed his brigade over a 25 mile stretch along the north bank of the Tennessee River, on a line roughly covering what is today U.S. Highway 72. Croxton's left flank rested near the Elk River's confluence with the Tennessee, while his right flank extended a few miles beyond Florence; his headquarters were at Center Star.[7]

Croxton had been ordered to watch Hood and try to delay any northward advance that the latter might attempt, keeping Thomas continually apprised of all developments. The difficulty of the assignment was relative. If Hood chose to remain south of the river, Croxton's job would be simple. If, however, Hood elected to move north (as it seemed he might) Croxton could do little to restrict him.[8] With barely a thousand troopers in his brigade, Croxton had requested and been promised the Ninth and Tenth Indiana and the Tenth and Twelfth Tennessee Cavalry regiments. The former lacked horses, however, and were subsequently pronounced unavailable. Only 450 of the Tennesseans reported for duty, but they were "so badly mounted and managed," that Croxton was barely able to garner 200 effective men from the lot; these he assigned to cover the river crossings west of Florence.[9]

On the evening of October 29, thanks to a black man who had somehow managed to cross the river in the dark of night, Croxton learned that Hood was near Town Creek, Alabama, midway between Decatur and Florence. Guessing that the Confederate might try to effect a crossing at Bainbridge that same night, he immediately sent word to Thomas, then ordered the Second Michigan Cavalry to reinforce the Bainbridge guard and sent an additional battalion to Raccoon Branch Crossing between Florence and Bainbridge.[10]

As it turned out, Hood did not attempt a crossing that night. Late in the afternoon of the following day, however, two brigades of General Edward "Allegheny" Johnson's division of Stephen D. Lee's corps (Stephen was no relation to Robert E. Lee) crossed the river three miles below Bainbridge, at

Brigadier General John T. Croxton (U.S. Signal Corps photograph no 111-B-1554 [Brady Collection] in the National Archives).

a point never before used as a ford.[11] Croxton promptly contested the movement and there was some brisk action until dark, with the Federal horsemen finally driven back two miles to the Huntsville Road. That night, Croxton established his line along Shoal Creek, where he remained through the following week, continuing to monitor Hood's movements and skirmishing daily with Confederate patrols.[12]

Brigadier General Edward Hatch (National Archives).

While Croxton was holding his vigil, Brigadier General Edward Hatch, a handsome, talkative, 32-year-old former sailor and Iowa lumberman, was hurrying east with his 2,500 horsemen. Formerly a part of Brigadier General Benjamin H. Grierson's West Tennessee Cavalry Corps, Hatch, who had marched from Clifton, Tennessee on October 29, had originally been ordered to report to Wilson while the latter was still in the field with Sherman at Rome, Georgia. However, when a Confederate movement into Tennessee began to appear increasingly likely, Hatch was rerouted and directed to join Croxton in patrolling the Tennessee River line.[13]

Hatch's division, consisting of the Sixth, Seventh, and Ninth Illinois and Second Iowa Cavalry, reached Pulaski on November 1. Major General Stanley, who had just reached Pulaski himself, immediately directed Hatch, the senior brigadier by three months, to join Croxton and assume overall command of the operation.[14]

Marching south from Pulaski on November 4, Hatch reached Lexington, Alabama, the following day and discovered that action was not long in coming. After opening communications with Croxton, he had a running fight with some of Brigadier General William Hicks "Red" Jackson's cavalry of Forrest's command. The Confederate horsemen were driven back some four miles and Hatch subsequently established his line on a northwest-southeast axis along the east bank of Shoal Creek, with Croxton anchoring the left at the Tennessee River.[15]

During this first half of November 1864, life along the river line for these Federal horsemen involved observing, skirmishing, and doing anything they could to disrupt Confederate activities.[16] Crossing a river as broad and as swift as the Tennessee with a large army was no mean accomplishment; nor was it done quickly. The crossing took place over a period of days, as facilities were available and as the army itself was deemed ready to be put across. From here, Hatch and Croxton sent out daily patrols in an effort to divine

Hood's intentions. "I know of no way of watching him so effectual as pressing his picket-line constantly," Hatch reported to Wilson.[17]

Despite their efforts, however, the information garnered from scouts, prisoners, deserters, and local civilians was as confusing and contradictory as it was plentiful. Intelligence suggested that Hood was up to something, but whether he was preparing to launch a large-scale raid or a full-scale invasion of Middle Tennessee remained unclear. Further, if he was indeed planning on a full-scale invasion, what his ultimate objective was equally unclear.[18]

By November 14, Schofield had assumed command at Pulaski. That night a foray by Croxton's troopers bagged a member of the Twenty-eighth Mississippi of Jackson's division. The prisoner informed his captors that Stephen D. Lee's corps and most of the cavalry, except for Forrest himself, were across the river and that the balance of the army would follow shortly.[19] Hatch regarded the information as reliable and in passing it on to Thomas, predicted a prompt advance by Hood, adding that

> at 10 o'clock last night the enemy had such an extended line of campfires, and so much brighter than usual, I was under the impression it was a ruse to cover a movement to the rear, but since this attack of Croxton's, believe the increase of campfires is owing to the fresh arrival of troops from the south side of the river.[20]

By the fifteenth, further evidence seemed to substantiate Hatch's prediction, but Thomas remained skeptical. For one thing, Sherman had begun his eastward march and Thomas still believed there was a good chance that Hood would decide to follow. Recent heavy rains had raised the river 18 feet at Florence; bridges had been swept away and it was extremely difficult to hold pontoons in place, particularly when Hatch's and Croxton's troops were cutting them away at night. All of this caused Thomas to think it unlikely that Hood would attempt to cross his entire army under such conditions. Nevertheless, Thomas directed Hatch and Croxton to maintain their vigil and be prepared for any eventuality.[21]

Schofield, too, had doubts. He had been a West Point classmate of Hood's and had little regard for the latter's high command capabilities. Schofield believed that Hood would not advance his infantry, but would instead send his cavalry on a raid while the infantry covered their line of retreat.[22] Edward Hatch, on the other hand, was convinced that a full-scale invasion was about to take place. Accordingly, he and Croxton put their troops to work felling trees, filling in gorges, and blocking streams to retard the expected advance as much as possible.[23]

While Hatch and Croxton were watching the fords along the Tennessee

River, Colonel Horace Capron had marched his cavalry brigade out of Nashville on November 1, under orders to reinforce Croxton. Arriving at Pulaski, however, Capron was diverted to patrol the surrounding country-side and root out some of the guerrilla bands that infested Middle Tennessee.[24]

There was little likelihood that a major Confederate force could slip around to the east undetected, but Thomas was concerned about his right flank. Accordingly, Schofield was directed to patrol the western sector; he complied by sending Capron's brigade out to Waynesborough, about 40 miles west of Pulaski.[25] Massachusetts-born and in his sixtieth year, Horace Capron was not only the oldest field-grade officer in Wilson's corps and Thomas's army, he was one of the oldest in the entire Union Army. As a young man, Capron had failed to make it into West Point, though the rejection did nothing to deter him from success in other fields. Active in cotton manufacturing and scientific farming, he was later appointed Special Indian Agent for Texas by President Millard Fillmore. After the war, Capron achieved further recognition for his writings on agriculture and Japan.

At the outset of the Civil War, Capron had received an appointment as lieutenant colonel of the Fourteenth Illinois Cavalry. He had commanded a brigade under General George Stoneman during the latter's disastrous raid to Macon the past summer and, like most of the cavalry officers in the west, suffered from Sherman's often unjust criticism.[26] In terms of quality, Capron's brigade, composed of the Fourteenth and Sixteenth Illinois, Fifth Indiana, and Eighth Michigan Cavalry was probably the weakest unit in Wilson's corps. Most of the horses in the brigade were unshod and broken down, while the men were armed with antiquated Springfield muzzle loaders, which were all but impossible to reload while the trooper was mounted. One officer declared that "after the first volley [they] were about as serviceable [sic] to cavalry as a good club."[27]

By November 18, Capron had established headquarters near Waynes-borough and had skirmished with some of Colonel Edmund Rucker's Brigade of Forrest's cavalry. Part of Rucker's command had managed to get across the swollen Tennessee River at Perryville following the Johnsonville raid, but the balance of Forrest's command had remained west of the river, pushing on to join Hood at Florence.[28] Capron had to contend with a more immediate need. The surrounding countryside was destitute of forage; rations were low and none were available closer than Pulaski. On November 20, he advised Wilson of his plight:

> I shall be able to eke out our subsistence for a day or two longer by gathering in for twenty miles around everything eatable for man or beast. What with the impassable roads, incessant rains, heavy scouting, and the necessity for bringing in their forage, our horses are fast being made unserviceable and useless.[29]

Although Capron's brigade appears
to have been somewhat worse off
than Wilson's other units, Capron
did not have a monopoly on problems. On November 16, Hatch had
to request additional artillery support, as his own battery, the First
Illinois Light Artillery, had but one
pair of Rodman guns. Moreover,
Hatch had many detached troopers
who were uselessly occupied in rear
areas, so he asked that they be returned to their parent units, where
they were sorely needed. Hatch also
called Schofield's attention to the
fact that his division had been on
continuous duty for 48 days and on
light rations since leaving Pulaski
two weeks earlier.

Colonel Horace Capron (reproduced
from the Collections of the Library of
Congress).

Hatch, too, was having diffi-
culty foraging, although not to the extent that Capron seemed to be experiencing. Overall, Hatch thought that his animals were "looking well," but, he
told Wilson, "such marching nearly all the time in mud, has produced many
serious cases of scratches or grease heel, which is the most obstinate thing
we have to contend with."[30] With characteristic boasting, Hatch vowed that
if he only had another brigade of cavalry, "the enemy should not have an ear
of corn outside their infantry lines."[31] Hatch's Second Brigade commander,
Colonel Datus Ensign Coon, reported that due to the scarcity of blacksmiths
and blacksmith tools, "Many of the horses were shod by use of the common
pocket-knife and hatchet." Despite this, Coon reinforced Hatch's observation about the overall well being of the horses, saying that "horses, however,
improved as the forage obtained from the country was abundant."[32]

By November 18, Forrest had joined Hood and within 24 hours his
squadrons were across the Tennessee River, clearing the way for the main
Confederate advance. Forrest had at his disposal some 5,000 horsemen in
three divisions, commanded by brigadier generals James R. Chalmers,
William H. Jackson, and Abraham Buford. Each division, in turn, was com-
posed of two brigades. Chalmers's brigades were commanded by colonels
Edmund Rucker and J. B. Biffle; Jackson's by brigadier generals Frank C.
Armstrong and Lawrence Ross. Buford's brigade commanders were Brigadier
General Tyree H. Bell and Colonel Edward Crossland.[33]

Forrest's command, too, was jaded from much recent, hard campaigning and needed refitting as much or more than Wilson's brigades. The
difference here was that the Federals had the resources to eventually meet
their needs, though admittedly there was a logistical problem to be over-
come. On the other hand, the well had nearly run dry for the Confederates.
On November 19, the same day that Forrest's horsemen were crossing the
river, Coon's brigade moved west across Shoal Creek (a north-south–flowing
stream) on a routine reconnaissance and ran into a foraging party of
Crossland's Confederate Kentuckians. A sharp fight ensued, which resulted
in Coon capturing a number of prisoners and headquarter wagons. Presently,
however, Brigadier General Armstrong, who had begun his war service as
a Federal and switched sides after First Manassas, heard the din of battle
and rushed his brigade forward to support the Kentuckians. After quickly
checking Coon's advance, Armstrong then drove the Federals back across
Shoal Creek, recapturing 40 prisoners, in addition to the wagons.[34]

On November 21, Hood issued a rousing message to his troops, proclaiming the start of the Tennessee campaign:

> Soldiers: You march to-day to redeem by your valor and your arms
> one of the fairest portions of our Confederacy. This can only
> be achieved by battle and by victory. Summon up in behalf of a
> consummation so glorious all the elements of soldiership and all
> the instincts of manhood, and you will render the campaign before
> you full of auspicious fruit to your country and lasting renown to
> yourselves.[35]

The northward movement was in three roughly parallel columns. Major
General Benjamin F. Cheatham's corps on the left, marching via Waynesborough, Lieutenant General Alexander P. Stewart's corps on the right,
heading toward Lawrenceburg, while Lieutenant General Stephen D. Lee
marched his corps between the other two. Forrest and his escort along with
Chalmers's division covered the army's left flank, marching via Mount Henry
and Pleasantville. The divisions of William Jackson and Abraham Buford
moved toward Lawrenceburg, then east toward Pulaski.[36]

As the Confederate northward movement began to develop, Hatch
reported to Schofield on November 20 that he believed the enemy would
move to Lawrenceburg, intending to interdict the road between Pulaski and
Nashville. In view of this, Schofield directed Hatch to move against Forrest,
keeping on his right flank, to prevent the Pulaski-Nashville road from being
cut. Schofield promised to have infantry support at either Lynnville or
Columbia. Schofield doubted that Forrest could get across the Duck River
below Columbia, but he was concerned about the railroad. "We must try to
prevent him from striking the railroad between Columbia and this place

[Pulaski]," Schofield told Hatch.[37] Accordingly, Hatch concentrated Croxton's brigade at Lexington. If it appeared that the Confederate movements were to threaten Pulaski, Hatch would respond accordingly. He and Schofield were both concerned, though, that Forrest could swing around his right flank unobserved. Indeed, Hatch thought Forrest might already have done so. If not, however, Hatch planned to guard against such a contingency by moving north.[38]

In the face of Hood's advance, Hatch retired slowly, first to Lexington, then to Lawrenceburg, 17 miles west of Pulaski, where he was attacked on November 22 by Armstrong's brigade. The fight was a sharp, all-day affair; Hatch managed to hold his line until dark, when he was finally turned out of position and forced back toward Pulaski.[39]

This action at Lawrenceburg marked the beginning of an eight-day race, replete with skirmishing and often severe fighting. As Thomas's senior deputy in the field, Schofield's objective was to delay the Confederate advance until Thomas was ready for a confrontation. For the moment, at least, the Confederates had the initiative. Hood, however, seems to have been unaware of his temporary advantage. Unfortunately for the Confederate cause, the vigor of Hood's northward movement failed to match the boldness of his vision. Stonewall Jackson he was not.[40]

As Schofield sifted through reports and attempted to divine Hood's intentions, he concluded that given the condition of the roads, his opponent would be unable to make much progress very quickly. Forrest, too, he thought, would be preoccupied with simply covering ground rather than looking for a fight.[41] Such thinking no doubt contributed to Schofield's sense of security, but did not leave the Ohioan entirely without concern. If Hood did somehow manage to get around his flank and cut him off at Columbia, 50 miles south of Nashville, there would be the devil to pay. Schofield's fear was that Hood could steal a march to Lawrenceburg before he knew what was happening. Accordingly, on November 20, Schofield expressed his views and concerns to Thomas, recommending a concentration at Lynnville on the railroad.

Thomas agreed and authorized the withdrawal. To avoid the appearance of desperation and panic, Schofield did not initiate his retirement for another 48 hours, starting Cox's division back on the twenty-second, followed by Stanley on November 23.[42] At the same time that he authorized Schofield's withdrawal, Thomas ordered Brigadier General R. S. Granger to evacuate the Athens-Huntsville-Decatur triangle and concentrate his command at the Stevenson, Tennessee, railhead, 100 rail miles southeast of Nashville. Hood's future movements would dictate where Granger would move from that point.[43]

As the Federals retired toward Lynnville, Forrest, with characteristic aggressiveness, had his troops swarming along the line of advance, nicely cloaking Hood's movements and seizing the initiative from Wilson's cavalry. For the time being, the Federals were on the defensive. Wilson's horsemen, outnumbered at this stage of the campaign, were backpedaling, doing their best to protect the flanks and prevent Forrest from sweeping around behind them.

Schofield also ordered the pontoon bridges across the Duck River prepared for defense, just in case Forrest did put in an appearance. Schofield expected that Capron's brigade would act as a deterrent against a swing around the left by Forrest. Shortly, though, Schofield received a two-day-old report from Capron, who was still in the vicinity of Waynesborough, that caused him some alarm. Stunned, Schofield fired back an answer, clarifying the role he expected Capron to play. He wrote,

> You seem to have entirely misunderstood your instructions, and I fully expect to hear of the capture of your command. Move back at once toward Mount Pleasant as far as the intersection of the Lawrenceburg Road, and from that point scout toward Lawrenceburg and Waynesborough and on the lateral roads.[44]

Capron promptly defended his actions, saying that he had remained in the vicinity of Waynesborough as long as he did because of forage and rations. Besides, he had observed no enemy movements in the area, save for the usual guerrilla activity.[45]

From the Federal perspective, this initial phase of Hood's Tennessee campaign was a welter of confusion and uncertainty. The Federal response to Confederate movements during this period (either known or suspected) is perhaps best understood by keeping in mind that assessments and decisions were made at three levels: first, at the upper level, by Thomas in Nashville; second, by Schofield and Wilson at the intermediate level; and finally, at the tactical level by the unit commanders who were actually engaging the enemy. Due to lag time between a report being sent, received, and answered, reactions were often out of sync with directives. Schofield himself was largely stationary (at least as the campaign got under way), but Wilson's unit commanders were almost continuously on the move, operating independently, miles removed from each other and Schofield. It was very much a "play it by ear" situation. The whole business was made worse by abominable weather. Cold rain, sleet, and sometimes snow created atrocious operating conditions for both sides. Roads were often little more than channels of mud, which later froze and made passage slow and difficult for wagons and artillery, and treacherous for horses.

In Nashville, Thomas attempted to fashion an appropriate overall strategy, given the often conflicting reports and rumors that reached him. With the most recent developments, Schofield was authorized to fall back from Pulaski to either Lynnville or Columbia as circumstances dictated. The important thing was to avoid getting cut off.[46]

At noon on November 21, Schofield advised Thomas that he would be moving to Lynnville with two divisions the next morning, leaving General Stanley behind in Pulaski with the other two divisions as a precaution against a raid by Forrest. Should it develop that Hood was advancing with his entire army, as it appeared likely he would, Stanley would fall back to Lynnville. By evening, the picture was clarified when Schofield received Hatch's 8 A.M. report, advising that Hood seemed to be heading for Columbia.[47]

Hatch, meanwhile, had reached Lawrenceburg late on the cold, snowy afternoon of November 21. During the night the temperature dropped and by 8 A.M. the ground was frozen rock-hard when Coon's pickets were attacked and driven back by Armstrong's brigade of Jackson's division. The fighting continued throughout the day. By midafternoon, one of Armstrong's batteries had succeeded in shelling Hatch out of town. Having little in the way of artillery support, Hatch could offer no counter battery fire. He retired east toward Pulaski before turning north to Campbellsville, still aiming to keep the Confederates from getting around his right flank.

Back in Nashville, Major Beaumont continued with the myriad organizational tasks of the new cavalry corps. On November 22, the same day Wilson had departed for the front, Beaumont brought his chief up to date on recent developments. Brigadier General Louis D. Watkins's freshly remounted Third Brigade of McCook's division, was reported en route from Louisville, though Beaumont did not expect it to arrive in time to participate in the current campaign. However, the Eleventh and Seventh Ohio Cavalry, respectively, 1,100 and 600 men strong, were expected to march for the front on the twenty-sixth.

That same afternoon, Wilson wired a series of orders to the indefatigable Beaumont. Brigadier General John Hammond was to be assigned to the command of a brigade that included the unassigned Indiana regiments, together with Fourth Tennessee. Beaumont was also directed to request Thomas to have General Granger return the cavalry detachments under his command. Captain John Green, one of the two Special Inspectors of Cavalry assigned to the corps, was instructed to work around the clock if necessary to have the Tenth and Twelfth Tennessee Cavalry regiments ready to send to Hatch. Wilson also wanted the Fourth U.S. Regulars sent directly to him as quickly as could be managed. Finally, Wilson told Beaumont to have Brigadier General Richard W. Johnson take command of the brigades of Capron and Hammond until such time as General Knipe arrived.[48]

Despite the demands of an unfolding campaign and the turmoil of formalizing a new corps organization, to say nothing of assigning units and requisitioning equipment, Beaumont also managed to find time to finalize the design and color schemes for division and brigade flags and badges, previously approved by Wilson. The new design and scheme was officialized in General Order Number 3. The corps flag would be a scarlet swallowtail, four by six feet, featuring crossed yellow sabers. Division flags—a slightly smaller, white swallowtail—would have crossed blue sabers and scarlet block letters identifying the division directly above the sabers. Brigade flags would be slightly smaller than that of the parent division, with a varying color scheme depending on the brigade number, and an identifying number below the crossed sabers.[49]

For the Federals, defending against the Confederate advance grew increasingly difficult. Circumstances changed almost on an hourly basis. On November 23, Schofield advised Thomas that he had heard nothing from Hatch or Wilson and was falling back from Lynnville to Campbellsville, where he expected to find Hatch. By 10:30 that night, however, he reported that Wilson had arrived, and there had been a communiqué from Hatch, who was of the opinion that Hood's infantry was marching from Lewisburg to Columbia.[50]

The same day, Beaumont gave Wilson a further update on progress. Colonel Robert R. Stewart of the Eleventh Indiana had been ordered to depart for Columbia on the twenty-fourth. Detachments belonging to Croxton's brigade were being readied as quickly as possible. Beaumont thought they were excellent troops. A supply of much-needed forage was due to arrive that night and division wagon trains were being readied on a priority basis. Beaumont concluded his report by saying he hoped Wilson would "give Forrest a small whirl on the Winchester style."[51]

From the junction of the Mount Pleasant and Lewisburg roads, where he had relocated his brigade pursuant to Schofield's orders, Capron advised Schofield on the twenty-third that he was scouting the right flank and had so far uncovered little enemy activity. Capron also reported that he had finally contacted Hatch. He sent a second communiqué to Hatch, advising the latter that his scout from Waynesborough in all directions had revealed no sign of the enemy in strength.[52]

On the morning of November 23, Hatch, continuing his retrograde, ordered Croxton, whose brigade had been in reserve the past 24 hours, to handle the rear guard assignment. In a day-long fight that subsequently developed, Croxton's brigade turned in another creditable performance before rejoining Hatch on the road to Campbellsville, 15 miles north of Pulaski.[53]

Moving out of Campbellsville the following morning, Hatch's leading brigade, consisting of the Third and Seventh Illinois and the Twelfth Missouri Cavalry, Colonel Oliver Wells commanding, was surprised by Buford's division. Wells recovered, however, and retaliated sharply, driving Buford back two miles. The fighting was intense (the Missourians alone lost 50 troopers) and Wells found himself overpowered and in trouble.[54]

Hatch's position here was critical. Five miles north of Campbellsville, the road bisected the Nashville and Decatur Railroad at Lynnville, midway between Pulaski and Columbia. If Forrest secured the road at Lynnville, Hood would be in an excellent position to interpose along Schofield's line of retirement. Accordingly, Hatch ordered Coon's brigade to hold the road until Wells could be recalled. Forming a north-south line facing west, Coon's troopers were barely in position before they came under strong fire. As the pace increased, Coon discovered that the Confederates were attempting to gain a foothold on the road below his position. The Second Iowa and Ninth Illinois regiments were rushed in to counter the move, but the hour belonged to Ross's Texans of Jackson's division, who shortly compelled Hatch to withdraw toward Lynnville.

Two miles beyond Campbellsville, the road wound through a narrow gorge where Hatch's column was seriously threatened when Coon's flank guards were driven in. Hatch himself barely escaped capture thanks to the quick thinking of his escort commander, Captain Elijah T. Phillips. Reacting quickly, Hatch ordered the nearest regiment, which happened to be the Ninth Illinois, to hold the gorge until the division had passed through. Fortunately for Hatch, the Ninth was a crack outfit. "They fight like devils," Hatch declared, proclaiming them the best regiment in the division.[55]

At 10 P.M., Hatch advised Thomas that he was four miles from Campbellsville, having been skirmishing most of the day. Croxton, he said, had reported being attacked by infantry. Despite what both Hatch and Croxton believed, they had not been up against infantry, but Forrest's troopers.[56]

On the twenty-fourth, Thomas telegraphed Schofield, asking if he had heard anything about Capron having been driven back by superior numbers. Still forced to contend with questionable news of enemy movements, Thomas said that still another report had a large part of Forrest's command already across the Duck River. This second report must have caused Thomas real concern; if it was true, it meant that Schofield was in some jeopardy. The report was not entirely without foundation. Fortunately, however, Schofield had already reached Columbia. His advance, the Third Division of the Twenty-third Corps under General Jacob Dolson Cox, a future governor of Ohio, had arrived at 7:30 A.M., following a hard march in the bone-chilling blackness. Cox had arrived just in time to beat back Forrest's horsemen who had surprised Capron's brigade and had driven it, reeling, back to Columbia.

What had happened was this: shortly after his communiqué of November 23 reporting an absence of enemy activity, Capron encountered Rucker's brigade near Henryville, a dozen miles northwest of Lawrenceburg. With their antiquated muzzle-loaders, Capron's troopers were no match for Rucker's command and were quickly driven back to Fouche Springs, on the road to Mount Pleasant, where Capron hoped to make a stand. By this time, however, Chalmers, accompanied by Forrest himself, arrived on the scene and Forrest, sensing a splendid opportunity, prepared to execute the kind of bold tactical maneuver that had made him the anathema of Federal commanders in the west.

With Rucker applying pressure from the front, Capron's command had fallen back to Fouche Springs, where the brigade planned to bivouac for the night, believing that for the moment that they were secure, although the pickets were still skirmishing with Rucker's advance. Forrest was up to something, naturally. Sending his old regiment, now commanded by Lieutenant Colonel David C. Kelley, around the Federal left, Forrest and his 80-man escort dashed around the Yankee's right flank.

Gaining the rear and completely undetected, Forrest suddenly swooped down on Capron's unsuspecting troops, many of whom were already in the process of preparing the night's bivouac. The surprise was complete, despite the fact that Kelley had somehow gotten lost and Forrest had to get the job done with only his escort, which, as it turned out, was quite sufficient. Forrest reported jubilantly, "I made the charge upon the enemy with my escort along producing a perfect stampede, capturing about fifty prisoners, twenty horses and one ambulance."[57]

In the meantime, Rucker, hearing the sounds of battle, advanced against the center of Capron's line, which quickly dissolved. Shortly, the entire Federal brigade was in full rout, bolting right through Forrest's escort in the process. By Forrest's order, Rucker rested his command until 1 A.M., then took up the pursuit. Hard on Capron's heels, he swept through Mount Pleasant, capturing 35,000 rounds of small-arms ammunition. He finally caught up with his quarry seven miles from Columbia, where Capron had reformed for another stand. Major Henry C. Connelly, Fourteenth Illinois Cavalry, described the action that followed:

> I was with the rear guard on the occasion referred to; it fell back and found the brigade in good position in line of battle. I rode to General Capron and expressed the opinion that he could not hold his position a moment against the troops pressing us in the rear and on the flanks, which we could easily see advancing rapidly to attack us. General Capron replied that he had been ordered to make a decided stand if it sacrificed every man in his brigade; that we must hold the advancing forces in check to enable the infantry to

arrive and get in position. I replied, "We are destroyed and captured if we remain here." At this moment General Capron gave the
order to retire. While passing through a long lane south of
Columbia, Forrest's forces charged the brigade in rear and on both
flanks with intrepid courage. Our command was confined to a narrow lane, with men and horses in the highest state of excitement.
We were armed with Springfield rifles, which after the first volley
were about as serviceable to a cavalryman thus hemmed in as a
good club. The men could not reload while mounted, in the excitement of horses as well as soldiers. The only thing that could be done
was to get out as promptly as possible, and before Forrest's forces
should close in and capture the command.[58]

Chagrined at having Capron's brigade on the ropes and failing to destroy
it, Forrest dogged the retreating Federals into Columbia. Fortunately for
Capron, the leading elements of Schofield's army, the Third Division of the
Twenty-third Corps, was just then approaching Columbia. The Third's
commander, Major General Cox, heard the fighting to the west and promptly
moved to Capron's support, a timely move as it turned out. Not only did
Cox rescue the Federal horsemen, but his quick-thinking action also secured
the vital Duck River crossings at Columbia for Schofield.[59]

Since the onset of Hood's advance, the Federal line had been pushed
back some 30 miles; it rested along the south bank of the Duck River.
Thomas had hoped he would be ready to assume the offensive by this time,
but such expectations hinged on the arrival of A. J. Smith, who, Thomas
had been assured, would leave St. Louis by November 10. As it worked out,
however, Smith's advance did not even reach St. Louis until the twenty-
fourth, by which time Hood was already threatening Columbia.

So, the first phase of Hood's invasion might be said to have ended with
Schofield safe at Columbia, but concerned about the immediate future. As
for Hood, he was shortly to receive a telegram from General Beauregard,
advising him that Sherman was definitely advancing toward the coast, no
doubt to reinforce Grant. Accordingly, said Beauregard, it was essential that
Hood "should take offensive and crush enemy's force in middle Tennessee
soon as practicable, to relieve Lee."[60]

Five
Columbia to Franklin

I do not know where Forrest is; he may have gone east, but, no doubt will strike our flank and rear again soon. Wilson is entirely unable to cope with him. —Schofield to Thomas, Franklin, Tennessee, November 30, 1864.[1]

On reaching Columbia, Wilson deployed his brigades on both flanks of the Federal line. With a total force of just under 4,500 troopers, however, he lacked the strength to adequately cover all of the river crossings, so attention was focused on the most likely spots.

Schofield's primary concern was a movement around the Federal left (east) flank. Accordingly, the bulk of Wilson's command fanned out to the east to cover the river crossings and roads above Columbia. Hatch and Croxton were stationed some six miles east on the road to Shelbyville, while Capron, reinforced at first by the Fifth Iowa under Major J. Morris Young and later by the Seventh Ohio commanded by Colonel Israel Garrard, were posted at Rally Hill on the Lewisburg Pike. Hatch was further directed to send his first brigade under Colonel Robert R. Stewart to patrol the fords above Columbia and send a detachment of the Sixth Illinois under Captain William D. Glass on a reconnaissance toward Shelbyville.[2] Brigadier General Richard W. Johnson's arrival from Pulaski on November 24 gave Wilson an opportunity to create a Sixth Division, which for the time being would consist of Croxton's brigade, together with Horace Capron's reinforced command.[3]

In addition to affording Wilson an opportunity to reorganize and reposition some of his units, the brief 48-hour respite at Columbia also provided one of the campaign's lighter moments. While inspecting Croxton's brigade, he discovered that the Second Michigan Cavalry was commanded by a woman. Upon questioning Croxton, Wilson learned that the woman was the wife of the regimental commander Lieutenant Colonel Benjamin F. Smith and had been with the regiment for some time. Such zeal was most commendable, Wilson declared, but the woman would have to go. Much to Croxton's relief and over Mrs. Smith's indignant protests, Wilson directed that she be relieved from further service and returned to Nashville at once.[4]

While he prepared for Hood's next move, Wilson continued to fire off and receive organizational memos from Beaumont. On the twenty-fifth, Wilson directed Beaumont not to delay sending units to the front as long as they were at least of regimental size. Regiments were not to be broken up, but Beaumont need not concern himself with organization beyond that level. Wilson would make dispositions once they arrived. All units sent to the front should be well supplied with ammunition. General Grierson, commanding the Cavalry Corps, District of West Tennessee, was ordered to have his units made ready at St. Louis, rather than waiting until they reached Nashville.[5]

On the same day, Beaumont issued Special Order Number 20, directing Colonel Thomas J. Harrison, Eighth Indiana Cavalry, to report to Wilson for duty; Brigadier General John Hammond was directed to take command of a temporary brigade consisting of the Fourth Tennessee and Ninth Indiana Cavalry.[6] Thomas, meanwhile, continued to receive updates from his field commanders and reacted accordingly. On November 25, General Granger reported from Huntsville that both Athens and Decatur had been evacuated. To the Federal command in Nashville, it seemed that Hood was preparing to concentrate on Middle Tennessee, but Thomas remained concerned about threatening moves elsewhere. Accordingly, Major General John B. Steedman in Chattanooga was ordered to have 5,000 men ready to respond in the event that Hood tried to cut the Nashville-Chattanooga Railroad.[7]

As far as Thomas was concerned, the key ingredient in his own strategy was still A. J. Smith's infantry, the leading elements of which were due to reach Nashville within 48 hours. The main body was en route somewhere between St. Louis and Paducah. It couldn't be soon enough to suit Thomas; the delay was giving him fits.[8] In addition to Smith, the reinforcements from the Mississippi region also included the cavalry brigade of Colonel Edward F. Winslow, which was part of Grierson's division and had been over in Missouri along with Smith's Sixteenth Corps. Smith was on his way, but Winslow was reported to still be in Missouri.[9]

On the twenty-sixth, Thomas received word from Schofield to the effect that Confederate infantry had been seen on the Lewisburg Pike southeast of Columbia. Any available infantry units should be sent to him promptly, Schofield said, adding that "I have drawn my force in the interior line [at Columbia], and will fight him there."[10]

By mid-afternoon of November 26, Wilson advised Schofield that he had set up headquarters near Rally Hill, 15 miles east of Columbia. Croxton and Capron continued to monitor the crossings of the Duck River toward Lewisburg, while Stewart's brigade and some of Jacob Cox's infantry were watching the situation west of Columbia.

Putting a large body of men, vehicles, and animals across a river is a dangerous and tricky proposition, one that every army in history has had to deal with. The many studies of Civil War campaigns have probably failed to develop as fully as they should an appreciation of the difficulties inherent in a large army crossing a major river. As far as the Duck River was concerned, there were a number of fords both east and west of Columbia. Some of these fords were more suitable than others, but, although the weather was improving and the river was falling, heavy rains had made the roads leading to many of the fords nearly impassable. On the afternoon of November 26, for example, General R. W. Johnson advised Wilson that a detachment of the Eighth Michigan Cavalry reported that the road to the crossing of the Lewisburg Pike at Duck River was "very bad ... and impassable for wagons and artillery." Furthermore, the report added, "the fords where the main roads cross Duck River are [also] deep and mostly impassable."[11]

While his patrols watched the river crossings, Wilson continued shuffling regiments around, trying to bring his command up to the kind of fighting standard that he felt was imperative to meet not only the exigencies of the moment, but those of the future as well. Of all the things that Wilson worked to achieve within his corps, none was more important than uniformity of weapons. In the weeks following the Franklin-Nashville campaign, this matter would be addressed vigorously. For the moment, however, the units in the field had to make do with what they had, which included Maynards, Sharps, Colts, and Spencers.

Although the Federal cavalry had thus far fought bravely enough, Forrest still had the best of things. In fairness, it should be pointed out that Forrest had the initiative because Hood did. Moreover, in this beginning phase of the campaign, the Confederates had the advantage of greater numbers for both infantry and cavalry. Finally, Wilson was new to his command—he had been on the job only one month—and had not had an opportunity to develop the kind of infrastructure, the kind of close-knit working relationship with his units that Forrest had long ago established.

Fortunately, Wilson was blessed with an able crop of subordinates. With the exception of John Hammond, all were veteran cavalrymen and, like Wilson, realized the latent potential of the western cavalry. They knew what their troops were capable of accomplishing, given the right leadership and organization, and they were anxious to work toward the fulfillment of that potential. Hammond and Hatch were the only two members of the group Wilson had known previously, remembering both men from Vicksburg days. Hatch had impressed him then as a leader of mounted troops. In fact, Wilson considered Hatch a better cavalry officer than the more celebrated Grierson.[12]

Edward Hatch had acquired a reputation as something of a braggart, but his determination, daring, and enterprising style more than made up for any boasting he may have done. Hatch reportedly once remarked that "he would be willing to die if he could "have the command of Sheridan's cavalry for just one day." In response, one of his staff officers inquired if Hatch "wouldn't like to live just another day to brag about it?"[13]

John Hammond had been a long-time member of Sherman's staff. Born in New York, he began his military career as a private in the Fifth California Volunteer Infantry and rose through the ranks to be brevetted brigadier general barely a month before. When illness prevented him from accompanying Sherman on the march to the sea, he was sent back to Nashville to recuperate. Recovering, he requested and was assigned to a cavalry command under Wilson. Though lacking experience as a field commander, his determination to turn in a good performance made him a valuable subordinate.[14]

Thirty-seven-year-old Richard W. Johnson was an old-line regular and a veteran of both infantry and cavalry service. Johnson's family had moved from Virginia to Kentucky just prior to his birth, providing yet another illustration of the divided loyalty frequently found in the border states. Johnson's older brother was then serving as a surgeon in the Confederate army, but R. W. was a solid Union man and a good officer. Wilson, in fact, considered him his best subordinate: "General Johnson is the best commander I have with me," he told Beaumont.[15]

Colonel Thomas J. Harrison had previously commanded the Eighth Indiana Cavalry and for a time was missing in action during a raid on the Atlanta railway system the past summer. He was just now reporting back to duty. Originally, Harrison was assigned to command Hatch's first brigade, but was later named to replace Capron. Finally, to complete the reshuffling, Colonel Robert R. Stewart, Eleventh Indiana, was named to replace Colonel Oliver Wells, Twelfth Missouri, as head of Hatch's first brigade.

In the meantime, the delay in getting A. J. Smith's Sixteenth Corps to Nashville had necessitated a change in strategy. Thomas had hoped to try to contain Hood south of Duck River until Smith arrived. "If you can hold Hood in check until I can get Smith up, we can whip him," Thomas told Schofield in a November 27 dispatch.[16] Thomas remained uncertain, though, as to Hood's future movements. "If Hood moves on the Chattanooga road I will send Smith to Murfreesborough," he told Schofield, who was growing increasingly uncomfortable on the south side of the river. Fearing his line was spread too thin,

Brigadier General Richard W. Johnson (reproduced from the Collections of the Library of Congress).

and with Thomas's blessing, Schofield prepared to evacuate Columbia. Originally, he planned to cross the river on the twenty-sixth, but heavy rains caused the move to be aborted, though not before Schofield's personal baggage wagon was upset and the contents soaked. The effort was repeated the next night with more success; by the morning of November 28 Schofield had his army drawn up in new positions along the north bank of the Duck River.[17]

Hood, meanwhile, had failed to catch Schofield south of the river. He had lost round one, not so much because of what his opponent had done, but because of his own less-than-energetic advance. Even so, he was still in a position to cut off his old classmate, though time was rapidly slipping away.

What Hood proposed to do was make a demonstration against Schofield's center, while simultaneously slipping around his opponent's left flank and thereby placing his army between Schofield and Nashville. Two divisions of Stephen Lee's corps, together with most of the artillery, would demonstrate against the Federal center, while Cheatham and Stewart, supported by Forrest's cavalry, executed the flanking movement.[18] Forrest put the plan in motion on November 28, with Chalmers crossing the river at Carr's Mills, seven miles east of Columbia, and Jackson at Holland's Ford, a few miles farther upstream. Buford, on the extreme right, crossed at the junction of the Lewisburg Pike, while Forrest and his escort crossed at Owen's Ford.[19]

By mid-morning of November 28, Croxton and Capron mistakenly reported Confederate infantry crossing at Huey's Mill. Wilson was incredulous. "I can scarcely credit this though will find out at once," he informed Schofield. By mid-afternoon, he had learned that it was Forrest's cavalry that was crossing in force and driving back his pickets. In view of this development, Wilson decided to concentrate at Rally Hill and so advised Schofield at 2 P.M. Ten minutes later, he followed this with a second dispatch, elaborating on the earlier report and requesting that Schofield direct Stewart's brigade to rejoin the cavalry corps from his patrol position west of Columbia.[20]

By late afternoon, the Federal horsemen had not been able to thwart Forrest's advance and, indeed, were being roughly handled. At 4:30 P.M. Wilson advised Schofield that the Confederates were across the river in force and were apparently bound for Spring Hill. "You had better look out for that place," Wilson warned Schofield, advising him that he was aiming to concentrate his brigades at Hurt's Crossroads, just north of Rally Hill on the Lewisburg Pike, by nightfall.[21]

The situation had changed in two hours, prompting Wilson to ask Schofield to have Stewart and Hammond join him by way of Spring Hill, a route that would offer less chance of running into Hood's infantry. Now certain that there was little to be feared from a Confederate movement around the army's right flank, Wilson wanted all of his brigades on hand.[22]

In truth, the situation on the Federal left was more than a little worrisome. Not only were the Confederates across the river in force, but they had come booming and one of Wilson's brigades had narrowly escaped disaster in the process. Once again, as it had been during the race for Columbia, it was Capron's brigade that was the victim. Hatch and Johnson commenced their retirement toward Hurt's Crossroads, pursuant to Wilson's plan, but as Johnson reached the Lewisburg Pike about dusk, he encountered the Seventh Ohio and portions of the Fourteenth and Sixteenth Illinois of Capron's brigade in full retreat.

What happened was that Capron, still on the south side of the river and watching the ford at Hardison's Mill, had been driven across the river. He had also been left isolated when Hatch and Croxton pulled back from the river crossings to the west of his position. This left a wide gap for Forrest's troops, Ross's Texans in particular, to surprise the rear elements of Capron's brigade and send it reeling north. Left behind were elements of the Eighth Michigan, Fourteenth and Sixteenth Illinois, and the Fifth Iowa Cavalry, commanded by Major J. Morris Young.

As Capron's brigade streamed back in disorder, General R. W. Johnson, having just arrived on the scene, quickly took charge. Deploying Croxton's brigade across the pike, Johnson then sent a company of nearby Ohioans back down the road to stall the expected Confederate pursuit. His quick thinking on this occasion was a good illustration of why Wilson held Johnson in such high esteem.

The pursuit anticipated by Johnson, however, failed to materialize, due in part to the Confederate preoccupation with the fragments of Capron's brigade left at the river, who now found their way blocked by Ross's Texans. Undaunted, Young managed to fight his way through to the safety of Johnson's lines in one of the really stirring episodes of the campaign. Young wrote:

> As soon as the enemy's fire was drawn the dismounted men were to immediately fall back, mount and follow out the Fifth Iowa Cavalry, which was to go through with sabers. In fifteen minutes, these dispositions being completed, the command was given "forward." In fifteen minutes more we struck the enemy in line barricaded and posted in outhouses and buildings just evacuated by Colonel Capron. We received their fire and instantly sounded the "charge," riding them down and scattering them in all directions. At 10 P.M. I reported the brigade entire to Major General Wilson.[23]

Wilson's failure to anticipate how vulnerable Capron would be when Hatch and Johnson were pulled back from the river crossings, and left him isolated and exposed, was a costly oversight. Fortunately for the young Federal commander, the Confederates did not take advantage of the situation as they might have, thanks to the bold action of J. Morris Young and R. W. Johnson's prompt and cool response.

The withdrawal from Duck River also witnessed another light moment of the campaign. Wilson, a confirmed teetotaler, discovered that one of his officers had been imbibing. A check soon produced a sergeant with a large demijohn of whiskey. Wilson promptly ordered the man to

> dash it down, which he proceeded to do with a cheerful "Aye, aye, sir," just as the column was passing down the slope of a hill where the stone was laid bare. The crash and jingle of the glass, audible to the entire staff, was followed by frowns and by silence which were ominous, but it was soon evident that there was no more liquor left in the column.[24]

While Wilson dealt with the crisis in his quarter, a nervous Schofield was attempting to get a clear picture of what was happening and what he ought to be doing. Indeed, if Hood's old classmate was a little edgy, it would not be surprising. Schofield's mission was to stall until Smith showed up, which Thomas kept saying was imminent. Knowing this and knowing that Hood had the advantage in numbers for the moment, Schofield played his cards close to the vest. He would fight if necessary, but until Smith arrived, he believed it prudent not to risk more than was absolutely necessary. So the idea was to hold and delay, but not too long. Timing was critical. If Hood was able to cut him off, it would be all over; Wilson's assessment of the situation suggested that this was the way things were shaping up.

Despite the urgency of Wilson's report, however, Schofield was still uncertain whether the enemy troops crossing the river were infantry or just cavalry; therein lay his immediate quandary. He was inclined to believe they were cavalry, but if he assumed infantry and began a general retirement toward Franklin to avoid being flanked, his brigades, strung out along the pike, would be vulnerable to an attack from both rear and flank if all this proved to be only a feint on Hood's part. The question was how long should he wait?

At mid-morning on November 28, even as Wilson's pickets were reporting Confederate activity at the fords east of Columbia, Thomas forwarded to Schofield a communiqué he had received from Grant the night before, stating that Savannah newspapers were reporting how Forrest would soon be harassing Sherman, a report that Wilson's troops would no doubt have found wryly amusing. Thomas added that if this proved to be true, Grant wanted him to take the offensive against Hood, a refrain that would become all too familiar to Thomas over the next two weeks.[25]

As the day progressed, Schofield updated Thomas as to the state of affairs, reporting first that the Confederates were crossing the Duck River in force near the Lewisburg Pike. This news was followed at 4 P.M. by a somewhat odd communiqué in which Schofield asked where Thomas proposed to fight if the Confederates continued their advance along the Lewisburg

Pike. No doubt Schofield was simply asking where we would make our stand in that event, but the wording was curious and more than anything else probably reflected the Ohioan's mounting uneasiness.[26] Schofield was certain that his position here at Columbia would soon prove untenable, necessitating a withdrawal to Franklin, 25 miles south of Nashville. The wagon bridge across the Harpeth River at that place had been washed away, leaving only the railroad bridge which was not at all suitable for moving wagons across. "Wouldn't it be well to replace [the wagon bridge] with pontoons?" he asked Thomas, who replied in the affirmative, directing Schofield to send the pontoons he used at Columbia on ahead to Franklin.[27]

At 6 P.M., Schofield informed Thomas that Confederate cavalry had captured Rally Hill. Wilson, he said, was attempting to reach the Franklin Pike before they did, but had warned Schofield that the enemy might be aiming to get between them at Spring Hill. It might be "well to send A. J. Smith's force to that place," Schofield suggested to Thomas.

Thomas, who was still hoping to get his entire force together before attempting to seize the initiative from Hood, responded at 8 P.M.

> If you are confident you can hold your present position, I wish you to do so until I can get General Smith here. After his arrival we can withdraw gradually across Duck River and fall upon him with our whole force, or wait until Wilson can organize his entire cavalry force, and then withdraw from your present position. Should Hood then cross the river we can surely ruin him.[28]

The lag time in communications continued to at least prove confusing, if not to complicate the decision-making process. Schofield's late afternoon dispatch regarding Wilson's efforts to drive back the enemy who had crossed the river was apparently misplaced or delivered late. Accordingly, Thomas did not have an opportunity to respond to it until after his 8 P.M. communiqué to Schofield, who likely now felt that his situation was a little better understood. "If Wilson cannot succeed in driving back the enemy, *should it prove true he has crossed the river*" (emphasis added), Thomas told Schofield, "you will necessarily have to make preparations to take up a new position at Franklin, behind Harpeth, immediately, if it becomes necessary to fall back."[29]

As subsequent events were shortly to demonstrate, November 29, 1864, proved a memorable day in the history of the Civil War. With Wilson's pickets pushed back from the river line by Forrest's cavalry, Hood's engineers began laying pontoon bridges at Huey's Mill and Davis's Ford, some five miles east of Columbia, during the night of the twenty-eighth. By dawn, the job was finished and by mid-morning nearly 20,000 veterans of Cheatham's and

Stewart's corps were across the Duck River and marching north, aiming for Spring Hill. Hood himself, strapped to the saddle, rode with the lead division. The day itself had come on splendidly, too: bright and pleasant, a welcome relief from what they had had to do their soldiering in of late. Behind them in Columbia remained the corps of Stephen Lee (minus one division), together with most of the army's artillery, which even now was maintaining a steady if desultory fire against the Federal position. Lee's assignment was to keep Schofield in the dark and, it was hoped, tied down while Hood and the main body executed the flanking movement.[30]

There was little sleep the night of November 28-29 for either Thomas, Schofield, or Wilson. At 1 A.M. Wilson fired off a dispatch to Schofield from Hurt's Crossroads reporting that the enemy's cavalry was across the river and that his infantry would soon follow on pontoon bridges. "I think it very clear that they are aiming for Franklin," he advised Schofield, "and that you ought to get to Spring Hill by 10 A.M.... Get back to Franklin without delay," he added, closing his dispatch in a tone that bordered on being peremptory.[31] At 3:30 A.M. Schofield received a communiqué from Thomas, advising him that his dispatches of 6 and 9 P.M. the previous day had been received. In view of the present circumstances, Thomas wanted Schofield to withdraw to Franklin, delaying Hood as much as possible until he was safely entrenched at Franklin. Smith had still not arrived, Thomas added.[32]

The arrival of daybreak on this same pleasant autumn morning witnessed Hood's infantry crossing the river on their newly laid pontoon bridges. Schofield, troubled by Wilson's reports of a Confederate flanking movement but still feeling uncertain about the situation, ordered a strong infantry reconnaissance of the river line above Columbia. By mid-morning, the reconnaissance had confirmed the presence of Confederate infantry north of the Duck River, which called for prompt action on the part of the Federals.[33] Even as the infantry reconnaissance was on its way to check out the situation to the east, Stanley, pursuant to Schofield's orders, had started up the Franklin Pike toward Spring Hill. He had with him the divisions of brigadier generals George D. Wagner and Nathan Kimball with some 900 wagons and 40 pieces of artillery.[34]

Around noon, however, after learning that Hood's infantry was across the river in force, Schofield directed Stanley to have Kimball's division, the second in line of march, halted at Rutherford's Creek and faced east as a precaution against a flank attack.[35] Right at that moment, the Federal army was in a somewhat awkward position with half of it en route to Spring Hill and the other half still in Columbia. Although increasingly concerned over the possibility of being attacked in the midst of a withdrawal, Schofield could not completely ignore the threat posed by whatever force Hood apparently still had at Columbia, whose artillery was even now making its presence felt. All he could do was be prepared to meet any exigency. Schofield later wrote:

> I decided to take the chances of a pitched battle at any point the enemy might select between Duck River and Spring Hill, as well as that of holding the latter place with one division against any hostile force which might reach it before dark.[36]

Wilson has been criticized for his decision to fall back from the Duck River, thereby depriving Schofield of his source of information about what was happening on the left flank. Yet Wilson supplied Schofield with a fairly accurate picture of conditions and offered recommendations as to an appropriate response. Those recommendations were perhaps couched in a rather brash style, but Schofield could scarcely say he had not been kept informed. Indeed, he fully approved of Wilson's actions, telling him (in a 6:30 P.M. communiqué on November 28) that he had "received your several dispatches giving the enemy's movements and your plans, and have given the orders you suggest. All right."[37]

In any event, Wilson began his withdrawal along the Lewisburg Pike, and by daylight of November 29 was being hard pressed by Forrest, Armstrong's brigade in particular. Fortunately for the Federals, the countryside was heavily wooded, giving the blue troopers a slight advantage in defending against the Confederate advance. Wilson's system of fire and withdrawal worked well in the wooded terrain. While one brigade acted as a rear guard, the balance of the command fell back to a new position, after which a fresh brigade took over the rear guard and the procedure was repeated.

At one point, after being directed to take his turn, Croxton, always the battler, inquired if his chief intended to fight. "Only when necessary to delay the enemy," Wilson told him. "I think I understand you," Croxton answered, "and all I have to say is if you don't intend to fight for all you are worth, please get your 'horse cavalry' out of the way and give me a clear road!" Wilson later recalled that Croxton's "perfect confidence in himself and his men was so clear from this remark that I felt no doubt our movements that day would be both deliberate and successful."[38]

By 9 A.M. the Federal horsemen had been pushed back to Mount Carmel Meeting House, five miles from Hurt's Cross-Roads. At this juncture, Coon's brigade, positioned behind a rail fence barricade, relieved Croxton's hard-pressed rear guard and found itself wrapped up in the midst of a heavy, hour-long firefight.

Ordered to withdraw, finally, Coon did so in a double line of regiments and was attacked by Forrest's troops charging down the pike in columns of fours. Again, it was the Ninth Illinois, covering the withdrawal, which bore the brunt of the attack. As the Confederates, driving hard after the Illinois troops, passed between Coon's regiments, they were caught in a raking cross-fire that quickly shattered the pursuit and temporarily forced the Confederate horsemen to fall back.[39] Then, almost abruptly, the pressure on the Federal squadrons fell off and Wilson continued his withdrawal unmolested, reaching Douglass Church, four miles from Franklin, at mid-afternoon. Here, Wilson was joined, finally, by Hammond and a portion of Stewart's brigade. The latter brought with him news of heavy fighting around Spring Hill.[40]

At this juncture, Wilson was temporarily isolated. Schofield, he assumed, had reached Spring Hill, but at what cost was impossible to say. Stewart's report indicated nothing more than that there was fighting around Spring Hill. For the moment, Forrest seemed to have disappeared. Wilson had patrols out, attempting to reestablish contact, but by dark he had begun to fear that his opponent might be headed for Nashville, a fear that seems to have taken precedence over Schofield's situation. "You had better look out for Forrest at Nashville tomorrow noon," Wilson advised Thomas. "I'll be there before or very soon after he makes his appearance."[41]

Accordingly, Wilson, with Hammond's brigade, remained at Douglass Church, while Hatch and Johnson crossed the Harpeth River and bivouacked for the night on the Franklin-Triune Road. When an after-dark reconnaissance revealed no enemy activity along the recently busy Lewisburg Pike, Hammond joined Hatch and Johnson north of the Harpeth River, where Wilson continued to watch for Confederate activity to the immediate east and south.[42]

What had transpired during the afternoon and evening hours of November 29 would have given Wilson considerable pause had he known of the drama being played out just a few miles to the west of where his squadrons were watching for signs of a flanking movement by Bedford Forrest. The story of Hood's failure to bag Schofield at Spring Hill is one of the Civil War's great "what ifs." The details of that Confederate slip-up have been well documented in other studies of the Franklin-Nashville campaign. Since the focus of this particular study is the Federal cavalry's role in that campaign, it would be redundant to examine the Spring Hill episode once again, except insofar as is necessary to provide a general background for an overall understanding of the campaign.[43] Stanley had started for Spring Hill at mid-morning on November 29. After dropping off Kimball's division at Rutherford Creek, pursuant to Schofield's order, Stanley resumed his march in what he later described as a "beautiful fall forenoon." Approaching Spring Hill, he was intercepted by a courier from the small Federal garrison there, advising him that Confederate cavalry were attacking from the east. The vanguard of Stanley's huge wagon train, together with some of its escort had already reached Spring Hill, but that would hardly be enough to repel the Confederates, so Colonel Emerson Opdycke's First Brigade of Wagner's division, then only a mile or so from town, was promptly ordered to move ahead and establish a defense while the rest of Stanley's troops came on in support. No laggard, Opdycke, a 36-year-old Ohioan, double-quicked his men into Spring Hill just in time to beat back Brigadier General Buford's skirmishers, who were even then approaching the wagon train.[44]

Spring Hill had suddenly become a hamlet of some considerable activity on this late and fair autumn day. In addition to the recently arrived wagon train and its escort, there were also elements of Stewart's brigade, en route to join Wilson, along with a stray company of Croxton's brigade. These units were the first to contest Forrest's advance before finally falling back to the breastworks Opdycke's men were hastily throwing up around the wagon park. The Federal horsemen subsequently moved on to join Wilson, to whom they reported the fighting at Spring Hill.[45]

The way all of this had come about was due to the imaginative Forrest, who was seldom without a feint up his sleeve, and in this instance it succeeded magnificently. While Ross's Texans occupied Wilson's horsemen, driving them back, Forrest had suddenly turned west on the Mount Carmel Road, aiming for Spring Hill with his main force.[46] As it turned out, Forrest came uncomfortably close to capturing Spring Hill, but the Federal skirmishers he encountered delayed him just long enough to allow Stanley's infantry to arrive and dig in. By mid-afternoon Forrest had been engaged for some three to four hours, when a dispatch from Hood arrived (he had heard the firing) and ordered Forrest to hold on, that infantry was on the way. But by this hour, Stanley had sufficient infantry on hand to deal with Forrest, and besides, most of the Confederate horsemen were beginning to run out of ammunition. Thus, Forrest chafed and waited impatiently for Hood's infantry to show up, there being little more that he could do.[47]

One other significant development occurred that should have altered the picture dramatically. Forrest's troops captured a courier, en route from Thomas to Schofield, directing the latter to establish a strong defensive position at Franklin. Thus, Hood was now in possession of the Federal plan and the appropriate response would have seemed clear. Actually, it was—to a certain degree.

Upon first hearing the sound of a fight at Spring Hill, Hood had directed Cheatham to support Forrest. However, when he arrived on the scene late that afternoon and viewed the Federal activity along the Franklin Pike from a high point, Hood ordered General Patrick Cleburne's division of Cheatham's corps to face west and take control of the pike. Unfortunately, Hood's order was issued without Cheatham's knowledge and from that point on, the Confederate command structure simply broke down.[48] There was nothing like a concerted strategy for dealing with the situation—actually, the opportunity—the Confederates found themselves facing. Both Cheatham and Stewart, as well as their respective division and brigade leaders, were justifiably confused. Hood himself appears to have been under the impression that the situation was well in hand; Schofield was going to be bagged, either that night or certainly by morning.[49]

What transpired instead was an effort by Cleburne to secure the pike, an effort that subsequently resulted in a tough fight with Stanley's entrenched Federals at Spring Hill. As it was, Cleburne's veterans very nearly carried the day before being checked by Stanley's artillery. The Confederate momentum was further checked by Cheatham's order to cease the attack while he concentrated his corps for an all-out drive on Spring Hill.[50]

While Cleburne was thus engaged, Cheatham's other two division commanders, John C. Brown and William Bate, were attempting to divine their particular role in this confused scenario. Cheatham, Stewart, Brown, and Bate all sought clarification from Hood, but rather than eliminating the ambiguity, this only made matters worse. When an annoyed Hood inquired why the pike had not been taken, Cheatham explained that he had called it off out of fear that the Federals were in a position to flank him. Hood's response (apparently not realizing that Cheatham's objective was different from his own) was to order Stewart to support Cheatham. This order only served to muddy the waters even further, because Stewart had earlier been ordered to secure the pike *north* of Spring Hill. Hood and Cheatham appear to have been carrying out mutually exclusive strategies. Hood's objective seems to have been securing control of the pike, while Cheatham, due in part to Hood's original orders to him, was focusing on Spring Hill. Given the prevailing climate it is no wonder the division and brigade commanders were confused as to their role.[51]

The net result of this total breakdown of communication—which is what the fiasco at Spring Hill was really all about—was that Franklin Pike remained open and Spring Hill was still in Federal hands. Darkness found Hood's brigades moving into bivouac, the glow of their campfires clearly visible from the nearby pike. Hood himself prepared to retire for the night, seemingly confident that the morrow would yield a great prize.[52]

About 3 P.M., roughly the time Hood was casting covetous glances at the Franklin Pike and getting under way with his effort to secure it, Schofield had finally concluded it was time to withdraw from Columbia, despite the fact that Stephen Lee's Confederates were still giving every indication that they fully intended to strike the Federal position. Leaving Jacob Cox's division behind as a rear guard, Schofield started for Spring Hill with two brigades. Cox was ordered to follow after dark. As they approached Spring Hill, Schofield grew more apprehensive as it became increasingly clear that the Confederates were uncomfortably close. Even so, the Federal column tramped along the pike undisturbed, save for scattered skirmishing with some of Forrest's cavalry, which if nothing else managed to add to Schofield's mounting sense of alarm.[53]

By 7 P.M. Schofield had reached Spring Hill, mightily concerned that his army was in dire peril, spread out as it was between that point and Columbia. Then came word that the Confederates had blocked the pike at Thompson's Station, a few miles north of Spring Hill. This report had arrived in the person of a frightened railroad engineer, who had come rolling into Spring Hill following an encounter with Ross's Texans at Thompson's Station, during which the engine had become detached and streamed south. Disappointed at not corralling the engine, the Texans nevertheless quickly set fire to the depot and bridge. Their presence had Schofield very concerned, thinking that they might well be Hood's infantry.[54]

At about the same time that a worried Schofield was arriving at Spring Hill, Jacob Cox was beginning his withdrawal from Columbia. Extricating his command was not all that simple, as Stephen Lee's artillery continued its brisk cannonading, to which the Federals responded with spirited counter-battery fire of their own. Sensing that the Federals were pulling out, Lee tried to force a crossing of the river, but a brigade under Brigadier General James Reilly was able to contest the crossing vigorously enough to allow the withdrawal to proceed unimpeded.[55]

As Cox's tired soldiers tramped up the pike in the chilly blackness of the autumn night, the enemy's bivouac fires beckoned from just beyond their marching route. In fact, a few of the weary and unwitting Northerners, thinking they were Yankee fires, strolled over to warm themselves, only to be quickly taken prisoner. Nevertheless, by midnight Schofield's entire command was reunited in Spring Hill.[56]

Relieved to have reached Spring Hill intact but still fearful that the enemy controlled the pike north of town, Schofield resolved to waste no time testing those waters. Cox's newly arrived division became the advance of the army, followed by the wagons under General Thomas Ruger's protection, then Stanley with the rear guard. Near Thompson's Station, from whence the errant locomotive had escaped, the Federals encountered Confederate horsemen belonging to William Jackson's division, along with Ross's Texans. Forrest's troops managed to burn a few wagons and capture some livestock, but otherwise were few enough in number and lacking in ammunition to do much more than annoy the Franklin-bound Yankees.[57]

Thus it was that a much-relieved Schofield, with his advance units, reached Franklin about daybreak. The remainder of the army tramped in through the morning, with Opdycke's rear guard trudging in about noon, having skirmished most of the way from Thompson's Station with Forrest's troopers. Not one to look a gift horse in the mouth, Schofield promptly got to work establishing a defensive position on the south bank of the Harpeth River. At the same time, he ordered bridges built that would accommodate both wagons and infantry.[58]

Although Cheatham, Bate, Brown, and perhaps even Forrest were all culpable to some degree, Hood himself bears the primary responsibility for the Confederate failure at Spring Hill. It is perfectly clear that Hood fully intended to secure the Columbia-Franklin Pike and sever Schofield's line of retreat. Hood issued orders to this effect, but failed to make certain that those orders had been properly executed; indeed, Hood almost seemed lack-adaisical about the whole affair. It has been suggested, however, that even if Hood had succeeded in gaining control of the pike, Schofield could have used alternate routes to reach Franklin.[59]

In any case, the Federals were now at Franklin and Schofield was feeling somewhat better about things, if for no other reason than the fact that he was only some 25 miles from Nashville. At mid-morning he fired off a dispatch to Thomas, reporting that the situation was stable for the moment and asking if he was to hang on there "until compelled to fall back?" Wilson was there, too, Schofield advised Thomas, adding, however, that Forrest seemed to be everywhere and "Wilson was entirely unable to cope with him." Twenty-four hours later, however, Schofield's view of Wilson and his horsemen would change dramatically.[60]

Six
Franklin

At the moment of the first decisive repulse of the enemy's infantry I received the most gratifying intelligence that General Wilson had driven the rebel cavalry back across the river. This rendered my immediate left and rear secure for the time being. —Schofield, Report of Operations, November 14–December 1, 1864[1]

W hile some of Schofield's weary troops went to work planking over the railroad bridge to accommodate passage of the huge Federal wagon train to the north side of the Harpeth River, others prepared a horseshoe-shaped defensive perimeter, with both flanks anchored at the river. There was not, Schofield realized, much time to lose. The Confederates would be along directly. Schofield doubted that his opponent would attack the Federal position head on, though that was of course a possibility. What he feared most was another movement around his left flank, out to the east of Franklin. He feared a repetition of Columbia, where Hood had come uncomfortably close to cutting off the Federals.

Accordingly, in the pre-dawn on that Wednesday, the last day of November 1864, Schofield fired off an order to Wilson, saying, "I want you to cover my immediate flank and rear, today at least, with a portion of your troops. I will be near this place, and I hope on the north bank of the Harpeth."[2]

Despite the presence of Wilson's horsemen to the east, Schofield remained less than reassured about the security of his left flank, particularly given the events of the past 36 hours. At mid-morning he sent a situation update to Thomas, in which he pointed out that Forrest was on his flank somewhere and Wilson was unable to check him. Thus, said Schofield, Hood was pretty much free to cross the Harpeth River wherever he elected to do so. Did Thomas wish him to hold?[3]

Thomas did indeed wish him to hold: for three days, providing the risk wasn't too great. If this could be managed, it would give A. J. Smith's newly arrived command time to get disembarked, organized, and brought forward. Finally, Thomas inquired, what did Wilson think he could contribute to holding Hood?[4]

Schofield, who must have been astonished that Thomas would even ask whether Hood could be held for three days, said he did not believe it was possible. "I can doubtless hold him one day, but will hazard something in doing that," Schofield informed Thomas, adding that he thought Wilson "could do very little."[5]

Wilson, meanwhile, had reached Douglass Church, on the south side of the Harpeth River, some four miles east of Franklin, during the afternoon of November 29. He was joined there by John Hammond's brigade, along with three companies of the Eleventh Indiana from Stewart's command. Both were welcome additions, particularly given that Wilson and his unit commanders believed they were outnumbered two to one. The reality, however, was that the two commands were close to parity at that point, with each side having between 4,500–6,000 troops, depending on the source consulted. The odds, however, were about to shift dramatically in Wilson's favor.[6]

Upon arriving at Douglass Church, Wilson disposed his command so as to be prepared for the most likely contingencies. Hatch and Johnson crossed the Harpeth at Hughes' Ford and went into bivouac at Matthews Farm, two and a half miles east of Franklin on the Triune road with orders to feed and groom their horses. Sometime after dark, Colonel George Spalding arrived with the Twelfth Tennessee after skirmishing all the way from Spring Hill. Normally a part of Stewart's brigade, Spalding's Tennesseans were temporarily assigned to Coon's brigade.[7]

Stewart, who had been watching Schofield's right flank at Columbia, had been prevented from rejoining the corps because of the enemy activity between himself and Wilson. Wilson had received no direct word from the missing brigade, but had been advised by the Indiana detachment that had come in at Douglass Church that Stewart was likely heading for Franklin. Accordingly, Wilson sent off a dispatch to Stewart, directing him to cross the Harpeth River and move east along the Triune road until he caught up with the rest of the corps, which Wilson figured would be moving toward the Nolensville Pike by that time.[8]

Hammond, meanwhile, was held at Douglass Church to cover the approach to Franklin itself. However, when there was no indication of Confederate movement by dark, Wilson withdrew Hammond across the Harpeth and sent him east toward the Nolensville Pike at Triune with orders to monitor the countryside for signs of enemy activity. Wilson had at first planned to delegate this assignment to Johnson, but changed his mind because Hammond's brigade was in better shape.[9]

The Nolensville Pike, today's U.S. Highway 31-41, would have been a logical axis for Forrest to use if in fact his intention was to sweep around the Federal flank and strike for Nashville, a fear that Wilson continued to harbor. Indeed, he was obsessed with the fear that Forrest would somehow manage to skirt his flank and reach Nashville unopposed. Such a happening would be most embarrassing.[10]

At 1:15 A.M. on November 30, Hammond reported from Petersburg, three miles out of Triune, that the road was "horrible, rocky and muddy, but no sign of the enemy. I will select a good position and picket the river strongly, and keep watch until I hear from you." During the next four hours, Wilson, having not yet opened communications with Schofield, advised Hammond that the "enemy cavalry is probably yet in the direction of Mount Carmel. Should you be attacked, delay the enemy all you can and notify me promptly."[11]

Wilson had barely fired off this order to Hammond when he heard from Schofield. After passing on Hammond's report and indicating his own intention to cover the Nolensville Pike with all of his cavalry, Wilson received a peremptory order to hold his position. "I want you to cover my immediate flank and rear, to-day at least, with a portion of your troops," Schofield directed, adding that "I will be near this place [Franklin] and I hope on the north bank of the Harpeth."[12]

Accordingly, early on November 30, Johnson was directed to send Croxton's brigade back across the river to Douglass Church. To the bearded Croxton it must have seemed like a familiar situation, reminiscent of his watch-and-delay assignment along the Tennessee River a month earlier. Here, Croxton's orders were to cover Franklin as long as possible, then fall back across the Harpeth. At the same time, Hammond was ordered to retire to Wilson's Mill (no relation to General Wilson) on the road to Brentwood.[13]

East of Franklin, the Harpeth River was wide, but fordable at several places. Consequently, it seemed that any flanking movement on Hood's part would likely come from above, rather than below the town. Nevertheless, as a precaution, Johnson was directed to furnish a unit to patrol that sector and sent the Fifth Iowa out to the Hillsborough Pike, some seven miles west of Franklin.[14]

While Wilson was making his troop dispositions, Forrest, with the divisions of Buford and Jackson, moved up along Hood's right flank. Buford's troops linked up with Stewart's infantry, with Jackson's men on the far right flank, just across the Harpeth River, which looped and bent around Franklin in a southeasterly direction for some distance, before resuming a more easterly flow. Thus, while Schofield's main line was on the south side of the Harpeth along an east-west axis, Wilson's position was actually east of the river.[15] For the first time in the campaign Forrest was at a numerical disadvantage, as

Chalmers's division had been sent to operate on the far left flank of Hood's army, leaving Forrest to challenge Wilson's 4,000-plus with a little more than half that many.[16]

Although the main Confederate attack at Franklin did not commence until late afternoon, the opposing horsemen were in action several hours earlier as a prelude to the main event. About 10 A.M., Croxton was attacked by Jackson's division, initiating some four hours of skirmishing between the two commands. About mid-afternoon, however, Confederate cavalry was reported crossing the river to his left, forcing Croxton to fall back across the Harpeth at McGavock's Ford, leaving the Second Michigan to cover his withdrawal.[17] Croxton had barely reached the north bank when reports of additional Confederate crossings were confirmed. In view of this development, Wilson promptly disposed his command to repel the enemy attack. At this juncture, he had but three brigades available for action: Hatch, still missing Stewart's first brigade, had only Coon's brigade on hand, while Richard Johnson had the brigades of Croxton and Harrison. Hammond was still patrolling the Nolensville Pike near Brentwood and was not a factor in the upcoming clash. In all, Wilson could muster no more than 4,000 troops with which to oppose the advance of Forrest's 2,500–3,000 men in the divisions of Jackson and Buford.[18]

Wilson formed his line in a rough semicircle with Croxton on the right, covering Franklin. Hatch, with Coon's brigade, was in the center, while Harrison watched the left and rear. Wilson described the setting and his concern as the situation unfolded:

> The field was broken by hills covered with woods and small clearings, not specially unfavorable to mounted men; but the occasion was a grave one. It indicated either the advance of Hood's whole army as at Duck River, or a turning movement by his cavalry, and in either case, from the fact that the National infantry and artillery were still on the south side of the river, it was absolutely necessary for their safety that my orders should be carried out to the letter.[19]

Meanwhile, to the west of where the cavalry action was about to take place, Hood was preparing to send the divisions of Cheatham and Stewart against Schofield's entrenched army. The plan seemed suicidal. Lee's corps (with most of the army's artillery) was still en route from Columbia, so the assault brigades would not even have the benefit of artillery preparation. It would be like Pickett's charge at Gettysburg without artillery support. Forrest pleaded for a flanking movement, using his cavalry and one division of infantry, but Hood was adamant. They would attack head on and that was that! (Ironically, Hood himself had pleaded with Lieutenant General James Longstreet for a flanking movement on the second day at Gettysburg.)

Hood's decision to launch a frontal assault at Franklin was probably influenced by several factors, not the least of which was his anger over the miscue at Spring Hill. There was also his physical condition. Hood was a man in a great deal of pain and the laudanum he took to suppress that pain could certainly have affected his judgment. Finally, Hood may have somehow sought to emulate Lee's rejection of a flanking movement on the second day at Gettysburg. Whatever the reasons, the loveliness of that final day of November 1864 was about to be stained by carnage seldom equalled in this war.

It was about 4 P.M. when Hood sent his brigades forward. On the Confederate right, Buford's horsemen moved in support of Stewart's infantry, leaving Forrest with only Jackson's division to challenge Wilson's troops.

Jackson's division, led by Ross's Texans, forded the Harpeth, driving back Coon's pickets and capturing the high ground that lay half a mile or so beyond the river. Coon sent the Sixth Illinois to support the pickets and readied the remainder of his brigade for action.

Meanwhile, on Wilson's right, Croxton had been advised by Colonel Joseph Dorr, commanding the Eighth Iowa, that enemy infantry was attempting to cross the river to the right of his position, near Franklin. Wasting no time, Croxton promptly directed the Second Michigan and First Tennessee regiments to hold the main line while he moved with the Iowans and his old regiment, the Fourth Kentucky Mounted Infantry, to deal with this new threat. The report, however, proved false, and Croxton was soon able to reunite his command.[20]

Shortly, Wilson ordered a general advance of his entire line. Using their seven-shot Spencer carbines to good advantage, the Federals moved forward and charged the high ground. With a strong effort they drove the Confederates from their recently secured position. Ross ordered a countercharge by the Ninth Texas, which was subsequently driven back with heavy loss. The Third Texas, brought on in support, managed to temporarily check the Federals, allowing the Confederates to retire. A Chicago newspaper correspondent attached to Croxton's brigade described the attack from the vantage point of the Second Michigan Cavalry:

> We were standing on an elevation, a little to the rear and left of this Michigan regiment [the Second], which gave us a full and complete view of the battle. We saw them slide from their saddles and rush forward a few rods to the aclivity of a gentle slope that shielded their horses from the fire of the enemy, and here they fell upon their faces, hugging the ground so closely that it was almost impossible for the enemy to see them, while their commander, Lieutenant-Colonel [Benjamin] Smith, seated upon a log in close proximity to his crouching line, with his bridle rein strung upon his arm,

seemed to be engaged in trying to light his pipe. Through the woods, along their front, as far as the eye could reach, nothing was to be seen but the heavy gray columns of the enemy moving slowly but confidently forward. Presently they halted, when a column of Louisiana cavalry,[21] apparently about 2,000 strong, swung round by the left, dismounted, and forming in line of battle, came rushing forward, pouring from their Enfield rifles volley after volley, while the woods resounded with the wild scream of the Texas ranger. Turning our face for a moment to the right we discovered General Croxton sitting upon his horse a few feet from us, with one leg thrown over the pommel of his saddle, looking at the scene. Thinking that he had not seen the heavy line of the enemy that was now moving up, and partially hidden from view by an undulating swell of the ground, we exclaimed, "General, those men will be annihilated." Turning his head slowly toward us and taking us to be a resident of the country, he observed, "Don't be alarmed my Tennessee friend, those are my whitefish boys; you'll hear them speak in a minute or two." He had scarcely finished speaking when Michigan arose to her knees, and, in that praying position poured into the enemy a sheet of fire which could be hurled from no other arm than the Spencer carbine. For a full minute an incessant stream of fire poured from the muzzles of those carbines, drifting upon the heavy columns of the enemy a sheety spray of lead, such as no human power could resist, halting, then staggering the advance. The line wavered for a moment, and then, under a rallying shout, it bounded forward a few feet against the storm of leaden hail. Again it halted, broke and fled. For nearly two hours, column after column was hurled upon that Michigan regiment, and each in turn was driven back with terrible slaughter. At length there was a pause; silence broken only by the fitful rustling of the forest leaf. In the distance, the enemy could be seen dismounting and massing columns for another charge—one that would trample beneath its feet the power that had so stubbornly resisted their advance. We turned to point them out to General Croxton, but he was gone. Onward came that black mass of the enemy, flaunting their banners with maddened desperation, and again did Michigan empty her carbines. Then came the ringing shout of their commander: "Up Michigan, right about, double quick, mount." Now was the moment of peril—the moment of danger. Not less than four thousand rifles[22] were ready to sweep away the line when it rose from its leafy couch, but at the very instant that the command was given to fall back, the eighth [*sic*] Iowa cavalry, under the command of Colonel Dorr, dashed through a thicket and struck the enemy upon the right flank with an enfilading fire that roilled it up into a mass of confusion. Amazed and bewildered, the rebels directed their glance for a moment in the direction of this unexpected attack, and in that moment Michigan was in the saddle and all was safe.[23]

With the approach of darkness, the Confederate horsemen recrossed the river. Some of Jackson's units were out of ammunition, and in any event,

Forrest lacked the strength of numbers to either overwhelm or outflank Wilson's squadrons.[24]

So however else things had gone for them during the campaign, this day belonged to the Federal horsemen. Wilson was jubilant. "We have had a glorious day," he informed Hammond at 8:45 P.M. "Have driven the enemy across the river at every point." At the same time, however, having heard nothing from Hammond since early that morning and concerned that he might not have received the last instructions sent to him, Wilson directed Hammond to begin his retirement along the Brentwood Pike.[25] Wilson had ample reason to feel the flush of victory here along the banks of the Harpeth River. Later, however, he was quick to point out that the absence of Chalmers's division was a key factor in that victory. "Had his whole cavalry advanced against me," Wilson wrote in later years, "it is possible that it would have succeeded in driving us back."[26]

There can be little doubt that dividing the cavalry was a serious error in judgment on Hood's part. Serious though it was, on that day it stood second to his later decision to send some 20,000 men against Schofield's entrenched Federals. Indeed, one might call it the nadir of Hood's career. The presence of Chalmers on the right flank might well have given Forrest just enough leverage to carry the day against Wilson's troops, but whether that in itself would have significantly altered the outcome of the battle is difficult to say. In light of what befell the main portion of the Confederate army in front of Franklin, it would seem that this was a day that John Bell Hood had placed beyond the reach of victory.

About 4 P.M., on a warm and glorious Wednesday, the last day of November 1864, even as Wilson's brigades were clashing with Jackson's troops, the Army of Tennessee began its surge toward the Yankee lines in the golden hue of the war's final autumn. On they came, nearly twice the number George Pickett had led up Cemetery Ridge at Gettysburg. It was a sight to behold: 18 brigades, more than 100 regiments, some 20,000 Confederate infantrymen, advancing in massed ranks across the gently rolling plain to do the bidding of their Confederate Ahab; to smite the white Yankee whale who had avoided the harpoon at Spring Hill, but who, by God, would be savaged here at Franklin!

So they went, their lines slamming against the the outlying Nationals of Wagner's division, which had overstayed its watchdog position and was quickly overrun, the men fleeing back toward their main line. Then it was Opdycke's reserve brigade of Wagner's division that rushed in to stem the tide, but these Confederates of the Army of Tennessee were a determined bunch and were soon on top of Schofield's main line.

Fighting was intense everywhere, but heaviest on the left and center.

Men were literally dragged over the breastworks by their opponents in a furious hand-to-hand struggle that was as vicious as any in the war.

> It is impossible to exaggerate the fierce energy with which the Confederate soldiers, that short November afternoon, threw themselves against the works, fighting with what seemed the very madness of despair. There was not a breath of wind, and the dense smoke settled down upon the field, so that after the first assault, it was impossible to see any distance. Through this blinding medium, assault after assault was made, several of the Union officers declaring in their reports that their lines received as many as thirteen distinct attacks.[27]

The autumn afternoon deepened into twilight and finally full darkness with no let-up in the Confederate effort. Major General Edward Johnson's division of Lee's corps made the final assault around 7 P.M., underscoring the futility of the afternoon. Sporadic firing continued for another two hours before Hood finally called it off and withdrew his shattered brigades.

That this had been one of the most bitter struggles of the war is supported by the testimony of the survivors. A veteran of the Sixty-fifth Illinois and of 27 general engagements felt that Franklin "was the hardest fought field I ever stood upon."[28] Opdycke reported that he "twice stepped to the front of the works on the Columbia Pike to see the effect of such fighting. I never saw the dead lay near so thick. I saw them upon each other, dead and ghastly in the powder-dimmed star light."[29]

It had been a costly afternoon for the Army of Tennessee: 1,750 killed, 3,800 wounded, 702 missing. In addition, the army had lost five general officers killed outright; six had been wounded, including one mortally; and one had been captured.[30] The Federals, too, had suffered. Schofield lost 289 killed, 1,033 wounded, and 1,104 missing. As with Lee at Gettysburg, Hood had paid a heavy price while gaining nothing, except perhaps to reaffirm his opponent's admiration for the courage and élan of the Confederate fighting men.[31]

At 7:10 P.M. Schofield fired off a telegram to Thomas, reporting that "the enemy made a heavy and persistent attack with about two corps, commencing at 4 P.M. and lasting until after dark. He was repulsed at all points, with very heavy loss, probably about 5,000 or 6,000 men.[32]

The night was well advanced before the desultory firing had ceased, allowing Schofield to begin his withdrawal across the Harpeth, pursuant to Thomas's directive issued earlier that afternoon. Unlike at Columbia, there was little to fear from Confederate molestation that night and the Federals effected their crossing with little harrassment. Meanwhile, after notifying Schofield of his success, Wilson reformed his units and posted strong pickets along the river in anticipation of a counterattack, after which he proceeded to Schofield's headquarters in person.

Though he had heard heavy firing from the direction of Franklin all afternoon, it was not until he walked into Schofield's headquarters that he learned of the titanic infantry battle that had been waged while his own troops were in the process of driving Forrest back across the Harpeth. Years later, Wilson described the scene that greeted him that evening:

> Schofield and Stanley were together and, after reporting the result of my fight with Forrest, I was greatly surprised to hear that a fierce battle had occurred between our infantry and Hood's army, that charge and countercharge had followed in rapid succession, that our works had been carried and recaptured, that deeds of extraordinary courage had characterized the fighting on both sides, that the enemy had finally been repulsed with the loss of many officers and men, and finally that Stanley himself, while in the midst of the melee, had been shot through the back of the neck, but had retained his position on the field till all was safe. Stanley in his bloody coat, with his neck wrapped in bandages, was before me and the wonder was that he had escaped alive.[33]

Interestingly enough, Schofield, who just a few hours before had denigrated his cavalry support, now did a complete about-face. After thanking Wilson for his splendid victory east of Franklin, he told his young cavalry chief, "If you had not succeeded in doing that, our victory here would have been in vain, for with Forrest upon our flanks and rear it would have been impossible for us to have withdrawn our train, artillery and troops from this position."[34]

Wilson was now directed to hold his command in readiness until daylight, then retire toward Nashville, covering the army's left flank. Accordingly, at 5:30 A.M. on December 1, with no further pressure from Forrest, Harrison and Coon marched their brigades cross-country to the Wilson Pike, then turned north, while Croxton traveled just east of and parallel to the Franklin Pike.[35] Reaching Wilson's Mill, they were joined by Hammond and Stewart. Stewart, in the lead, had halted to feed and groom his horses, thus delaying Hammond's forward progress. In any case, the two brigades suddenly found themselves under attack by Forrest, who had pushed his command across the Harpeth at daybreak in pursuit of the Federals.

The attack was made by Buford's command, but the Federals proved too strong and the effort was quickly repulsed. Forrest then pulled back and Hammond and Stewart followed the rest of the corps through Brentwood, then cross-country to Thompson's Chapel on the Nolensville Pike, where Wilson established a strong defensive perimeter for the night.[36]

Wilson had his brigades in motion before daylight and by evening the corps had reached Nashville, crossed the Cumberland River, and gone into bivouac at Edgefield. The advance of Schofield's main body reached the Tennessee capital about noon. After burying the dead and caring for his wounded, Hood, refusing to be swayed from his purpose by the carnage at Franklin, marched his army toward Nashville, where he established a position six miles south of the city on December 2.[37]

So the first stage of Hood's campaign to rescue the Confederacy had come to naught. Indeed, the army that had crossed the Tennessee River a fortnight earlier now barely qualified to be described as an army, at least from the standpoint of numbers. Hood had shot his bolt, but he wasn't finished yet. Thomas, on the other hand, had gained the time he needed to put together a powerful striking force of his own that included Wilson's cavalry corps, which had continued to grow despite the exigencies of the campaign. It seemed doubtful that Hood would attempt to assault Nashville; if he did, his tatterdemalion brigades would be decimated on the anvil of this fortress city. If Hood stayed put, Thomas would seek him out.

Seven
Hood's Dilemma

The only remaining chance of success in the campaign, at this juncture, was to take position, intrench about Nashville, and await Thomas' attack, which, if handsomely repulsed, might afford us an opportunity to follow up our advantage on the spot, and enter the city on the heels of the enemy.—John Bell Hood, *Advance and Retreat*[1]

F ollowing his sharp but unsuccessful skirmish with John Hammond's brigade at Owen's Cross-Roads on December 1, Forrest moved with Buford and Jackson to Brentwood, where he effected a junction with Chalmers's division. Chalmers was immediately sent north along the Franklin Pike in a final effort to delay the Federal retreat, but both Schofield and Wilson were by then safely behind the Nashville defenses, so Forrest had no choice but to call off the pursuit.[2]

On the morning of December 2, Forrest dispersed his command to cover the approaches to Nashville as completely as his limited means permitted. Chalmers was sent out to cover the extreme left of the army's position. Buford was ordered out to Mill Creek on the Murfreesboro Pike, while Jackson's assignment was to cover the Nashville and Mill Creek pikes.[3]

By mid-afternoon, Hood and the main contingent of the army began to arrive, with Hood setting up his headquarters at the Travelers Rest home of John Overton, six miles south of Nashville. The army set about establishing a semicircular line of entrenchments, some five miles in length, extending from the Nashville and Chattanooga Railroad tracks on the east to the Hillsboro Pike on the west. Hood's line was about half the length of the Federal entrenchments across the way.

As at Franklin, Nashville was served from the south by a series of turnpikes, as well as three different railroads. The former, especially, would play a significant role in the forthcoming battle. Clockwise from the west and radiating out from Nashville like the tentacles of a giant, ten-fingered hand were the Charlotte Pike (closest to the Cumberland River), then the Nashville and Northwest Railroad, followed by the Hardin, Hillsboro, Granny White, and Franklin pikes. Just beyond the Franklin Pike was the Tennessee and Alabama Railroad, then the Nolensville Pike, the Nashville and Chattanooga Railroad, and finally the Murfreesboro Pike.

Cheatham's corps held the army's right flank from the railroad tracks to approximately the Franklin Pike, where it connected with Stephen Lee's corps, which covered the ground between the Franklin and Granny White pikes. On the army's left, A. P. Stewart's corps extended from the Granny White to the Hillsboro Pike. Chalmers's horsemen took up station on the extreme left of the army, occupying a line from the Hardin Pike to the Cumberland River. Hood lacked the resources to match the Federals yard for yard. Accordingly, between Chalmers's right and Stewart's left, directly opposite Thomas Wood's Fourth Corps, a considerable gap existed.[4] Why Hood chose to place the battered remnants of his army in harm's way following the carnage at Franklin is a question that will never be answered to everyone's satisfaction. Hood's reasoning has been the subject of considerable criticism and speculation. The late Thomas L. Connelly suggests that "Hood's behavior was caused by a combination of ignorance and irrationality," which is probably about as close as we are likely to get in understanding John Bell Hood's motives.[5]

There is something compelling somehow about a Confederate invasion of Kentucky and beyond—what Connelly called the "Ohio Dream." There is a certain romance connected with this "Hail Mary" strategy, this last-ditch effort to pull the South's chestnuts out of the fire.[6] However, Hood's long-range vision of the campaign and what it might have achieved seems to have been hazy at best, notwithstanding his postcampaign apologetics. Marching to the Ohio River and perhaps turning east to assist Lee may well have been a part of his strategy, but if so it was vague and loosely conceived. His day-to-day decisions suggest a man who functioned more by instinct and gut reaction than by careful reasoning. Moreover, one cannot help but wonder how much Hood's actions were influenced by the pain of his wounds and by how much his mind might have been beclouded by the opiates taken to relieve that pain.

In defense of his strategy after the fact, Hood argued that a continuation of his northward movement was impossible without reinforcements from the trans–Mississippi department and he could not afford to turn back without creating a grave morale problem in the army. Hood wrote:

> Unless strengthened by these long-looked-for reinforcements, the only remaining chance of success in the campaign at this juncture, was to take position, intrench about Nashville, and await Thomas'

attack, which, if handsomely repulsed, might afford us an opportunity to follow up our advantage on the spot, and enter the city
on the heels of the enemy.

I could not afford to turn southward, unless for the special purpose of forming a junction with the expected reenforcements from
Texas, and with the avowed intention to march back again upon
Nashville. In truth, our army was in that condition which rendered
it more judicious the men should face a decisive issue rather than
retreat—in other words, rather than renounce the honor of their
cause, without having made a last and manful effort to lift up the
sinking fortunes of the Confederacy.[7]

Although General Beauregard had urged General Edmund Kirby Smith
to send Hood reinforcements from the trans–Mississippi department, there
was little likelihood of that happening. Whether Hood fully recognized that,
or whether in his naïveté he clung to the hope that somehow reinforcements
from the west would arrive to swell his depleted ranks is not clear.[8]

How much John Bell Hood truly understood of what he faced when
he took up position in front of Nashville is also unclear, but the evidence
suggests little. One thing, however, is abundantly clear: He had not come
this far to turn his back on the fortress of Nashville, which seemed to have
become something of an obsession for him. So the battle would be joined,
an epic encounter that historian Stanley Horn has christened the decisive
battle of the Civil War.[9]

Between Florence and Columbia, Hood had conducted a reasonably
sound campaign. Between Columbia and Nashville, however, the campaign
was marred by three serious flaws: the miscue at Spring Hill, the frontal
attack at Franklin, and the decision to entrench in front of Nashville in a
position that, given his limited resources, was virtually indefensible. To these
Hood added a fourth error in judgment. As the army was leaving Franklin,
Hood had ordered Cheatham to send Major General William Bate's 1,600-
man division to destroy the railroad between Nashville and Murfreesboro,
some 28 miles east of Franklin. Hood believed that the presence of his army
had caused Thomas to evacuate the garrisons at Murfreesboro, Knoxville,
and Chattanooga, which would allow him to occupy Murfreesboro and open
communications with Lee.[10] However, upon reaching Murfreesboro, Bate
discovered that instead of being evacuated as suspected, the town was
strongly defended by a garrison estimated at 6,000–10,000 under the command of Major General Lovell Harrison Rousseau.[11]

Bate advised Hood accordingly and the latter responded by sending
Forrest with the divisions of Jackson and Buford to reinforce Bate. Thus,
the Army of Tennessee, reduced to fewer than 25,000 effectives after the
punishing losses at Franklin, was now further weakened by the departure of

a division of infantry and two-thirds of its cavalry. The absence of these troops in the forthcoming battle proved costly. At any rate, Bate was advised on December 5 that Forrest would be in overall command of the operation and "that the defeat of that portion of the enemy at Murfreesboro is of first importance."[12]

In the meantime, while Bate was marching to Murfreesboro, Forrest had been busy skirmishing with Federal pickets, tearing up the Nashville and Chattanooga Railroad, burning bridges, and capturing several stockades and blockhouses in the area. A trainload of black troops and supplies en route from Chattanooga was captured and destroyed, although most of the troops managed to escape.[13] Forrest received Hood's order on the morning of December 5 and promptly headed for Murfreesboro, leaving Chalmers to cover the army's extreme left and a small detachment from Bell's brigade to picket on Cheatham's right, between the pike and the Cumberland River.[14]

After wrecking the railroad at LaVergne and effecting the surrender of its 80-man garrison along with two pieces of artillery, wagons, and stores, Forrest pushed on, uniting with the lead elements of Bate's command some four miles from Murfreesboro. After posting one of Jackson's brigades to cover the Wilson Pike, Forrest proceeded to drive Rousseau's pickets back into Murfreesboro.[15]

When the main body of Bate's infantry arrived on the following morning, Forrest immediately formed a line of battle and advanced against Murfreesboro. However, after two hours of skirmishing with little appreciable gain, Forrest called a halt. With one of Jackson's regiments, he scouted the Federal position, which proved too strongly defended to justify a direct attack. That evening, Forrest was further reinforced by the brigades of Sears and Palmer, raising his combined force to some 6,000.

About mid-morning on December 7, Palmer reported a strong column of the enemy advancing along the Salem Pike. The Federal force, 3,300 strong under Major General Robert H. Milroy encountered little opposition from Forrest until it reached Overall's Creek, several miles south of Murfreesboro, near the memorable Stones River battleground. At that point, Milroy ran into Bate's infantry. A stiff fight ensued, one in which Milroy compared the roar of musketry to the "thunder of a volcano."[16]

This hour belonged to the Federals, however, as most of Bates's infantry broke and, in the words of a much-chagrined Forrest, "made a shameful retreat." Both Forrest and Bate attempted to rally the men, to no avail. Forrest, however, had already sent an urgent order to Jackson, who brought his horsemen up in a hurry and, after checking Milroy's advance, forced the Federals to fall back on the Murfreesboro defenses.[17] Abraham Buford's division, meanwhile, had managed to penetrate the Murfreesboro defenses from the opposite end and cause considerable damage before Rousseau was finally able to drive him out.[18]

Hood later reported that the "infantry had behaved badly." Having concluded that Murfreesboro could not be stormed successfully, he withdrew Bate's division on the ninth, replacing it with Colonel Charles Olmstead's brigade of the late Patrick Cleburne's division. Forrest, meanwhile, was directed to resume his destruction of the railroad between Nashville and Murfreesboro.[19]

Grant was not the only one concerned about an end run. On December 11, Forrest sent Buford north to patrol the area east of Nashville, as a precaution against the possibility of a Federal flanking movement.[20]

By December 12, the infantry attached to Forrest's command had completed its destruction of the railroad between LaVergne and Murfreesboro. On the following day, Jackson, operating south of the town, captured and burned a trainload of some 60,000 rations arriving from Stevenson, Alabama. The haul also netted some 200 prisoners of the Sixty-first Illinois Infantry.[21] Forrest's assault on the Federal property around Murfreesboro was conducted with his usual effectiveness. Unfortunately, the net result of his efforts there would be more than offset by his absence in front of Nashville.

While Forrest was busy tearing up the railroad around Murfreesboro, Chalmers, with his two brigades commanded by Colonels Edmund Rucker and Jacob Biffle, attempted to fill in the four-mile gap between his left flank and the Cumberland River.[22]

Chalmers needed most of his troops for picket duty, but on December 3, he sent Lieutenant Colonel David C. Kelley, the minister-turned-cavalryman, with 300 men to blockade the Cumberland below Nashville. Kelley picked a likely spot on a bluff some 12 miles below the city. Putting his two field pieces to good use, he soon managed to stop and capture a pair of transports laden with horses and mules, probably earmarked for Wilson. Federal gunboats quickly interrupted his little party, but Kelley nevertheless managed to come away with 56 prisoners and 197 horses and mules.[23]

On December 10, apparently solicitous about his right flank, Hood ordered Chalmers to send Biffle's brigade to patrol that sector. Chalmers, who had a tough enough assignment as it was, complained. To compensate for the loss of Biffle, Hood gave him a brigade of infantry, a hard-fighting unit that had suffered heavily at Franklin and was now reduced to some 700 effectives.[24]

On the evening of December 15, Hood advised Forrest that Thomas had attacked. In the face of this development, one might fairly assume that Hood would have recalled his cavalry commander immediately. Forrest, however, was directed to hold his command in readiness and was not actually ordered to rejoin the army until the next day.[25]

Up to and including the Battle of Franklin, Hood had been able to meet the Federals on something resembling even terms. By the time he reached Nashville, however, that ratio had undergone significant changes. With an army of fewer than 25,000 effectives, Hood faced Thomas, who now had more than 50,000 of all arms troops at his disposal.[26] Moreover, the Federals were well provisioned and safely positioned behind a superb set of defenses. By contrast, Hood's troops were short of almost everything, from hats to shoes. Each brigade had some sort of shoe shop where they attempted to fashion makeshift footwear out of raw cattle hides. The effort alleviated the condition to some extent, but there remained a great many barefoot men in the Army of Tennessee. Some supplies and clothing trickled in on the Central Alabama Railroad, but the quantity was well out of proportion to the army's needs.[27]

Finally, the weather may have inconvenienced the Federals, but it produced real hardship and suffering among Hood's troops. Between the almost continuous rain, snow, and sleet, with little to eat, covered with threadbare clothing, and often with no shoes, it was a challenge of the first order merely to survive, let alone prepare to receive an attack. It is to the Army of Tennessee's everlasting credit that it not only survived this period, but did so as a combat organization that fought back gallantly for two long days before succumbing to overwhelming odds.

Eight
Interlude

General Grant expresses much dissatisfaction at your delay in attacking the enemy. If you wait till General Wilson mounts all his cavalry you will wait till doomsday, for the waste equals the supply.—Halleck to Thomas, December 9, 1864[1]

Although Thomas had the bulk of his infantry on hand by early December, he had become convinced that it would be unwise to move against Hood without adequate cavalry support. An old horse soldier himself, he concurred with Wilson's urging that the mounted regiments be given time to refit before undertaking an offensive.[2] Accordingly, once they were settled in their quarters at Edgefield, Wilson and his staff pressed forward with the task of readying the corps for its part in the forthcoming campaign. Wrote Wilson:

> The first week of December was the busiest and most important period in the reorganization of the cavalry forces. Clothes were drawn for the men, the horses were rested, reshod and well fed, extra shoes were fitted, new arms were issued, old ones were repaired, and equipments of every kind were put in order. As fast as horses were received, they were issued where they would do the most good, and while they came in large numbers dismounted men from the rear came more rapidly in numbers sufficient to constitute two extra brigades of fifteen hundred men each. These were organized and used on foot as infantry till horses could be got for them.[3]

Fulfilling his promise to keep Grant's headquarters apprised of the situation in Middle Tennessee, Wilson wrote to Grant's military secretary, Adam Badeau, in early December, declaring that he was "making good progress in getting my command ready for the field. Ten days will make a wonderful change." Then, with his characteristic confidence and optimism, Wilson added, "Tell General Grant that Hood is doing good service for the

Union and ought not to be disturbed for the present.... If he will only wait a few days I would not give much for his hide."[4] Wilson also took advantage of the opportunity to remind Grant's headquarters that he was still awaiting President Lincoln's approval of Sherman's order giving his new command official corps status. Wilson declared, "He should either do this at once, or make an order establishing a cavalry department, for the simple reason that nothing less than full authority can enable me to thoroughly regenerate it, and to give the staff proper rank."[5]

By far, however, the most immediate and serious problem confronting Wilson was a shortage of horses. When he assumed field command near Columbia, Wilson had some 4,500 mounted troops. During the next two weeks, the corps received approximately 3,000 remounts besides harvesting an additional 1,500 from the surrounding countryside during the retreat to Nashville, but due to the arduous nature of the campaign, about 1,500 had to be sent back to the remount depots to recuperate. Many horses were still unshod and most of those arriving from the depots were needed to replace broken-down animals, so there was little net gain in numbers.[6] If the procurement of horses constituted a major challenge, maintaining them in serviceable condition proved no less difficult. The stress of continuous campaigning, particularly under adverse weather conditions, wore out the horses much faster than the riders. By the time Wilson's brigades reached Edgefield, the effects of the past month were plainly visible.

Forage also posed a problem. After three and a half years of war, the countryside had little left to offer and the weather exacerbated the problem. Since the burning of the big supply depot at Johnsonville by Forrest in November, the quartermaster was finding it difficult to keep up with demands for hay or "long forage" as it was then called. According to some, this shortage of hay was having an adverse effect on the horses. However, the chief quartermaster, Brigadier General Robert Allen, pointed out that the horses would not suffer if fed a full ration of grain for a few weeks, provided they were properly cared for. General Allen angrily declared that some officers "shamefully abuse their horses and charge it to hay."[7]

At the outset of the Civil War, many if not most of the volunteer cavalrymen in the Union army had little or no idea about how to be a horse soldier, how to ride and fight as troopers, or how to care for their horses. Although the school of the saddle gradually taught these men about the responsibilities of being a cavalryman, including an awareness that their value as a mounted soldier depended on having a serviceable horse between their legs, many men and officers remained dilatory in providing care for their mounts.[8]

General Henry Halleck was of the opinion that the cavalry was wasting far too many horses. Early in December he complained to Grant that 22,000 animals had been issued to the western cavalry since September 20. If this number, without any campaign, had already been reduced to 10,000, Wilson's cavalry would never be fully remounted.[9] Halleck's criticism was unjustified, however. A good portion of Sherman's cavalry had been on almost continuous duty since the fall of Atlanta, including the recent campaign that had brought Hood's army to the gates of Nashville. Moreover, Thomas was quick to point out, not only had a great many horses been killed in battle, but many had died of diseases such as glanders and distemper. Finally, what Halleck failed to take into account was that many of the 22,000 horses he alluded to were remounts that had not had an opportunity to fully recover from the rigors of the Atlanta campaign before being pressed back into service.[10]

Halleck had plenty of supporters and some were more severe in their criticism. Sherman, in fact, declared that he had "not seen in this war a cavalry command of 1,000 that was not afraid of the sight of a dozen infantry bayonets."[11] An infantry veteran visiting the Ninth Illinois Cavalry in camp at Edgefield remarked that the "artillery makes the noise, the cavalry makes the show, and we do the work."[12] In the past there had been plenty of justification for the foot soldier's time-honored gripe about the show-off, do-nothing horsemen. But, as Wilson put it, neither the oft-heard reward offered "for a dead cavalryman nor the cry of 'grab a root' was ever heard in the East after the Battle of Winchester nor in the West after the Battle of Nashville."[13]

The challenge of rounding up enough horses to mount all of the regiments in Wilson's growing corps was made considerably easier by Secretary of War Edwin M. Stanton's December 1 communiqué to Thomas, authorizing the latter to "seize and impress horses and every other species of property needed for military service in your command." Thomas was further advised that he "need not hesitate an hour about exercising this authority at Nashville, Louisville, and wherever property can be had."[14] The authority was formalized with the publication of General Order Number 5, dated December 3, 1864. Memorandum receipts were to be issued for each animal taken. Upon presentation of the receipt to an army quartermaster, a government voucher, not exceeding the $160 price set by the Cavalry Bureau, would be given to the individual whose horse had been impressed.[15]

The order was understandably welcomed by Wilson, who promptly dispatched four regiments into lower Kentucky, a region traditionally rich in prime horseflesh. In addition, a 50-man detachment under Lieutenant Joseph Hedges, Fourth U.S. Cavalry (regulars), was ordered to comb Nashville and environs and collect every hack, omnibus, and carriage horse deemed suitable for cavalry purposes. For reasons unexplained, the Adams Express Company seems to have been exempted from the order.[16]

The roundup was highly successful; Wilson reported collecting some 7,000 horses within seven days after receiving the authorization. He wrote:

> Every horse and mare that could be used was taken. All street-car and livery stable horses, and private carriage and saddle horses, were seized. Even Andrew Johnson, the vice-president elect, was forced to give up his pair. A circus then at Nashville lost everything except its ponies; even the old white trick horse was taken but it is alleged that the young and handsome equestrienne, who claimed him, succeeded in convincing my adjutant general that the horse was unfit for cavalry service.[17]

Wilson's troopers were so thorough that the civilian populace in these areas was soon howling to Secretary Stanton:

> The general impressment of horses by the military is so oppressive here that we cannot think it meets your approbation. All horses are taken without regard to the occupation of the owner or his loyalty. Loaded country wagons with produce for market are left in the road; milk carts, drays and butcher's wagons are left in the street, their horses seized. We know not the immediate necessities of the service, but we are certain that great wrong is being done in carrying out the order. If there be such we pray you look into it.[18]

Stanton refused to be swayed, however, and the impressment of horses continued. But even with these steps, there were simply not enough animals available to mount every trooper in the cavalry corps. Consequently, on December 10, Wilson ordered his division commanders to take "instant measures to mount regiments complete by dismounting partially dismounted regiments. Those to be mounted will be selected from the best armed and disciplined regiments in the command."[19]

While the need for horses was the corps's biggest deficiency, Wilson also had to contend with a tremendous backlog of requisitions for new arms and equipment. Wilson wanted every man armed with a Spencer carbine, but the demand exceeded the supply. So difficult were they to come by, in fact, that there was a standing order, freeing from camp duty for one week any soldier who was enterprising enough to procure a Spencer for himself.[20] Fortunately, many of the men were already armed with Spencers and there was a liberal sprinkling of other repeating weapons, including Burnsides, Colts, Maynards, Sharps, and a few Henrys. In addition to the carbine, most regiments were also equipped with revolvers, and a few carried sabers.[21]

Besides the seemingly endless problem of finding enough horses, weapons, and accoutrements, there were regiments to be reassigned, incoming personnel to be processed, and a host of lesser administrative duties required to keep a military command functioning properly. Thomas and Wilson both had an especially difficult challenge in this regard; each was forced to create a military organization out of disparate units hastily assembled to repel an invasion. While some of these regiments had been assigned with each other in the past, they had not previously been brought together in any command beyond the division level.

Tennessee governor and U.S. vice president Andrew Johnson's undisciplined volunteer cavalrymen were a military and political headache for Wilson. During the Civil War it was virtually impossible to maintain a volunteer regiment at full strength. Most governors, including Andrew Johnson, preferred to authorize new regiments rather than fill up the ranks of the older units because creating a new regiment afforded the governor an opportunity to repay an old debt or extend a political favor by appointing someone to a regimental command. The system was particularly costly and wasteful with the volunteer cavalry because it took much longer to turn a raw recruit into an effective horse soldier. It would have been far more efficient if the new recruits had been absorbed into existing regiments and trained alongside veterans.

Wilson had originally incurred Johnson's hostility when, as chief of the Cavalry Bureau, he successfully opposed Johnson's efforts to raise 12 regiments of one-year volunteer cavalrymen from Tennessee. However, in the interim between leaving the Cavalry Bureau in the spring of 1864 and assuming command of Sherman's horse wing the following October, Wilson discovered, much to his chagrin, that Johnson had somehow managed to secure the necessary authorization to enlist his 12 regiments of one-year horsemen.

Discipline in these units was practically nonexistent. Many were frequently absent without leave and not a few were nothing more than "drunken rowdies who used their authority to terrorize the people among whom they were stationed." These particular Tennessee regiments were anything but a welcome addition to Wilson's new corps, which had plenty of legitimate problems without having to contend with this rabble. Nevertheless, they were under Thomas's overall jurisdiction, and as cavalry, became Wilson's responsibility.[22] Wilson soon discovered that in most cases the discipline problems in the Tennessee regiments could be traced directly to the officers, who, in many instances, were more guilty than their men. The governor alone held the power to appoint or dismiss such individuals, and his cooperation in resolving the problem was deemed essential. Accordingly, at Thomas's suggestion, Wilson called on Johnson and presented his problem.

The vice president, however, became angry at Wilson's candid and blunt remarks about the conduct of his Tennesseans. Disgusted with Johnson's reaction, Wilson, with a sarcastic apology for having troubled his excellency, excused himself and started to leave. When Johnson inquired as to why he was leaving, Wilson told him he was thoroughly disillusioned. He said:

> I came here thinking that you were a statesman and a patriot, but I am sorry to find that you are merely a politician of the common sort. I read your speech in the Senate against secession and I said to myself, here is a man worthy to be President, but this interview convinces me that I am wrong.[23]

Wilson later recalled that the vice president immediately softened and announced his intention to cooperate fully. However, even though Johnson exhibited a cordial and cooperative attitude throughout the remainder of the campaign, Wilson remained unconvinced of his sincerity. The incident was perfectly in character for Wilson, but it was also an incredibly injudicious statement for a career Army officer to make to a man in Johnson's political position. In point of fact, the vice president evidently never forgot or forgave Wilson; upon assuming the presidency, Johnson used the power of his office to stymie Wilson's career.[24]

At any rate, Wilson's solution to the problem of the Tennessee cavalry regiments was simple and effective: the regiments were broken up and distributed among the other regiments and brigades where the men were subject to effective discipline. Vacancies at the regimental command level were now filled by capable veterans such as Colonel George Spalding of Michigan, who ultimately turned the Twelfth Tennessee Cavalry into a highly effective combat unit.[25]

The continuing interdepartmental struggle to get Grierson's cavalry to Nashville might have been funny had it not been for the gravity of the situation in Middle Tennessee. The two divisions of cavalry properly belonging to the Army and Department of Tennessee had for some time been concentrated in southwest Tennessee and northern Mississippi. Designated the Cavalry Corps, District of West Tennessee, these units were commanded by Brigadier General Benjamin H. Grierson. His unit commanders were Hatch and Colonel Edward F. Winslow. Normally, Grierson's horsemen operated out of either Memphis or Vicksburg, defending Federal installations in the region against Forrest, raiding down into Mississippi, or chasing after guerrilla bands that liberally infected the area.

Early in September 1864, the bulk of Edward Winslow's brigade was sent across the Mississipi River into Missouri and Arkansas to assist Federal forces in the area in repelling a large Confederate column under General Sterling Price. On October 24, Major General O. O. Howard, commanding the Department and Army of the Tennessee, advised Grierson of Wilson's

Colonel Edward F. Winslow.

appointment and of the latter's intention to reorganize all of Sherman's cavalry. Grierson was to send Hatch's division to join Wilson in the field (then near Rome, Georgia) as quickly as possible. Grierson was further instructed to spare no effort in retrieving Winslow's command from Missouri and prepare his own division for a raid through northern Mississippi and Alabama preparatory to joining Wilson in the field.

Grierson replied that he had already ordered Hatch to join Wilson and that he was still trying to bring Winslow back. He was not, however, having much success because the Federal command in Missouri was reluctant to part with Winslow's troops. With regard to readying his command for a raid, Grierson pointed out that except for a mixed detachment left over from Winslow's and Hatch's commands, he had no other troops available.[26]

By virtue of Special Order Number 7, Cavalry Corps, Military Division of the Mississippi, issued on November 6, 1864, Grierson was appointed to command of the Fourth Division, which was to include Edward Winslow's brigade, together with such other troops as would thereafter be assigned. The order directed Grierson to collect the various detachments of his command and join the cavalry corps at Nashville, moving by way of Louisville. Grierson was further instructed to leave one regiment at Vicksburg and two or three at Memphis for purposes of scouting and reconnaissance.[27]

On the face of it, the transfer of these troops ought to have been a relatively uncomplicated, straightforward procedure. Instead it evolved into what was perhaps Wilson's most vexing administrative problem. Three factors were involved: First, there was the logistical difficulty of bringing troops back from Missouri and Arkansas. Added to that was a jurisdictional disagreement over which military department really had authority over the units in question. These two factors were further complicated by Grierson's apparent failure to appreciate the sense of urgency in Wilson's orders. All these problems combined to produce a bureaucratic snag of the first order.

Impatient over the delay in bringing these units into the fold, Wilson sent Brigadier General Joseph F. Knipe to Memphis on November 16 to oversee the transfer of Grierson's baggage and wagons to Nashville. Knipe discovered that Grierson, seemingly in opposition to orders, had sent a detachment of recently returned cavalry from St. Louis to Memphis for refitting, rather than sending them directly to Nashville. That was irritating enough, but he then learned that Grierson was gone—as far as Wilson could tell, without authorization.[28]

What had happened was that Grierson discovered that a detachment of some 400 dismounted men from Winslow's brigade had arrived at St. Louis. His adjutant obtained an order from the department commander, Major General William S. Rosecrans, to have these troops sent downriver to Memphis for refitting. Grierson's decision was based on his understanding that the remainder of Winslow's brigade would be returning crosscountry to Memphis from Missouri and Arkansas, rather than to St. Louis. Thus it made more sense to reunite the brigade at Memphis.[29] The problem, however, was that Grierson's logic, however well-intentioned, conflicted with Wilson's orders for these units to be sent directly from St. Louis to Nashville. Thomas had further reinforced that directive by requesting that Rosecrans send all cavalry units earmarked for Middle Tennessee via the Cumberland River to Nashville.[30]

Totally exasperated, on November 20 Wilson sent his personal representative, Lieutenant Henry E. Noyes, to St. Louis, Memphis, "or wherever else it may be necessary," armed with full authority to get Grierson's troops started to Nashville. Along with Noyes went Wilson's personal letter to Grierson, sharply reprimanding him for his actions and demanding an explanation for what Wilson regarded as unauthorized absence.[31]

Arriving in St. Louis on November 23, Noyes met Colonel Edward Winslow, who was recuperating from a leg wound sustained in the Battle of the Big Blue a month earlier. The rest of the division, Noyes learned, was expected to arrive about the first of December. Winslow proved most cooperative in helping to arrange the speediest possible transfer of his command to Nashville, as did General Rosecrans. However, when he reached Memphis on November 28, Noyes found that Grierson was absent and that Major General C. C. Washburn, commanding the District of West Tennessee, was at first disinclined to part with any of Grierson's cavalry. Finally, after two conferences and with Winslow's help, Noyes managed to pry loose the three regiments that had formerly constituted Winslow's old brigade: the Third and Fourth Iowa and the Tenth Missouri. The three were veteran regiments and highly regarded.[32]

When Grierson returned and learned that he had come under verbal fire, he wrote to Wilson, defending his actions, which he regarded as being perfectly reasonable. He had, it seems, gone to Springfield, Illinois, to see about filling vacancies in the ranks of three Illinois cavalry regiments. His authority for the leave had been a directive from headquarters, District of West Tennessee. Further, Grierson pointed out, the fact "That your orders and those of Major General Thomas concerning the cavalry have not been carried out is certainly no fault of mine...."

Although Wilson was clearly miffed, it was questionable as to whether official action against Grierson was justified. In being absent from St. Louis, he had acted in accordance with a departmental directive. His decision to send troops to Memphis was not justified. When the division began its return march it was about equidistant from both St. Louis and Memphis. Admittedly, it would have been shorter to march overland from Memphis to Nashville, but orders had specified a concentration at St. Louis, where the large remount depot was better equipped to supply fresh horses that were almost certain to be needed. It could be argued that since the issuance of Special Order Number 7 on November 6, Grierson was a member of the cavalry corps and subject only to orders issued from Wilson's headquarters. The situation, however, was not so clear-cut. Strictly speaking, Grierson reported to Wilson, but he also operated under the immediate jurisdiction of generals Washburn and Dana, a reality he could scarcely ignore.[33]

Sherman's carte blanche order gave Wilson every right to tap Grierson's cavalry for his new corps. Ordinarily, that would probably have been the end of it. However, a November 7 presidential directive assigning control of all Federal troops along the east bank of the Mississippi to Major General E. R. S. Canby created a most inopportune administrative problem because it encompassed the units at Vicksburg and Memphis. Since Grierson's cavalry had been operating out of these locations, generals Washburn and Dana considered them subject to the new directive, as did Canby.[34] Thomas and Wilson, on the other hand, regarded Grierson's command as an extension of Sherman's army and thus under Thomas's overall command. In any event, as a result of the dispute, two closely allied but independent commands wound up being at cross-purposes when they ought to have been complementing each other. This was a perfect illustration of why Wilson wanted the same kind of presidential authority that had been given to Canby. He was convinced that such authority would have added more muscle to Sherman's directive and thus strengthened his own position.[35]

Grierson's situation was certainly awkward to be sure, juxtaposed as he was between two commands. He seems, however, not to have been overly concerned about dealing in a forthright manner with the issues involving his

Brigadier General Benjamin H. Grierson (U.S. Army Commands photograph no. 98-X-1 in the National Archives).

division. He could, for example, have made an effort to keep Wilson better informed about the returning cavalry units and secured Wilson's permission to visit Springfield. In fact, given the exigencies of the time, getting his troops to Nashville ought to have been a higher priority than recruiting in Illinois. In any case, the entire episode created friction between Wilson and

Grierson. As a result, Grierson was subsequently replaced as commander of the Fourth Division by Emory Upton.[36]

In the meantime, on November 30, Lieutenant Colonel Frederick W. Benteen,[37] Tenth Missouri Cavalry, commanding the brigade in Winslow's absence, brought his long-sought, campaign-weary troopers into St. Louis, having marched and fought over some 2,000 miles in 12 weeks.[38] Benteen was delayed in St. Louis because an unusually heavy concentration of ice in the Mississippi had snarled river traffic. It was not until December 9 that Benteen's men were finally put aboard steamers for the trip to Nashville, their horses on barges lashed alongside the ships. The journey proved to be cold, time consuming, and somewhat hazardous. One steamer was disabled by an internal explosion and several others became ice-bound. In both situations, men and horses had to be put ashore to complete their trek by rail.[39]

Meanwhile, the portion of Winslow's command that had remained in Memphis during the Sterling Price campaign had since been supplemented by returning detachments of sick, wounded, and dismounted (including those sent down from St. Louis by Grierson). This command was set to embark for Nashville when General Napoleon J. T. Dana suddenly countermanded the order, relented, then finally stopped the departure for good. Dana also instructed Winslow to detain Benteen's contingent if at all possible.

So the jurisdictional dispute persisted. In this case, Dana was using as authorization for his action a December 6 order from General Halleck, directing him to launch a cavalry strike against the Mobile and Ohio Railroad as a means of severing Hood's supply line. Dana felt that the entire division was needed to do the job, but Winslow protested, pointing out that his command had specifically been ordered to Nashville.[40]

Winslow was upset with this new development. On December 15 he wrote to Noyes, expressing disapproval and frustration over the continued separation of his brigade. He hoped that Wilson's influence would prevail and suggested that perhaps Grierson had not been as helpful as he might have been. "I am powerless here, or anywhere, in this matter," Winslow wrote, "but had my efforts here been properly seconded by Brigadier-General Grierson, I am perfectly confident that we should now be in Nashville."[41] Halleck finally settled the matter by releasing Benteen's detachment, but he did permit Dana to retain the Memphis contingent until after the strike against the Mobile and Ohio Railroad had been effected. At that time the balance of Winslow's command was to be sent promptly to Nashville.

This situation illustrated a flaw in the Federal command structure. To begin with, clarification was needed to establish exactly who had jurisdiction over Grierson's cavalry. Assuming, as Wilson and Thomas did, that they belonged to Sherman's command, then Halleck's order ought to have been directed to Thomas's headquarters, which would then have been referred to Wilson for execution. In any event, Winslow was not the only one displeased with how Grierson had handled the situation. On December 13, Brevet Major General Emory Upton arrived from the east. Wilson promptly named him to replace Grierson as commander of the Fourth Division.[42]

Only 25 years old, Emory Upton was already one of the most accomplished officers in the Union army, having served with marked distinction in both the infantry and artillery. An outstanding field commander and student of military history and tactics, Upton's influence on the United States Army would be felt long after his time.[43] Wilson and Upton had much in common: physical size, age, ability, dedication to duty, fierce determination, and boundless self-confidence. They had been friends since West Point; Wilson had graduated in 1860, Upton in 1861. Wilson stood sixth in his class; Upton was eighth in his. Later, they served together in the Shenandoah Valley, Wilson as commander of Sheridan's Third Cavalry Division, Upton as commander of the First Division, VI Corps.

During the Battle of Winchester, Upton received a severe thigh wound that laid bare the femoral artery. Sheridan ordered him evacuated, but Upton refused. Instead, he had his surgeon apply a tourniquet and remained on the field, issuing orders from a stretcher until darkness ended the fighting. "This," Wilson was later to declare, "was the most heroic action that came under my observation during the war."[44]

When Wilson went west to command Sherman's cavalry, he asked for his old friend, but the wound prevented Upton from reporting for duty until mid–December. Although totally lacking in cavalry experience, Upton was completely confident in his ability to succeed and promptly set about bringing his scattered regiments together.[45] Upton visited Benteen's detachment on their steamers at Cairo, Illinois, then went on to Memphis to see about the rest of Winslow's command. As a result of Halleck's order, however, Upton learned that he would not have access to the rest of his division until after the strike on the Mobile and Ohio Railroad, which had sortied from Memphis on December 21 under Grierson's command.[46]

On December 22, more than two months after the issuance of the original order, Benteen's detachment, the first contingent of Winslow's brigade, debarked in deep snow at Portland, Kentucky, just below Louisville. From there the detachment marched through Louisville to join the gathering units of Upton's new division, then bivouacked at Camp Upton near the Louisville and Nashville Railroad. Winslow and the rest of his brigade did not complete their assignment with Grierson until early January. Thus they were unable to reach Camp Upton until the middle of the month.[47]

Brevet Major General Emory Upton (U.S. Signal Corps photograph no. 111-B-5255 [Brady Collection] in the National Archives).

While Wilson was struggling to get his divisions mounted, armed, and organized, Thomas was waging a backstage war with Grant and the Federal high command in Washington, even as he prepared to take the offensive against Hood. Lincoln, Stanton, Halleck, and finally Grant had all begun to grow visibly worried when Hood and his tatterdemalion brigades arrived in front of Nashville. Mainly, they feared that Hood would somehow slip around Thomas and march up into Kentucky or even Ohio. Consequently, with each passing day that Thomas failed to attack, this concern, especially on the part of Grant, assumed the proportions of genuine alarm, bordering on panic. Wilson labeled the notion of a Confederate winter march to the Ohio River as "about the wildest and the most desperate and hopeless undertaking possible to imagine."[48] Wild and desperate perhaps, but the entire campaign had been a long shot to begin with. What more could Hood lose by trying for the Ohio River?

Oddly enough, the situation seemed to worsen in direct proportion to the distance one happened to be from the threatened area. Everyone, except those directly involved at Nashville, was wild with concern. As Wilson put it, "No apprehension was felt at Nashville, there was not the slightest excuse for any at Washington."[49] The threat, although real, was greatly exaggerated by those not in a position to make an informed judgment. The Army of Tennessee had suffered a frightful mauling at Franklin. Rations and clothing were practically nonexistent. Blankets were threadbare—when they were even available—and a great many men were without footwear of any kind. By comparison, the Federals were adequately supplied, growing in numbers each day, and securely entrenched behind what was probably the most strongly fortified city on the North American continent at that time.[50]

Despite their hungry, battered condition, Hood's army remained a viable force with plenty of sting left. So long as that remained the case, it represented a genuine threat. What neutralized that threat, insofar as those in charge at Nashville were concerned, was the unrelenting Federal vigilance. Wilson had the Seventh Ohio Cavalry patrolling the Cumberland River line as far west as Clarksville. John Hammond's brigade was covering the river east to Carthage. Additionally, a fleet of ironclads and gunboats supplemented these patrols, thus making it virtually impossible for Hood to sneak by unnoticed.[51]

Despite these precautions and Thomas's reassurances that the situation was firmly under control, Grant and officials in Washington remained unconvinced and edgy. Colonel Henry Stone, a member of Thomas's staff, described the pressure his chief was subjected to during this period:

> From the 2d of December until the battle was fought on the 15th, the general-in-chief did not cease day or night, to send him [Thomas] from the headquarters at City Point, Va., most urgent and often uncalled-for orders in regard to his operations, culminating in an order on the 9th relieving him, and directing him to turn over his command to General Schofield, who was assigned to his place—and order which, had it not been revoked, the great captain would have obeyed with loyal single-heartedness.[52]

Wilson, characteristically, pulled no punches in his criticism of the pressure
brought to bear on Thomas:

> He [Thomas] was twitted with being slow. He was threatened with
> removal. Orders, indeed, were drafted to that end, and, as if to spare
> him no humiliation, it was proposed that he should turn over his
> command to Schofield, his inferior in rank, and report to him for
> duty. Not satisfied with this, Grant ordered [Major General John
> Alexander] Logan from City Point to Nashville. And then, as the
> crowning evidence of lost equipoise, of confusion in counsel, and
> want of confidence either in Thomas, Schofield, Logan, or in all of
> them, Grant himself left his army in Lee's front at Petersburg and
> got as far as Washington on his way to Nashville.[53]

The stream of dispatches indicative of Washington's mounting worry
commenced on December 2, when Stanton wired Grant expressing Lincoln's
concern over the situation in Middle Tennessee. "This looks like the
McClellan and Rosecrans strategy of do nothing and let the rebels raid the
country," Stanton informed Grant, politely advising him that the president
wished this to be considered.[54] Within half an hour after receiving Stanton's
communiqué, Grant wired Thomas urging him to attack before Hood had
an opportunity to fortify. Stanton had evidently planted a seed in Grant that
wasted no time taking root. Two and a half hours later, Grant wired Thomas
again, prodding him to attack before Hood destroyed the railroads. With
this second message, however, Grant was considerate enough to point out
that since he was not personally present he might "err" as to the best method
of handling the situation. It was the last time he would be so generous.[55]

Except for Schofield, Thomas had been solidly supported in his conduct of the campaign, although Wilson felt that it would have been wiser
to concentrate at either Franklin or Pulaski. He had urged Thomas to bring
in the Murfreesboro garrison, strip the Chattanooga railroad of troops, and
push forward to meet Hood.[56] Thomas would probably have liked nothing
better than to move against his opponent, but without A. J. Smith's support
and given the logistics of getting his command organized, there was no way
he could have considered taking the offensive any earlier than he did. Wilson,
strangely enough, seems to have overlooked the fact that his own command
was hardly ready to undertake an offensive movement by the time Hood
reached Pulaski or even Franklin. Indeed, much of the criticism leveled
against Thomas was over the delay in getting Wilson's cavalry ready.

It is to Thomas's everlasting credit that he had the courage of conviction to withstand the interference of Grant and Washington until Wilson
was ready. The blue-clad horsemen would play a pivotal role in the forthcoming battle. Thomas replied to Grant's two communiqués that same night,

explaining that he lacked sufficient infantry and cavalry to mount an offensive, but planned to do so when Wilson's First Division arrived from Louisville in two or three days. Thomas reminded Grant that his command was composed of the "two weakest corps of General Sherman's army and all the dismounted cavalry except one brigade, and the task of reorganizing and equipping has met with many delays, which have enabled Hood to take advantage of my crippled condition."[57]

On December 6, Grant again wired Thomas, advising him not to wait for more cavalry. Later that same day, Thomas sent off a dispatch to both Grant and Halleck, explaining that he hesitated to attack with fewer than 6,000 cavalry because Forrest was reported to have twice that number.[58] Halleck apparently showed the dispatch to Stanton because on the seventh, he wrote to Grant, thundering his disapproval of Thomas's rationale. "Thomas seems unwilling to attack because it is hazardous, as if all war was anything but hazardous. If he waits for Wilson to get ready Gabriel will be blowing his last horn."[59]

On December 8, Grant again tried to coax Thomas into taking the offensive. To the lieutenant general at City Point, Virginia, it seemed clear that Hood was trying to cross the Cumberland, although the basis for this insight is not clear. "Why not attack at once?" Grant asked Thomas.

> By all means avoid the contingency of a foot race to see which, you or Hood, can beat to the Ohio.... Now is one of the finest opportunities ever presented of destroying one of the three armies of the enemy. Use measures at your command, and you can do this and cause a rejoicing that will resound from one end of the land to the other.[60]

The following day it was Halleck's turn. Grant was very much dissatisfied with the delay, he informed Thomas. Do not wait for Wilson, said Halleck, or "you will wait till doomsday, for the waste equals the supply. Moreover, you will soon be in the same condition that Rosecrans was last year—with so many animals you cannot feed them."[61] That afternoon, Thomas advised both Grant and Halleck that he had planned to attack on the tenth, but a severe storm of freezing rain struck during the early morning hours of the ninth and rendered all movement virtually impossible. To both, Thomas declared that he had done everything possible, but that if Grant saw fit to relieve him, he would "submit without a murmur."[62]

Grant indeed saw fit to do so. Ironically, even as Thomas declared his intention to "submit without a murmur," orders to that effect were in fact being prepared, directing Thomas to turn his command over to Schofield, to whom he was then to report for duty. The order was signed but, fortunately, never executed.[63] Disturbed as he was with Thomas, Grant nevertheless remained hesitant about replacing him. On December 8 he had informed Halleck that if Thomas didn't strike immediately he ought to be relieved. Halleck replied that if Grant wished Thomas replaced he should give the order, but that it was his responsibility. Halleck felt certain that no one in Washington actually wanted Thomas removed from command.[64]

This was a rather unexpected turnabout. After believing the consensus was to remove Thomas, Halleck was now saying that no one in Washington wanted Thomas removed. Grant must have chafed at finding himself suddenly standing alone on this issue and decided to back off for the moment. He told Halleck:

> I am very much unwilling to do injustice to an officer who has done as much good for the service as General Thomas, and will therefore suspend the order relieving him until it is seen whether he will do anything.[65]

The storm that struck Middle Tennessee on December 9 was widespread and severe. Wilson reported, "Rain, snow, and sleet in abundance followed by intense cold covered the ground that night with such a glare of snow and ice as to render it impossible to move cavalry not especially roughshod for the occasion." Some of Thomas's staff officers found it virtually impossible to even ride to headquarters.[66]

On the evening of December 10, Thomas called a meeting of his commanders in his room at the St. Cloud Hotel. After reporting on Grant's insistence that an immediate attack be launched and his own plans to hold back until the ice had melted, Thomas asked for opinions. Being the junior commander present, Wilson spoke first. Given the icy conditions then prevailing, he vowed that if the situation was reversed, his dismounted troopers could defend the Confederate positions with "nothing more dangerous than baskets of brickbats."[67] According to Wilson's account of the meeting, his declaration produced smiles of agreement and, one by one, generals Wood, Smith, and Steedman each lent complete support to Thomas's plan of action.[68]

At the conclusion of the conference, Thomas asked Wilson to remain a moment longer. When the two men were alone, Thomas, in an uncharacteristic display of emotion, expressed his chagrin at the unrelenting pressure from the east:

> Wilson, the Washington authorities treat me as if I were a boy. They seem to think me incapable of planning a campaign or of fighting a battle, but if they will just let me alone til thawing weather begins and the ground is in condition for us to move at all I will

show them what we can do. I am sure my plan of operation is correct, and we shall lick the enemy, if he only stays to receive our
attack.[69]

Wilson later recalled that he came away from that meeting holding an even
higher opinion of the soldierly qualities of George H. Thomas.

The pressure continued from the east where a fear that Hood would
not wait for Thomas to attack but would sortie out and cause all sorts of
trouble was what had Grant nearly frantic. Grant wired Thomas on
December 11, writing:

> If you delay attack longer, the mortifying spectacle will be wit-
> nessed of a rebel army moving for the Ohio River, and you will be
> forced to act, accepting such weather as you find. Let there be no
> further delay. Hood cannot stand even a drawn battle, so far from
> his supplies of ordnance stores. If he retreats and you follow, he must
> lose his material and much of his army. I am in hopes of receiving
> a dispatch from you to-day announcing that you have moved. Delay
> no longer for weather or reinforcements.[70]

Thomas, who must have been exasperated beyond belief and thoroughly
weary of the continual plodding, answered Grant's communiqué six hours
later, patiently explaining that he would

> obey the order as promptly as possible, however much I may regret
> it, as the attack will have to be made under every disadvantage. The
> whole country is covered with a perfect sheet of ice and sleet, and
> it is with difficulty the troops are able to move about on level ground.
> It was my intention to attack Hood as soon as the ice melted, and
> would have done so yesterday had it not been for the storm.[71]

Thomas's plan originally called for Wilson to break camp at Edgefield,
cross the Cumberland, and move into position on the right flank, preparatory to attacking Hood on the tenth. The storm postponed the attack, but
by the night of the eleventh, the weather had moderated enough to permit
the troops to begin moving into attack positions. Wilson, accordingly,
advised his division commanders that they were to begin crossing the
Cumberland on the morning of December 12.[72]

As outlined in Special Field Order Number 1, Hatch and Knipe were
to cross their divisions on the pontoon bridge while Croxton moved via the
planked-over railroad bridge. Johnson was to follow Hatch, but was
instructed to use the railroad bridge should it happen to be vacant by that
time. Ordnance trains and ambulances would follow the troops. Each man
was to be provisioned with rations for three days and forage for one.[73] One

witness who observed the cavalry's movement into battle position recalled "From early dawn all day, like some gigantic half-human monster, those blue columns moved steadily on."[74]

By nightfall on December 12, Thomas finally had his command ready, but, as he explained to Halleck, another delay was yet necessary:

> I have the troops ready to make an attack on the enemy as soon as the sleet which now covers the ground has melted sufficiently to enable the men to march. As the whole country is now covered with a sheet of ice so hard and slippery it is utterly impossible for troops to ascend the slopes, or even move over level ground in anything like order. It has taken the entire day to place my cavalry in position, and it has only been finally effected with imminent risk and many serious accidents, resulting from the number of horses falling with their riders on the roads. Under these circumstances, I believe an attack at this time would only result in a useless sacrifice of life.[75]

Unconvinced, Halleck tried a new approach on December 14, perhaps hoping to appeal to Thomas's conscience and soldierly qualities. Hood's position, claimed Halleck, was threatening to jeopardize the entire Federal plan of action to end the war! In addition to threatening the Ohio River country, Hood was forcing General Canby to retain large contingents of troops along the Mississippi River, troops that were sorely needed elsewhere. "Every day's delay on your part, therefore, seriously interferes with General Grant's plan," Halleck warned Thomas.[76] Patiently, the long-suffering Thomas replied that the weather had finally moderated, the ice was at long last beginning to melt, and the attack would be launched on the morning of the fifteenth.[77]

Unbeknownst to Thomas, however, on the thirteenth Grant had sent Major General John Logan from Washington to Nashville to replace Thomas. Logan's instructions were relative: He was to notify Grant immediately upon reaching the Tennessee capital and was to assume command only if Thomas had not yet launched his attack.[78] Even this course of action, however, failed to calm the nervous Grant, who suddenly concluded that the situation merited his personal attention and entrained for Nashville himself on the afternoon of December 14, convinced that the possibility of a great disaster loomed in Middle Tennessee.[79]

As Grant and Logan headed west, Thomas called a second conference at the St. Cloud Hotel on the afternoon of the fourteenth. With a few minor adjustments, the plan of attack outlined for the tenth would be followed on the morning of December 15. As spelled out in Special Field Order Number 342, the plan called for A. J. Smith's corps to move against the Confederate left flank, supported by Wilson's cavalry. Thomas J. Wood's Fourth Corps would advance on Smith's left against the center of Hood's line. Whether because Thomas felt it merited a rest after the withdrawal from Pulaski to Nashville or perhaps for more personal reasons, Schofield's Twenty-third Corps was assigned a relatively minor role covering Wood's left flank. Responsibility for the Nashville fortifications was assigned to Major General Steedman, who was to hold the remainder of his command ready to provide support wherever needed.[80]

Like Thomas, Wilson left nothing to chance. Since his cavalry would be working in conjunction with and in support of A. J. Smith's infantry, Wilson conferred with Smith personally to make certain that each understood the other's plan of operation. At the same time, Wilson made sure that his own commanders were fully conversant with their respective roles. "I personally showed my division and brigade commanders the ground over which they were to advance, assembled them at my headquarters, and verbally reiterated my instructions. To make sure that there should be no misunderstanding, I then furnished each with a written copy of the orders for his government."[81]

With the plan finalized and the orders issued, Wilson retired to his own tent, where, as the hour approached midnight, he wrote to a friend on Grant's staff:

> Everybody else has made his last will and testament or written to his wife or sweetheart, but having nothing to dispose of, and neither wife nor sweetheart to write to, I give you about four minutes before preparing myself for four or five hours of sleep.
>
> All arrangements are made for battle in the morning, and much seems in our favor. If we are ordinarily successful, and Hood ordinarily complacent, we shall have but little time for letter writing during the next two weeks. The weather has moderated, the rebels are quiescent, and our troops in good condition.[82]

If Wilson was truly expecting complacency from Hood, it would seem to have been a dangerous calculation on his part. Given Hood's irrational behavior in the past, which Wilson certainly ought to have been aware of by that time, it would have been far better to anticipate the unexpected. As the thing played out, of course, the unexpected did not occur. But on the night of December 14, the eve of battle, one could not tell what the morrow would bring.

In any event, it only remained for daylight to set things in motion. Among the rank and file, tired of the drudgery and routine of camp life, there was a ripple of excitement and anticipation. A member of the Ninth Illinois Cavalry recalled that they "were not sorry when the order came to exchange our disagreeable camping-ground for the more dangerous and exciting scenes of the coming battle."[83]

Nine
Nashville

Dang it to hell, Wilson, didn't I tell you we could lick 'em, didn't I tell you we could lick 'em?—Thomas to Wilson[1]

A heavy blanket of fog hung over Nashville and the surrounding countryside as Federal buglers sounded reveille in the damp, bone-chilling, 4 A.M. blackness of Thursday, December 15, 1864. Thomas was up early. Checking out of the St. Cloud Hotel, he rode to a high hill just east of the Hillsboro Pike, where he would have an excellent view of the battle that, finally, was about to get under way.[2]

Along the extensive Federal line, regiments and brigades moved out of the Nashville fortifications to their prescribed battle stations. "On every hand," wrote a member of the Ninth Illinois Cavalry, "was seen the active movement of a large army. The sun had barely risen, but was obscured by dense fog that hung over the city like a pall, the ground yet icy, but slowly giving way to the more humid atmosphere."[3] As the assault troops moved out of the fortifications, they were replaced by General Charles Cruft's provisional division of new recruits, General J. F. Miller's Nashville garrison, and, finally, General J. L. Donaldson's armed quartermaster contingent. Thomas, characteristically leaving nothing to chance, took the precaution of establishing a solid reserve line of defense.[4]

By 9 A.M., the fog had begun to lift, revealing the entire panorama of the unfolding battle. Colonel Henry Stone of Thomas's staff described the scene:

> When about 9 o'clock, the sun began to burn away the fog, the sight from General Thomas' position was inspiring. A little to the left on Montgomery Hill, the salient of the Confederate lines, and not more than six hundred yards distant from Wood's [General Thomas J. Wood's Fourth Corps] salient, on Lawrens Hill, could be seen the advance line of works, behind which an unknown force of the enemy

lay in wait. Beyond, and along the Hillsboro Pike, were stretches of stone wall, with here and there a detached earth-work, through whose embrasures peeped the threatening artillery. To the right, along the valley of Richland Creek, the dark line of Wilson's advancing cavalry could be seen slowly making its difficult way across the wet, swampy, stumpy ground. Close in front, and at the foot of the hill, its right joining Wilson's left, was A. J. Smith's corps, full of cheer and enterprise, and glad to be once more in the open field.[5]

With the movement of the assault troops into position, skirmishers were simultaneously pushed forward and the Federal artillery opened up on the Confederate positions, maintaining a steady bombardment and provoking some lively counterbattery fire in return. General Wood recalled that this fire "from the enemy's batteries, added interest to the scene and showed that he was keenly watching our operations."[6] Indeed, the Confederates were not the only ones who observed the proceedings. Several major Civil War battles were fought before an audience of civilian spectators, looking on as if witnessing the performance of some grand outdoor drama. They had looked on at Bull Run and Gettysburg, and now they lined the hills around Nashville, many hoping to witness a great Confederate victory.[7]

Thomas's initial attack—a diversionary movement—would be executed by General James Steedman, whose 7,600-man command consisted of nine regiments of black infantry, a battalion of white troops, and two batteries of artillery.[8] Steedman, who had advanced down the Murfreesboro Pike under cover of the fog, launched his effort against Cheatham's sector, on the right flank of the Confederate line, about 8:30 A.M. The attack began well enough with the Federals pushing forward boldly, driving Cheatham's skirmishers back. However, as Steedman's advance reached the main line, it got caught in a punishing cross fire and quickly faltered. Some units reportedly broke and ran because of poor leadership.[9] In any case, the attack fell apart and Steedman pulled back to regroup. Later that morning he launched a second sortie, but it had little effect on the outcome of this battle, the key to which was going to be the Confederate left flank. Aside from these two efforts, however, the left of Thomas's line remained mostly inactive for the remainder of the day.[10]

Despite the failure of Steedman's efforts, some of the Federals were convinced that they had deceived Hood, causing him to shift troops from the left and center to reinforce his right flank. In truth, however, Hood was in no way deceived by the maneuver. The transfer of Wilson's cavalry from Edgefield on the thirteenth had convinced him that the main Federal effort would be against his left flank. As a consequence, having discerned Steedman's attack for what it was, Hood actually began shifting troops from his right and center to strengthen the left later that afternoon.[11]

Fog had also delayed the advance of both Wilson and A. J. Smith. Then a mix-up further delayed Wilson's movement until 10 A.M. Wilson had conferred with Smith the previous evening and made arrangements for the latter's infantry to move into position by passing around behind the cavalry. However, there was either a misunderstanding, or Smith failed to inform his subordinates because Wilson's horsemen were held up for nearly two hours while John McArthur's division plodded across their front and into position. Smith attributed the delay to diverging roads and stubborn enemy skirmishers. McArthur, however, claimed that he waited for the cavalry to move out. When they failed to do so, he decided to move on his own volition, which suggests that perhaps Smith had not done a good job informing him of the plan agreed to with Wilson. In any event, the Federal offensive lost two hours of daylight, a loss that proved crucial by day's end.[12]

With the exception of Steedman, who had originally been slated for a largely passive role, Thomas adhered to his battle plan of December 10. A. J. Smith was to assault the Confederate left: Wilson would operate on Smith's right and attempt to get around and behind the Confederate flank. Wood's Fourth Corps was to advance on Smith's right, conforming his movements to those of Smith's. The entire maneuver was to operate like a giant wheel to the right, with Wood acting as the pivot. Schofield, who was assigned to a supporting role, had Jacob Cox's division on the Hillsboro Pike behind Wood's right flank, while General Darius Couch was stationed behind A. J. Smith.[13]

Wilson's main effort was assigned to Edward Hatch's Fifth Division, which was to be the link with Smith's infantry. John Croxton would advance on Hatch's right. On Croxton's right, R. W. Johnson's Sixth Division was directed to clear the Charlotte Pike, maintain communications with Croxton, and generally secure the right flank of the cavalry corps. Finally, Knipe's Seventh Division was available for support wherever needed.[14]

Owing to the terrain and the necessity of conforming to the movements of the infantry, Hatch's entire division save for one regiment in each brigade was ordered to attack dismounted. Croxton's brigade, however, remained fully mounted, as did one brigade each in the divisions of Johnson and Knipe.[15]

Wood's Fourth Corps, the largest in Thomas's command, was ready at 6 A.M., but was delayed until noon by the maneuvering of Smith and Wilson. Wood, however, pushed his skirmishers out and maintained a brisk fire with the Confederates during the hiatus. By noon Smith was finally in position, had established contact with Wood, and the giant wheeling movement of 30,000 men got under way.[16]

Wood's main objective, a high point called Montgomery Hill, was believed to be heavily defended. Other than for a few skirmishers, however, it was largely empty; Hood had evacuated the position several days earlier. Unaware of this fact, Wood ordered a heavy artillery bombardment, then sent in the second brigade of General Samuel Beatty's division under Colonel Sidney Post. Although there was little to oppose the Federal advance, Wood described the assault as though it had overwhelmed the entire Confederate army. "At the command, as sweeps the stiff gale over the ocean," wrote Wood, "driving every object before it, so swept the brigade up the wooded slope, over the enemy's intrenchments; and the hill was won."[17]

On the right, as A. J. Smith advanced, his line gradually swung to the left until it was nearly a north-south axis, paralleling the Hardin Pike. Pushing forward, Smith soon encountered a pair of Confederate redoubts (numbers 4 and 5) guarding Hood's left flank. Unlimbering his artillery, Smith ordered a bombardment to silence the Confederate batteries, while his infantry prepared to assault the enemy works.[18] The Confederate left flank, which ran parallel to the Hardin Pike, actually featured five redoubts. For all intents and purposes, numbers 1, 2, and 3 were part of the main line; 4 and 5, however, were set out across the Hillsboro Pike, some distance beyond the main line and, as such, were exposed and vulnerable.[19]

As noted, between the extreme Confederate left flank and the Cumberland River, Hood had only a token force under the command of General James Chalmers. Chalmers had Edmund Rucker's brigade posted between the river and the Charlotte Pike, while Colonel David Coleman, now commanding the remnants of General Matthew Ector's old brigade, occupied the ground between the Charlotte and Hardin pikes. The Seventh Alabama Cavalry on Coleman's right constituted a tenuous link with the main Confederate line.[20]

Although A. P. Stewart was in overall command on the Confederate left flank, the responsibility for holding the sector that would soon be threatened by Smith's infantry and Wilson's cavalry had been assigned to Major General Edward C. Walthall. At 33, Walthall was the youngest division commander in the army, as well as an extremely tough and capable leader. In addition to his own division, Walthall had just that morning been reinforced by the brigades of Coleman and Claudius Sears.[21] When Stewart learned of the Federal advance, he ordered Walthall to prepare for the onslaught. The latter responded by placing one company of infantry and a battery of artillery in redoubts 4 and 5 even though both were still incomplete. Walthall positioned the remainder of his command behind a stone wall running behind redoubts 3 and 4.[22]

Wilson's forward movement got under way almost simultaneously with the infantry's advance. Hatch was delayed a bit longer than the others because McArthur's troops were still passing across his front. When the way was finally clear, Hatch advanced rapidly, driving back the Confederate skirmishers, and was quickly on top of David Coleman's understrength brigade. Coleman had two companies of Texans in an advanced position east of Richland Creek, with the balance of his brigade behind breastworks along a ridge west of the creek.[23]

As the fog lifted and the Federals commenced their advance, Lieutenant J. T. Tunnell, commanding the Texans, saw a swarm of blue-coats bearing down on his position. He promptly reported the news to Coleman, who ordered Tunnell to hold as long as possible, then fall back on the main position, an order that the lieutenant responded to with alacrity. What Tunnell had seen was Colonel Robert R. Stewart's dismounted first brigade of Hatch's division. So swift was Stewart's advance, however, that Tunnell barely had time to fire a token round of resistance before falling back on Coleman's main line. Unfortunately for the Confederates, Tunnell's rapid pull-back left Chalmers's lone brigade under Rucker isolated and cut off from the rest of the line.

Capitalizing on the moment, Hatch immediately ordered the Twelfth Tennessee Cavalry under Colonel Spalding to exploit the rapid advance. Spalding responded by capturing Chalmers's headquarters baggage, including 14 wagons and 43 prisoners. Spalding's success later prompted Wilson to remark that "this fully vindicated my action in putting a Northern field officer in charge of a Tennessee regiment."[24]

Following his capture of Chalmers's wagons and troops, Spalding was directed to resume his pursuit. After disposing of Coleman's command, he was to swing left and cover the right flank of Coon's second brigade, which had already begun to wheel left in conformance with the movement of A. J. Smith's infantry.[25] Sweeping across the Hardin Pike, Coon's brigade soon found itself confronting redoubt 5. Battery I, First Illinois Light Artillery, opened up with an enfilading fire, supported by a battery of McArthur's rifled Parrot guns. The Confederate field pieces responded with brisk counterbattery fire for a time, but were eventually overpowered and silenced.

While it lasted, the duel prompted an officer of the Ninth Illinois Cavalry to remark that this "was the first time we had listened so close to that modern bird of war, the 'Steel-rifled Parrott [sic].' The eagle may be a more practical emblem of war, may show better on dress parades, but for effective service there is no comparison between the fowls."[26]

The exchange of fire lasted nearly an hour, during which time Coon's troops and Smith's infantry pressed forward to within 500 yards of the redoubt, at which point Hatch ordered a charge. As the troops surged forward, the Confederates, wrote Coon, "changed their little messengers of shell to grape and canister, accompanied by heavy musketry from the infantry support behind their works."[27]

There was keen competition among the Federal regiments to be the first to reach the enemy position. The distinction of being the first man inside the redoubt was awarded to Lieutenant George Budd, Company G, Second Iowa Cavalry. According to Coon, Budd "drew his saber upon the cannoneers and forced them to discharge the last load intended for the Federals on their own friends, then in plain view on the east side of the fort, not 500 yards distant."[28]

The cavalrymen contended that they beat the infantry into the fort, but Smith and McArthur claimed that their men arrived simultaneously with the cavalry. Hatch allowed as how that was probably true because two companies of the Eleventh Missouri Infantry had gotten intermingled with Coon's men during the assault.[29] McArthur, however, conceded the captured artillery pieces to Coon's men because "their gallantry on that occasion being conspicuous, although the fort had been rendered untenable by the fire from my batteries." In any case, the captured guns were quickly manned and turned on the retreating Confederates by Company Q, Ninth Illinois Cavalry, which had received mountain howitzer training.[30]

The Federals had barely secured the fort when they were fired upon by Confederate guns in redoubt 4, some 600 yards distant. However, with the balance of McArthur's infantry and Stewart's dismounted horsemen already closing in on number 4, Hatch again ordered Coon to charge.[31] Redoubt 4 proved to be a considerably more difficult undertaking. The fort was situated atop a 200-foot bluff and was protected by strong breastworks. The fort itself contained four smooth-bore Napoleons supported by 100 men of the Twenty-ninth Alabama, who had been ordered to hold at all costs.[32]

A member of the Ninth Illinois recalled that the position was "well fortified and so steep that men can barely go up, and, holding their Spencers almost at a 'present,' begin the ascent while the Confederate troops send round after round and volley after volley to hold back our rushing upward tide, but they generally shoot too high."[33]

Competition remained high among Coon's men as they advanced on number 4. "So eager were the officers and men to reach the second redoubt," wrote Coon, "that many fell to the ground exhausted. Many soldiers when too tired to walk, crawled upon their hands and knees up the steep bluff to the foot of the redoubt."[34] Again it was a race between infantry and cavalry. Not to be outdone, Coon ordered his exhausted troopers to "take those guns before the infantry gets up!" Somehow the brigade found the strength to respond. This time it was the Ninth Illinois who had the first man over the top, followed almost immediately by a representative of the Second Iowa. The Confederates put up a valiant fight, but were quickly inundated by the blue tide. Once more the captured guns were turned on the retreating enemy with good effect.[35]

Coon barely had a chance to reform his regiments when he received orders to take a third position. In the confusion of the moment, he mistakenly appropriated two of Stewart's regiments, the Eleventh Indiana and Twelfth Missouri. He later reported:

> I mistook two regiments of the First brigade for those of my own, and had the honor of leading them to the summit of a third hill, and shall ever remember with pleasure the gallant conduct of these men in holding that place, under a most galling fire from the enemy in front and on both right and left flanks, until the infantry came up, when they moved forward and took three pieces of artillery, from which they had driven the enemy a few moments before.[36]

The cavalry's successful assault of these fortified positions was especially gratifying to Wilson because it was accomplished within sight of infantry who "had never seen dismounted cavalry assault a fortified position before."[37]

Thomas, meanwhile, observed that A. J. Smith's movement had not carried to the right as far as anticipated, creating a gap between the infantry and Wilson's cavalry. Accordingly, Schofield was directed to move his Twenty-third Corps around and take position on Smith's right. By the time McArthur and Hatch had taken redoubts 4 and 5, Schofield had filled in the gap, allowing Wilson more latitude in his effort to get around and behind Hood's left flank.[38] Following the fall of redoubts 4 and 5, Smith subjected Walthall's line to a punishing artillery bombardment that was made all the more effective because Walthall had no remaining field pieces with which to offer counterbattery fire.[39]

The pressure on the Confederate left flank was increasing rapidly. When Coleman retreated before Hatch's initial attack, he was placed behind the rock wall on Walthall's extreme left. As the Federals swarmed across the Hillsboro Pike, Coleman was shifted to a new position near the Compton house. However, with the fall of redoubt 5, he was forced back, allowing the Federals to drive a wedge between his position and the rest of Walthall's line.[40] Walthall did what he could, which was very little, but he was a fighter and used to tough situations. At Franklin he had had two horses shot out from under him. Now he pulled Brigadier General Dan Reynolds's brigade out of line and sent them down to reinforce the hard-pressed left. As a result, Walthall's line was forced to shift right to fill in the gap and was thus stretched even thinner.

Reynolds enjoyed some success in slowing the oncoming Federals, but the combination of artillery fire from two nearby hills with the swarming Federal advance eventually drove his regiment back toward the Granny White Pike. In the end, it was simply a case of overwhelming numbers.[41]

So quickly overpowering was the Federal assault that it caused the Confederate line to curl back around to the left, creating in the process a rupture between Chalmers on the far left and the end of the infantry line. As a consequence, Chalmers's headquarters wagons and baggage, thought to be secure on the Hardin Pike, were overrun and captured before Chalmers realized what had happened.[42]

Chalmers's immediate opponent, R. W. Johnson, had also been ready to move early, but like Hatch, Johnson had been delayed by McArthur's infantry, so that it was near 11 A.M. before he finally got under way.[43] Johnson's assignment was to clear the Charlotte Pike as far as the Davidson house, eight miles south of Nashville, while at the same time protecting the cavalry corps from any rear or flank attack.[44]

Chalmers had only Edmund Rucker's brigade with which to contest the Federals and it was little enough. Early on December 15, Rucker's artillery and that of Colonel David Kelley—he still held his position along the Cumberland—dueled with the Federal gunboats of Commander LeRoy Fitch.[45]

Johnson's plan of attack called for Colonel James Biddle's second brigade to advance on foot, supported by Colonel Thomas J. Harrison's mounted first brigade. Biddle deployed his command and moved forward behind a strong line of skirmishers, but progress was intolerably slow. Johnson later claimed that his troops were unused to infantry tactics, a handicap that seems not to have affected Hatch's men. Johnson also pointed an accusing finger at the Fourteenth Illinois, whose advance was retarded, it seems, because the troops were encumbered with sabers.[46]

Recognizing that his attack was bogged down, Johnson quickly ordered Harrison's mounted brigade to bypass Biddle's command and take over the forward movement. Pushing forward promptly, Harrison directed the Fifth Iowa to dismount and engage the enemy skirmishers, while the Sixteenth Illinois flanked left and charged up a long slope to the ridge where Rucker had his artillery and troops posted behind stout barricades. Harrison's immediate objective was to capture Rucker's artillery, or kill the horses that pulled the field pieces before the Confederates were able to move them.

Harrison's line drove forward and Johnson later reported that he "never saw a charge more gallantly made or persistently pressed than this."[47] Even so, the effort fell slightly short of its intended mark. Nearing the crest of the ridge, Major Charles H. Beeres, commanding the Sixteenth Illinois, reached a stone wall that was too high to jump. Dismounting the regiment, Beeres ordered his men to tear down the wall, but the delay in doing so gave Rucker time to move his artillery.[48] Withdrawing down the Charlotte Pike, Rucker made a stand, but was soon forced to fall back again, finally taking up a stronger position along a ridge with his left flank anchored at the Cumberland River. His artillery, positioned around the nearby Davidson house, had an excellent field of fire.[49]

Sweeping forward with vigor, Harrison drove his brigade straight at the Confederate position, but quickly found the resistance stiffer than expected. A company of the Seventh Ohio, in the forefront of things, had its commanding officer and several others captured before Harrison halted his advance to wait for artillery support to arrive.[50]

When Battery I, Fourth U.S. Artillery arrived on the scene, it quickly silenced the Confederate guns. But for the moment, Harrison remained stymied by the strong Confederate position. Johnson accordingly requested and received help from Croxton. The plan called for Harrison to make a general demonstration against the Confederate position while Croxton, on Harrison's left flank, enveloped the Confederate right, forced it to bend around, and cut it off from the Charlotte Pike. At the same time, Johnson requested an enfilading fire on the Confederate line from naval gunboats on the Cumberland River. Johnson's strategy was to push Chalmers—Johnson believed he was up against Chalmers's entire division—into a pocket against the river. As it worked out, Croxton had been ordered to the Hillsboro Pike and was unable to lend a hand. With the daylight waning, Johnson bivouacked for the night, prepared to implement his strategy in the morning using part of Harrison's command to execute the role intended for Croxton. Chalmers, for his part, chose not to linger. Rucker was directed to withdraw east to the Hillsboro Pike, leaving the Seventh Alabama to hold on until daylight.[51]

About the time Rucker commenced his movement, Croxton, in compliance with Wilson's orders, had also started for the Hillsboro Pike. The two brigades maintained a running skirmish en route to their respective destinations. Like Croxton, Joseph Knipe had also moved to the Hillsboro Pike. However, three-quarters of a mile beyond the six-mile post, he turned east to the Granny White Pike, where he bivouacked for the night.[52]

The Federal objective had been to get as much of Wilson's cavalry as possible behind Hood, cut off his retreat, and hold him for the Union infantry. Wilson's horsemen, in effect, would become the anvil against which the Confederate army would be destroyed. In theory, it was a sound plan; in practice it had worked well as the first day's fighting drew to a close. The results of the day were encouraging. The cavalry corps had driven the Confederate left flank back nearly four miles and Wilson was justifiably proud. He wrote:

> It was an unusual day's work for cavalry. For the first time on any
> American battlefield all the available mounted force, a full army
> corps in strength, were massed on the flank of an advancing army,

making a turning movement of the first importance against an enemy occupying a strongly fortified position. For the first time in our country the horsemen on foot had charged side by side with the infantry, carrying the enemy's intrenchments, taking his field guns, and capturing the detachments told off for their support. For the first time they had planted themselves in force behind the enemy's flank on one of his main lines of retreat in exactly the position for which they had started. The night was, however, so cloudy and dark, the country so broken, and the troops so fatigued, that a further advance that night was impossible. There was nothing for the cavalry to do but make their bivouac sure. Having done this, they slept without unsaddling and were ready at the earliest dawn to resume operations. Having seen that they were invincible in cooperating masses, they believed themselves sure of victory the next day, and with this exultant feeling, they rested though most uncomfortably, till the next morning.[53]

After making his troop dispositions, Wilson rode to Thomas's headquarters. He found the Federal commander satisfied with the day's results, though regretting the fog and the delay caused by McArthur's infantry. Thomas also expressed satisfaction with the cavalry's performance in terms that Wilson later recalled "might well have made an older and better soldier blush."[54]

At 9 P.M., Thomas sent a telegram to Halleck reporting the day's success, an announcement that surely must have given Thomas great satisfaction. To his wife, waiting anxiously at the New York Hotel, Thomas wired, "We have shipped the enemy, taken many prisoners and considerable artillery."[55] Thomas's only orders to Wilson for the next day was to "resume operations without change of plan, and to press the enemy's flank and rear as soon as I could see to move, with all the force I could bring to bear."[56]

When he called on him later that night, Schofield recalled that Thomas was of the opinion that Hood would retreat during the night and that the next day's activities would be largely that of pursuit. Schofield, however, suggested that Hood would be waiting for battle and that the cavalry's advance should be held back until the enemy's intentions could be positively determined. Whether or not it was actually due to Schofield's suggestion, Wilson did receive an order instructing him to hold his position until it could be ascertained what Hood was going to do.[57]

The entire Federal army was fairly well scattered by the close of the day's fighting. Steedman alone retained any semblance of his original formation. Schofield's corps spent the night east of the Hillsboro Pike facing what was soon to be known as "Shy's Hill," where the Confederates were in the process of developing the strong point of their new left flank. Colonel Jonathan Moore's Third Division of A. J. Smith's corps filled the gap between the divisions of Cox and Couch.[58]

On Schofield's left, A. J. Smith finished the day on a nearly parallel line between the Hillsboro and Granny White pikes. Wood, who had been ordered to push on to the Franklin Pike, did not receive that order until sunset. Consequently he was able to advance only as far as the Granny White Pike before darkness brought him to a halt.[59]

By full dark, the original Confederate left flank had been completely withdrawn and established in roughly the position from which it would fight when the battle was renewed. Stephen D. Lee still held the center position of the original line, with orders to cover the Franklin Pike while Hood formed a new line. A. P. Stewart's battered units were then shifted to the center of the new line, establishing Lee as the new right flank. Cheatham's corps was shifted from the old right flank to the new left.[60]

By 6 A.M. on Friday, December 16, the entire Federal line had resumed its forward movement through a light fog. Advancing cautiously, Steedman found the Confederate position on his front evacuated, Cheatham's corps having moved to the left of the new Confederate line. Pushing on down the Nolensville Pike, Steedman quickly routed a detachment of Biffle's cavalry, then took up station on Wood's left flank. Behind Steedman, Brigadier General Charles Cruft moved a brigade forward to occupy Riddle Hill to cover the left and rear of Thomas's position.[61]

Continuing his own forward movement toward the Franklin Pike, Wood, after some fairly brisk skirmishing, drove back the remnant of defenders from Lee's original position. By 8 A.M Wood had reached the pike, but had to confront a strong line of skirmishers deployed in advance of Lee's new position. At this juncture, Wood, noting a gap between his right and A. J. Smith's left, brought up General Kimball's division to fill in.[62] Wood reported:

> This was promptly done, the troops moving handsomely into position under a sharp fire of musketry and artillery. Thus formed, the entire corps advanced in magnificent array, under a galling fire of small-arms and artillery, and drove the enemy's skirmishers into his main line. Farther advance was impossible without making a direct assault on the enemy's intrenched lines, and the happy moment for the grand effort had not yet arrived.[63]

A. J. Smith, meanwhile, had also moved forward cautiously, probing until he had located the new Confederate line. Advancing slowly in echelons from the right, he moved to within 60 yards of the enemy positions. As Wood had noted, the moment for the "grand effort" was yet to come; in the meantime, Hood's troops were subjected to a lashing artillery bombardment against the Confederate strong points of Peach Orchard Hill and Shy's Hill.

The Confederates responded with what little artillery they had, but it was scarcely a contest. General Bate, commanding on Shy's Hill, had some sharp-shooters armed with English Whitworth rifles who managed to make life uncomfortable for the Federal cannoneers, but that was about it.[64]

Wilson's men also got into action early when Chalmers drove Hammond's pickets off the Granny White Pike. Hammond quickly committed his entire brigade and promptly regained possession of the pike.[65] Hammond now held the most exposed position in the cavalry corps. Accordingly, about mid-morning, Coon's brigade was sent in to reinforce Hammond, with Stewart's brigade available if needed. Wilson held Croxton's brigade in reserve but close at hand. On the far Federal right, Johnson had been ordered to move cross-country to the Hillsboro Pike.[66]

Between the tenacity of the Confederate resistance and the dense underbrush in what was known as the Brentwood Hills, the Federal horse-men, fighting dismounted, were finding the going tough and slow. "It looked for a while," Wilson later recalled, "as though the cavalry might do more to annoy the enemy if it were on the other flank." He proposed this idea to Thomas, who agreed to consider it providing one more effort failed to yield the desired results.[67]

It was fortunate that Thomas chose to wait. By noon, Wilson's men had managed to work their way through the underbrush to a point where they now posed a very real threat to Hood's left and rear. The progress had restored Wilson's faith. He declared confidently, "There was no longer any doubt as to which flank we ought to be on, for all was now going well."[68] During the height of the fighting, some of Wilson's men captured a courier en route from Hood to Chalmers. According to Wilson, the dispatch read: "For God's sake drive back the Yankee cavalry from our left and rear or all is lost."[69]

Thomas was tightening the noose. Clockwise from the right, the Union line was composed of Wilson's horsemen, followed by Schofield, Smith, and Wood. As the second day of fighting got under way, Schofield's Twenty-third Corps had moved up to take station between Smith's infantry and Wilson's cavalry.

Like a boxer looking to land a knockout punch, Thomas continued to press the Confederate left. On Shy's Hill, General Bate had his job made all the more difficult when Coleman's brigade was removed from its sup-porting position behind the hill and sent down to try to hold off Wilson's horsemen. Cheatham's position on the Confederate left suffered a serious blow about noon when Hood, fearing that Lee's right flank was about to be turned, ordered three brigades of Cleburne's old division shifted to the right flank. This left only Brigadier General Daniel Govan's single brigade of Arkansas troops to hold a sector originally occupied by an entire division.[70]

Thus, weakened by the detachment of much needed troops from a line that was too thinly defended and hammered at from all sides, the Confederate left was on the verge of collapse. About 3:30 P.M., when Govan was left to cover a division-sized perimeter, Wilson's troopers began to break through, driving a wedge between Govan and Coleman.

Observing the success of his units, Wilson dispatched three successive staff officers to Thomas requesting that Schofield attack immediately. When no attack was forthcoming, Wilson grew apprehensive. It had been raining since noon and daylight was rapidly fading. Fearing that the success of his troopers would be wasted if they were not promptly supported, Wilson rode through the somber December day to Thomas's headquarters to plead his case in person. He found both Thomas and Schofield viewing the battle from a small hill that afforded an excellent view. With characteristic "ill-concealed impatience," Wilson urged Thomas to order the infantry forward. Thomas, with his characteristic calmness, studied the situation through field glasses and asked Wilson if he was certain that the troops making all the progress belonged to him. Assured that this was indeed the case, Thomas then commented that John McArthur's division seemed to have seized the initiative and was already moving forward. Turning to Schofield, Thomas directed him to attack immediately.[71]

The order having been given, Wilson headed back to his own command as rapidly as his gray mount Sheridan could carry him. It was after 4 P.M. by the time he returned and discovered that the "enemy had already broken and was in full but disorderly retreat by the only turnpike [Franklin] left in his possession."[72]

Meanwhile, as Thomas had observed, John McArthur had also grown impatient at the long delay. Like Wilson, he was afraid that if not pressed, the Confederates would have an opportunity to reorganize. Accordingly, McArthur notified A. J. Smith that he would attack unless he received orders to the contrary. Smith passed it on to Thomas, who vetoed the idea, but McArthur was never apprised of the refusal. Since he had not received a direct order to the contrary, McArthur now ordered Colonel William L. McMillen's first brigade to move forward and attack. The movement would be supported by McArthur's second and third brigades. McMillen's objective, Shy's Hill, was actually in Schofield's zone of responsibility, but because the latter did not seem inclined to attack the position, McArthur was making it his responsibility.[73]

It took McMillen an hour to position his regiments and secure ammunition for the artillery. By 3:30 P.M., about the time Wilson was conferring with Thomas and Schofield, McMillen was ready. His strong line of skirmishers moved forward, bayonets fixed, down the slope and up the steep incline toward the crown of Shy's Hill. Simultaneously, McArthur's second and third brigades moved against the rest of the Confederate line.[74] As McMillen's men neared the crest, they received a volley of musket fire from the flank that shredded the ranks of the Tenth Minnesota on the left of McMillen's line. Despite this, McMillen reported, the regiment "reached the rebel works in its front as quickly as the regiments on its right, which were less exposed."[75]

Pursuant to Thomas's order, Schofield committed his Twenty-third Corps to action. Accordingly, about the time McArthur's division was pressing the issue on Shy's Hill, Jacob Cox's division put further pressure on the Confederate left.[76] Meanwhile, Wilson's troopers had been pressing up from the south. About 3 P.M., half an hour or so before McMillen's advance got under way, Hatch, moving across a ridge that ran south along the Confederate left, brought up Battery I, First Illinois Light Artillery and opened up an enfilading fire on the Confederates.[77] Coon wrote of it:

> I ordered the Sixth and Ninth Illinois and Second Iowa, on my left, to commence firing at will on a fort some 500 yards distant, while two pieces of my artillery played upon it from the valley below. This, I am satisfied, had the desired effect, for the enemy commenced evacuating in a very few minutes.[78]

Hatch advanced his entire line. The Twelfth Tennessee reached the hill first, capturing 75 prisoners with a number of small arms and battle flags. There was a spirited disagreement over who was entitled to the spoils. Hatch claimed that the trophies and prisoners were taken by McMillen's infantry, though it was probably Cox's division. In the end it mattered little, as Wilson ordered all the prisoners turned over to the infantry so as not to delay the pursuit of the enemy.[79]

Hatch's breakthrough accelerated the disintegration of the Shy's Hill position, which quickly spread along the rest of the Confederate line. The men of Stewart's corps in the center, then Lee's corps on the right, pulled out and fled south. Lee managed to rally enough men to make a stand, and in doing so, allowed Hood's brigades to escape.[80]

To help alleviate the pressure on his tortured left flank, Hood ordered the Arkansas brigade of General Reynolds pulled out of Stewart's line and sent down to help Coleman hold off Wilson's horsemen. Like Lee on the right, Reynolds, supported by a section of artillery under Major Daniel Trueheart, held open a gap leading over to the Franklin Pike until Cheatham's men were able to pass through.[81]

Meanwhile, on the far Federal right, R. W. Johnson, after discovering that Rucker had evacuated his position, moved eastward to link up with the rest of the cavalry corps in compliance with Wilson's orders. About 2 P.M.,

Johnson ran into Rucker's new position near the Hillsboro Pike. Following a brief skirmish, Rucker again withdrew and Johnson sent word to Wilson requesting further instructions. By dark, however, there was still no word, so Johnson bivouacked his command on the pike near the Little Harpeth River.[82]

On the Federal left, Wood and Steedman had launched a 3 P.M. assault on Hood's right at Peach Orchard Hill. The line was held by Lee's corps, which met Wood's assault with such a withering blast of grape, canister, and musketry that Wood was forced to pull back. However, when the Confederate line finally did begin to rupture and break apart, Wood sensed the advantage of the moment and ordered a general advance. This time, the men of his Fourth Corps swept up and over the Peach Orchard position, but by that time, only a token remnant of defenders remained to offer opposition.[83]

Hood was at his headquarters, the home of Judge J. M. Lea, when word reached him that the Yankee attack had breached his lines. He always claimed complete surprise at this news and had, as a matter of fact, just finalized plans for his own offensive movement the next day. "Our line, thus pierced, gave way," Hood recalled, "and soon thereafter it broke at all points, and I beheld for the first and only time a Confederate army abandon the field in confusion."[84]

All that Hood could hope to accomplish at this point was to avoid total destruction. At about 4:30 P.M. he sent an urgent dispatch to Chalmers directing him to hold the Granny White Pike at all hazards so that the army would have an avenue of escape. Accordingly, Rucker's brigade with David Kelley's regiment took up a strong position across the pike, constructing a formidable barricade of logs, brush, and fence rails.[85]

With the Confederates now in full retreat, Wilson moved quickly to cut them off. Pursuit of a defeated enemy was traditionally one of the prime functions of cavalry. The problem was that most of Wilson's units had been fighting dismounted and it took time to bring the horses forward and get a mounted pursuit organized and under way. Wilson described the moment, as his emotionally charged horsemen, sensing the kill at hand, spurred through the storm-lashed darkness after their vanquished foe:

> As on the day previous, the ground was not only soft but heavily overgrown with timber and underbrush. The distance which separated the dismounted troopers from their led horses was considerable, and although every man hurried as though his life was at stake it was pitch dark before they were remounted and in pursuit. Not a minute was unnecessarily lost, but rapid movements across rough country and plowed fields in the dark were impossible.... But the enthusiasm of victory was now all on our side. "There was mounting in hot haste" and, although it was so dark that our troopers

could hardly see their horses' ears, Hammond and Hatch, in the order named, led their gallant horsemen in headlong pursuit. It was now raining hard and the rain was gradually turning into sleet. The night was cold and dismal, but both officers and men felt that the opportunity was all they could expect and that no effort should be spared to gather the fruits of victory. They noted the low roll of thunder, which they may have mistaken for the roar of distant cannon, and they were grateful for the momentary flashes of lightning, which showed them the highway and fitfully lit up the landscape on either hand, giving them a sight here and there of straggling detachments of the enemy hurrying forward to the rear.[86]

As Wilson's cavalry thundered down the pike overwhelming small bands of straggling Confederate infantry, they suddenly found the way blocked by Rucker's barricaded command. Pausing just long enough to ready themselves, the Federals, led by George Spalding's Twelfth Tennessee, charged headlong at the Confederate position. Though heavily outnumbered and with the pall of defeat hanging over them, Rucker's men nevertheless fought fiercely. They held off the Yankee horsemen long enough for the bulk of Hood's infantry to put some distance between them and their pursuers.[87]

Wilson thought this one of the "fiercest conflicts" of the Civil War, a "scene of pandemonium, in which flashing carbines, whistling bullets, bursting shells, and the imprecations of struggling men filled the air."[88] The fighting quickly spread to nearby fields. With only muzzle flashes to guide them, both sides were soon fighting hand to hand. In one of the wars ironic twists, Rucker and Spalding suddenly found themselves confronting each other.

"Who are you anyhow?" Rucker cried out. The answer came back in defiance: "I am Colonel George Spalding, commanding the Twelfth Tennessee Cavalry," thereupon Rucker rushed at Spalding, grabbing his rein, and calling out fiercely "Well, you are my prisoner, for I am Colonel Ed Rucker, commanding the Twelfth Tennessee Rebel Cavalry!" "Not by a damn sight," shouted the Union colonel, and giving his horse the spur, with a front cut in the dark, he broke the grip of his antagonist and instantly freed himself.

By some strange chance at this instant Captain Joseph C. Boyer of Spalding's regiment also became engaged with Rucker. He heard both challenge and answer and pushed boldly in to assist his colonel in the blackness of the night, fighting to the front like the hero he was. Without knowing exactly how it came about, Boyer closed in upon Rucker, wrestling the saber from him. Then occurred one of the most remarkable incidents of the war, for, while sturdy combatants were whacking each other with exchanged sabers, a pistol shot from an unknown hand broke Rucker's sword arm and thus disabled him, compelling him to surrender at discretion.[89]

Virtually every trooper in Wilson's command, including his staff officers, was involved to some degree during this wild pursuit down the Granny White Pike. Flushed with success and with their blood up, the cavalrymen pursued relentlessly, falling vigorously on any semblance of Confederate resistance. Yet despite their efforts, the bulk of Hood's shattered army managed to remain just out of reach.[90]

Wilson, who always maintained that the delay on the first morning of the battle prevented a more complete victory, felt compelled to call off the pursuit about midnight. By this time his columns were badly scattered, the men and horses exhausted from nearly 18 hours of continuous duty. Accordingly, orders went out to the unit commanders to bivouac for the night and resume the pursuit at dawn.[91]

A bit earlier, during the height of the pursuit, Wilson had heard the sound of horses behind him and turning, heard someone call his name. Recognizing Thomas's voice, Wilson acknowledged the greeting. Then in a completely uncharacteristic outburst Thomas fairly shouted, "Dang it to hell, Wilson, didn't I tell you we could lick 'em, didn't I tell you we could lick 'em?" Indeed, Wilson wrote, "The victory was all we could wish."[92]

So the Battle of Nashville was over and while a jubilant Thomas returned to Nashville feeling vindicated at last, a Confederate private found Hood "crying like his heart would break." The grand dream of reaching the Ohio River had ended in ignominious defeat. The once proud Army of Tennessee had been reduced to a battered rabble.[93]

Ten
Pursuit

It is very dark, and our men are considerably scattered, but I'll collect them on this bank of the stream—West Harpeth. Hatch is a brick.—Wilson to Thomas, December 17, 1864[1]

W ilson spent much of the night of December 16 in a nearby farmhouse, which doubled as a hospital and headquarters. Fired up and flushed with excitement, he had little time for or interest in sleep. Instead, he spent the time receiving dispatches and drafting orders for the next day's pursuit. His companion was the wounded Confederate Colonel Ed Rucker, whose arm had been amputated by Wilson's surgeon.[2]

Wilson had planned for R. W. Johnson's Sixth Division to push toward Franklin via the Hillsboro Pike on the west. Meanwhile, Hammond, Hatch, and Croxton would drive down the Granny White Pike. However, sometime after midnight word came from Thomas to use the Franklin Pike as a route of pursuit. Wood and Steedman were to follow Wilson and rendezvous with A. J. Smith and Schofield at or near Brentwood, where the entire army would advance directly on Franklin.[3]

Wilson thought it a bad idea. Marching cross-country through the mud to reach the Franklin Pike would eat up precious time. Besides, the two pikes converged this side of Franklin anyway, so why bother? It would be more effective, he told Thomas in a 3 A.M. dispatch, to crowd Hood by the "shortest roads, instead of losing any time to get on the other flank." Hood was known to be expecting reinforcement from Murfreesboro, which in all probability was Forrest. Wilson agreed that the infantry needed to "crowd the enemy vigorously on the Franklin Pike, and, if possible, prevent a junction of Hood and the forces now in the direction of Murfreesboro."[4]

But the plan stood. The four infantry commands received their orders shortly before midnight, but owing to the weather were unable to get underway before 8 A.M. on December 17. Half an hour after responding to

Thomas's directive, Wilson issued his own marching orders with some modification. Knipe and Croxton were sent east to the Franklin Pike. Knipe would be responsible for covering the pike itself and those roads to the west of it; Croxton's assignment was to cover the roads to the east. Hatch, with Wilson in company, was directed to continue south along the Granny White Pike, covering in addition those roads east of that pike. Johnson's orders were not changed: he pressed south along the Hillsboro Pike. The strategy here was to try and cut off Hood's line of retreat before he reached the Harpeth River.[5]

Flushed with victory, Wilson's troops were in the saddle and under way before daylight on a thoroughly miserable day: fog, rain, cold, and hock-deep mud. It would get no better.

The point of convergence for the Granny White and Franklin pikes was about five miles north of Franklin. Here, at Hollowtree Gap, Stephen Lee had developed a stout defensive position the previous night. And it was well that he did. Hammond's brigade of Knipe's division, with the Nineteenth Pennsylvania in the lead, encountered the Confederate position about mid-morning and attacked with a vigor that impressed Lee. Lee wrote, "Early on the morning of the 17th our cavalry was driven in confusion by the enemy, who at once commenced a most vigorous pursuit, his cavalry charging at every opportunity and in the most daring manner."[6]

But if Lee was impressed, Hammond's men found it a costly little fight. The Nineteenth Pennsylvania and Tenth Indiana sustained some 80 casualties, including 20 killed between them. Eventually, Wilson was able to threaten Lee's flanks and force him back to Franklin. There were three major waterways that stood between Hood's army and safety: the Harpeth River at Franklin, the Duck River at Columbia, and the Tennessee River at Florence. Lee's rear guard action at Hollowtree Gap bought Hood enough time to cross the first of the three rivers. This scenario was to be repeated time and again during the following ten days.[7]

Lee crossed the Harpeth unopposed, but did not tarry long in Franklin. The town was filled with wounded men from both armies left there after the battle of November 30. Not wishing to subject these men and the civilian population to any possible artillery fire, Lee left a small detachment to delay the oncoming Federals, then pushed on to Spring Hill.[8]

Lee's main body had barely left Franklin when Richard Johnson's Sixth Division arrived. Having forded the Harpeth west of town, the Sixth came storming in. The Seventh Ohio charged through Franklin, striking the small rear guard in the flank. Almost simultaneously, Knipe came up, followed shortly by Hatch. Like Lee, Wilson paused only briefly in Franklin before resuming the pursuit. Hatch and Knipe advanced in two parallel columns down the Columbia Pike, while Johnson struck south along the Carter Creek Pike to the west.[9]

Lee's rear guard was pressed as it withdrew from Franklin, at one point using the old Federal breastworks that had stood Schofield's troops in such good stead during the bitter fighting of November 30. At this juncture, Lee himself was wounded in the foot and eventually forced out of action. The command of his corps now devolved to Major General Carter Stevenson, who established a new defensive line just north of the West Harpeth River.[10]

On the Union left, Croxton had passed around Brentwood and headed east to the Wilson Pike before turning south. After swimming the Harpeth at McGavock's Ford, he headed down the Lewisburg Pike and halted for the night near Douglass Church, having encountered only small parties of the enemy, of which he captured some 130. In following this route, Croxton had retraced almost exactly his steps of November 30. What a difference a fortnight had made.[11]

Meanwhile, the atrocious weather persisted, the rain pouring down in torrents. Late that afternoon, with darkness rapidly closing in and a dense fog settling down over the rain-soaked countryside, Wilson's squadrons ran into Hood's rear guard just north of the West Harpeth River. In the rain and blackness, some of the Federals got themselves mixed in with Confederate stragglers so that it became impossible to distinguish one from the other. Given these conditions, even the usually aggressive Hatch hesitated to order an attack. The confusion and delay worked to the advantage of the Confederates, who managed to wheel a battery of artillery into position to reinforce their defense.[12] When Wilson galloped up, however, he promptly ordered Hatch and Knipe to form ranks and charge both enemy flanks. At the same time, he directed his own escort, the Fourth U.S. Cavalry, Lieutenant Joseph Hedges commanding, to form his regiment in a column of fours and charge straight down the pike at the Confederate center.

Hedges was primed to move when the newly arrived Confederate battery opened up with canister. Momentarily confused, Hedges moved his regiment off to the side of the pike while Hatch's Chicago Board of Trade battery returned counterbattery fire. Wilson had no intention of waiting for the enemy guns to be silenced, though, and ordered Hedges to move forward as ordered. With sabers drawn, the Fourth Regulars stormed down the rain-lashed pike while the dismounted troops of Hatch and Knipe moved against the Confederate flanks. Hedges's men quickly broke through the thinly defended Confederate line, the troops sabering cannoneers at their posts. Hedges himself outdistanced his men and was captured by the Confederates three times during the wild melee, but on each occasion managed to escape by yelling, "The Yankees are coming, run for your lives."[13]

Pressed hard from all sides, the Confederate line began to give way. Stevenson disgustedly reported that he was unable to control Chalmers's cavalry attached to his command. He declared:

> I may as well state that at this point, as soon as the enemy engaged us heavily, the cavalry retreated, leaving my small command to their fate. The enemy perceiving the shortness of my line, at once threw a force around my left flank and opened fire upon it and its rear. This was a critical moment, and I felt great anxiety as to its effect on my men, who, few in numbers, had just had the shameful example of the cavalry added to the terrible trial of the day before.[14]

Stevenson formed his command in a three-sided open square, from which they continued to fight savagely though giving ground to Wilson's superior numbers. While Hatch and Hedges continued to apply frontal pressure, Hammond's brigade, with Lieutenant Colonel Benjamin Gresham's Tenth Indiana in the lead, forded the West Harpeth upstream and struck Stevenson's retreating command in the flank.[15]

Wilson continued to press the pursuit until the near total exhaustion of men and horses dictated a halt. If the Federal effort had been all-out, the Confederates had also fought with a furious passion of their own. Once more the rear guard had managed to hold the Yankee horsemen at arm's length. Just south of Spring Hill, Stevenson's hard-pressed troops were reinforced by Clayton's division. The latter, having become aware of the plight of the rear guard, had turned and placed his own command across the pike to provide support.[16]

The affair on the West Harpeth was a savage, hard-fought action. Wilson described it as "another running night fight, in which all semblance of order was lost, where regiment got separated from regiment, troop from troop, and officers from men. There was no guide but the turnpike, and no rule but 'when you hear a voice shoot, or see a head hit it.'"[17]

At 6 P.M. on December 17, Wilson sent the following dispatch to Thomas:

> We have "bust up" Stevenson's division of infantry, a brigade of cavalry, and have taken three guns. The Fourth Cavalry and Hatch's division, supported by Knipe, made several beautiful charges, breaking the rebel infantry in all directions. There has been a great deal of night firing, volleys and cannonading from our guns—the rebels have none. It is very dark, and our men are considerably scattered, but I'll collect them on this bank of the stream—West Harpeth. Hatch is a brick![18]

Wilson's remark about Hatch reflected his respect for the man's soldierly qualities. Although Wilson thought Hatch a little too quick on the trigger at times, he valued his services highly. In fact, Wilson later wrote, "It was largely to [Hatch] that the principal success of both the first and second days in front of Nashville was due."[19]

While the Federal horsemen and Stephen Lee's rear guard were battling along the West Harpeth, the main body of Hood's army had managed to reach Spring Hill. Behind them, Thomas Wood's Fourth Corps sat helplessly on the north bank of the Harpeth River at Franklin, awaiting the arrival of a pontoon train.

If the Battle of Nashville had saved the reputation of George H. Thomas, the pontoon train that went astray in the aftermath of that victory was an acute embarrassment to the portly Virginian. What happened was a simple enough mistake, but one that nevertheless proved costly.

Late on December 16, the pontoon train had been ordered to join the pursuing army. Awakened from sleep to issue those orders, Thomas mistakenly specified the Murfreesboro Pike rather than the Franklin Pike. The officer in charge of the pontoon train apparently did not regard his instructions as odd and accordingly went off on a five-day journey that ultimately resulted in the pontoon train not reaching Franklin until December 21. By that time a frustrated Wood had managed to erect a temporary bridge and at least get a few of his troops across the rain-swollen Harpeth River.[20]

While the pontoon train was wending its way toward Franklin, Wilson was pulling out all the stops to cut off Hood's main body. A magnificent effort on the part of the Confederate rear guard was the only thing hat prevented him from doing so. Stephen Lee later remarked, "A more persistent effort was never made to rout the rear guard of a retiring column."[21]

By December 18, there were reports to the effect that Forrest had been killed. Prisoners, however, informed Wilson that Forrest, with Jackson's division and two brigades of infantry, had departed Murfreesboro for Columbia 48 hours earlier. If true, that meant that Forrest could be expected on the scene at any moment.

Regardless, Wilson resumed the pursuit early on December 18. R. W. Johnson moved south from Franklin along the Carter Creek Pike, before turning east on a dirt road into Spring Hill, where he arrived just in time to strike the rear guard in the flank. Johnson lacked the strength to hold them at bay until support arrived, however.[22]

In preparation for a renewed push on Hood's fleeing army, Wilson called a halt seven miles north of Columbia at 1 P.M. on December 18. Every horse was ordered fed and groomed. The men were to be issued three days' rations and all the ammunition they could carry. Unit commanders were directed to inventory casualties and furnish headquarters with a count of effectives present for duty. Eli Long's Second Division was also directed to join the cavalry corps as soon as possible, though it would not arrive in time to be a factor in the pursuit.[23] That night Wilson wrote a glowing report to Grant's headquarters:

> Our campaign is so far complete, and I know you will rejoice.... If the right steps are taken, and Dana operates properly from Memphis, Hood ought to be destroyed. I don't know how many trophies, nor how many prisoners we have, though I can safely say no corps of this army has more of the real evidences of victory than the one I have the honor of commanding.[24]

By December 18, A. J. Smith and Schofield had reached Franklin, as had Thomas himself. From here, Thomas ordered Steedman to march to Murfreesboro and turn over his transportation to General Thomas Ruger. Steedman was then to entrain for Stevenson, Alabama, where he was to be joined by General R. S. Granger with the garrisons from Athens, Huntsville, and Decatur, Alabama. Steedman's new assignment was to reoccupy those strategic points that the Federals had abandoned when Hood began his northward march. With the balance of his command, Steedman was to threaten Hood's rail lines west of Florence, Alabama.

Although the Federal pursuit had been vigorous and the chances that Hood might be caught this side of the Tennessee River remained good, Thomas was evidently concerned that the Confederates just might reach the river despite the best efforts of Wilson and Wood. Accordingly, on the evening of December 18 he wired Admiral S. P. Lee requesting the support of naval gunboats. Thomas thought that in addition to destroying any bridges Hood might use at Florence, the gunboats could also be used to ferry troops from western Tennessee.[25]

On December 18, Cheatham's corps replaced Stevenson's weary command as the army's rear guard. To this force was added Brigadier General Frank C. Armstrong's recently arrived brigade, which had been sent on ahead by Forrest. Forrest had learned of the disaster at Nashville on December 16 and had immediately moved to rejoin the army. His progress had been slow because many of the infantry under his command were without shoes. Thus, it was not until December 19 that he was finally able to reach the army at Columbia.[26]

The rain that had plagued both the hunter and the hunted through the first two days of the pursuit had temporarily abated, but on December 19 a new storm of rain and snow descended on the region. Wilson's supply train had been delayed; as a consequence, all the cavalry, except for Hatch's division, were out of rations and nearly out of ammunition. In view of this and because of the weather, Thomas directed that the cavalry corps, except for

Hatch, was to remain in bivouac that day. Hatch was ordered to get under way early to be clear of Wood's infantry, which in the meantime had closed up on Wilson's horsemen and actually bivouacked a short distance beyond the cavalry. Hatch found the going slow, however, and Wood had his people in motion ahead of the cavalry, but not for long.[27]

At Rutherford's Creek, Hatch's advance, followed by the leading elements of the Fourth Corps, was greeted with heavy fire from Confederates positioned on the opposite bank. The position was a naturally strong one. Steep banks rose from both sides of the creek, so swollen by recent rains as to make it impossible to ford without bridges or pontoons.[28] No crossing was going to happen, though, until the Confederates were dislodged from the opposite shore. Accordingly, Wood had his troops fell some large trees and build rafts to ferry some riflemen across. The current in the swollen creek was so swift, however, that the rafts were quickly swept away.[29]

For the veteran Wood, the situation at Rutherford's Creek was not only the low point of the campaign, it was one of the most discouraging days of his entire career. He wrote, "In these efforts was passed one of the most dreary, uncomfortable, and inclement days I remember to have passed in the course of nineteen and a half years of active field service."[30]

Meanwhile, when Hatch and Coon arrived and found the creek impassable, Hatch ordered the brigade to dismount and move upstream one mile. Coon was then able to cross a handful of the Sixth Illinois on the remnants of a burned-out railroad bridge, but the structure did not suffice for a crossing in force. Accordingly, Coon moved still farther upstream, where he finally managed to find a suitable site. The problem was that instead of crossing Rutherford's Creek they had actually forded Curtis Creek, a small stream that parallels the former before joining it. Although Coon's troops managed to develop some light skirmishing with the Confederates, darkness precluded anything more than that. The Federals were compelled to bivouac for the night and wait for the morrow before making another effort.[31]

The Federal pursuit had been hell on Wilson's horses. The rains had turned the countryside into quagmires of mud that adhered to the horses' legs, then froze when the temperature dropped. As a result of that and the general strain of the campaign itself, many of the cavalry mounts were breaking down. On December 20, Knipe and Johnson were sent back to Nashville with the dismounted regiments of their respective divisions, leaving Wilson with five brigades to continue the pursuit.[32]

During the night, the Confederates abandoned their position, enabling Wood's people to put two bridges across the creek during the morning hours of December 20. Farther along the creek, Coon's troops were up early and were soon at work repairing the railroad bridge to accommodate the division's wagons and Parrot guns. By noon, the operation was completed and Hatch advanced on Columbia with the Seventh and Ninth Illinois moving forward on foot, followed by the rest of the division, mounted.[33]

While Hatch and Wood were temporarily stymied at Rutherford's Creek, Forrest had been given the rear guard assignment, replacing Cheatham's corps. Hood apparently had some intention of making a stand at Columbia, but thought better of it by the time his battered brigades had reached that point. The object was survival, pure and simple. Accordingly, Forrest's mission was to hold off the Yankees long enough for the army to get south of the Tennessee River. Phase one of the assignment would be to hold the line of the Duck River at Columbia as long as possible, then retire toward Florence, Alabama, by way of Pulaski. To carry out his mission, Forrest had, in addition to his own horsemen, some 1,900 infantry, including 400 without shoes, under the capable Major General Edward Walthall.[34] Forrest quite likely had no peer when it came to getting the most out of what was available, a talent he demonstrated time and again over the next several days. To begin with, he had the shoeless men ride in wagons while the rear guard was on the move; when it was time to fight, they jumped out and took their place in line.[35]

When the Federals finally reached the Duck River late on December 20, they found that their quarry had crossed and continued its southward flight. Coon reported that the Confederates had left a small party of men and a piece of artillery in Columbia and the Seventh and Ninth Illinois skirmished with this group. "There was light cannonading from both sides," said Coon. Forrest, however, reported that the Federals appeared in front of Columbia on the evening of the twentieth and "commenced a furious shelling of the town." According to Forrest, he talked to Hatch under a flag of truce. Forrest pointed out that there were no troops in town and requested that the shelling stop. Hatch seems to have complied.[36]

The weather turned bitterly cold so that when the wayward pontoons finally arrived, getting them set up took longer than usual. As a consequence, it was not until December 23 that Wood and Wilson were able to get their commands to the south side of the river, and it was near noon on Christmas Eve before the Federal pursuit was resumed in earnest.

Still hopeful of catching Hood this side of the Tennessee River, Thomas clung to the strategy of having his infantry press forward along the pike, while Wilson's horsemen continued to operate on the flanks. Movement along the turnpike was bad enough, but the secondary roads were nearly impassable. Thus, the strategy, which might have worked under better conditions, was foiled by the weather. Had Wilson's horsemen been sent directly down the pike, it is possible that Hood's main body might have been caught and held up just long enough for Wood's infantry to arrive.[37]

On December 24, Wilson was finally able to resume the pursuit. Late that afternoon Croxton drove elements of Forrest's command across Richland Creek, capturing a few prisoners and a flag in the process. Croxton, however, was not pleased with the performance. He blamed the Eighth Iowa for failing to respond to five separate orders to cover the right flank. Had the order been obeyed, Croxton believed they would have captured the enemy's artillery and a great many more prisoners.[38] During this affair, which Forrest described as a "severe engagement," Hammond's brigade was operating on Croxton's right flank. A member of the Ninth Indiana wrote that "no one will forget the little knot of dead and dying artillerymen and horses by the road-side, maimed and mangled by bursting shell, a gory, ghastly sight."[39]

As part of this same action, Coon was attempting to provide support on the left flank and needed to cross Richland Creek. Once again, however, he was stymied by high water. All Coon could manage was to engage the Confederates in a half-hour of long-range skirmishing. With darkness closing in, the Confederates withdrew toward Pulaski and Wilson's troops bivouacked for the night.[40]

On Christmas morning, Thomas Harrison's brigade, with the Fifth Iowa in the lead, began skirmishing with Forrest's rear guard some eight miles north of Pulaski. The Iowans drove the Confederates through town, capturing intact the bridge across Richland Creek. Having secured the bridge, Harrison quickly picked up the pursuit, followed closely by the rest of the corps.

Approximately seven miles south of Pulaski, Forrest had taken up a strong defensive position at the head of a heavily wooded ravine, variously known as King's Hill, Anthony's Hill, and Devil's Gap.[41] Harrison came up, looked the situation over and concluded that the "enemy would retire from this position as he had from others on a flank movement from us." With this in mind, Harrison dismounted his brigade and, deploying (from left to right) the Sixteenth Illinois, Fifth Iowa, and Seventh Ohio, advanced against the Confederate position.

The cagey Forrest, who had carefully concealed six pieces of artillery, suddenly opened fire on the advancing Federals and followed this up by launching a surprise counterattack that overpowered Harrison's attenuated line and drove it back half a mile before Harrison was finally able to restore order. In the process, the Confederates also managed to capture a field piece belonging to the Fourth U.S. Artillery.

But Hatch, Croxton, and Hammond were rapidly moving up on the flanks. Finally, with daylight fading, Forrest wisely chose to withdraw. Wilson's men tried desperately to recover the captured field piece, but it remained in Confederate hands until the capture of Selma some four months later.[42]

On the morning of December 26, Hammond's brigade led the van of

Wilson's pursuit. Five miles beyond Anthony's Hill, the Second Tennessee made contact, driving Forrest's skirmishers back to Sugar Creek, where the Confederates had taken up another position. The Second and Fourth Tennessee attacked and, according to Hammond, "drove the enemy into his works." But the attackers were themselves driven back some 300 yards by a second counterattack in as many days. Hammond finally rallied his command and drove the Confederates back to their position, where it became something of a stand-off until late afternoon, when the Fourteenth Ohio Battery shelled the Confederates into retreat.[43]

Forrest, however, recounted a somewhat different version:

> On the morning of the 26th the enemy commenced advancing, driving back General Ross' pickets. Owing to the dense fog, he could not see the temporary fortifications which the infantry had thrown up and behind which they were secreted. The enemy therefore advanced to within fifty paces of these works when a volley was opened upon him, causing the wildest confusion. Two mounted regiments of Ross' brigade and Ector's and Granbury's brigades of infantry were ordered to charge upon the discomfited foe, which was done, producing a complete rout. The enemy was pursued for two miles, but showing no disposition to give battle my troops were ordered back.[44]

At this juncture, Wilson figured that Hood had had ample time to reach the Tennessee River. His suspicion was confirmed on December 26, when local citizens informed him that Hood was now south of the river. Wilson's only hope was to catch Forrest's rear guard before it escaped.[45]

Accordingly, Colonel George Spalding was given 500 picked troopers from those regiments that had seen the least service. He ordered to push forward as rapidly as possible in the hope of intercepting Forrest before he reached the Tennessee River. Spalding struck out and, pushing his troops to the limit, reached Bainbridge on the Tennessee River early on the morning of December 28, only to learn that the last of Forrest's command had crossed the previous night, taking the floating bridge with them.[46]

Had Admiral Lee's ironclads been able to move upriver and destroy the Confederate pontoons, Wilson might have caught his quarry. However, the water level had fallen so low that Lee was unable to get close enough to do the job. Wilson later claimed that Lee told him he did not have a pilot that could be trusted to navigate the tricky waters of the Tennessee River. Whatever the reasons, Wilson regarded them as inadequate and thought that a golden opportunity had been lost. "This was indubitably our last and best chance," Wilson declared, "but the independence of the navy and the natural timidity of a deep-water sailor in a shoal-water river defeated it."[47]

Meanwhile, Wood, following close behind Wilson, reached Lexington, Alabama, on December 28, where he was advised that the last of Hood's army had gotten safely across the river. Both Wilson and Wood marked time, pending instructions from Thomas, who officially ended the pursuit on December 29.[48] On the same day, Thomas also wrote to Halleck, bringing him up to date on the situation and explaining how the rigors of the campaign made it necessary to halt and refit. If Hood stopped at Corinth, Thomas would resume the pursuit after a brief pause for refitting. Should Hood continue south, however, then Thomas thought it would be best to wait until spring before continuing the campaign.[49]

At that point, Thomas's command was strung out between Columbia and the Tennessee River. Schofield was at Columbia, A. J. Smith was at Pulaski, Wood was at Lexington, Alabama, and Wilson was at Sugar Creek. The pursuit of a beaten army was one thing, but an organized campaign south of the Tennessee River was simply unfeasible at that juncture. Thomas wanted to concentrate along the river between Eastport, Mississippi, and Huntsville, Alabama, and strike south in spring.[50]

Accordingly, on December 29, Thomas directed Wilson to divide his cavalry corps, sending one division to Eastport with A. J. Smith's infantry and the balance to Huntsville with Wood's Fourth Corps. Wilson didn't like the idea and said so. The point of concentration ought to be Waterloo, Gravelly Springs, or Tuscumbia, Alabama, Wilson argued, in a December 30 letter to Brigadier General William D. Whipple, Thomas's chief of staff:

> In order that the cavalry forces under [Thomas's] command may render the service they should in the operation of the next year, it is essential that this Cavalry Corps be concentrated at some point as nearly as may be on the line of future operations, where full supplies of forage, arms, equipments, and horses may be furnished with facility, and where the necessary measures for discipline and reorganization may be carried into effect. A camp on the north bank of the Tennessee, somewhere near Waterloo or Gravelly Springs or Colbert's Shoals, would seem to possess all the requisites just enumerated.[51]

Thomas was persuaded and authorized his cavalry chief to concentrate at Eastport, or wherever seemed best. By the time he received the authorization, however, Wilson was already in Huntsville, so before the corps settled in, a second move was necessary. Thomas was also under pressure again, this time to launch an immediate follow-up campaign, for which he needed the cavalry in the Eastport area as quickly as possible. Wilson advised him that he would comply promptly, but that his command was in bad shape and needed time to reorganize and refit.[52]

Meanwhile, although Thomas had officially called off his pursuit of Hood, a thrown-together force of 600 cavalry under the command of Colonel William Jackson Palmer left Decatur, Alabama, on December 28 following Hood's line of retreat. Operating as part of General Steedman's command, Palmer's force was made up of detachments from the Fifteenth Pennsylvania, Second Tennessee, and the Tenth, Twelfth, and Thirteenth Indiana Cavalry.

Palmer drove off a force of Confederate cavalry under General Philip Roddey near Leighton, Alabama on the thirtieth. Here, Palmer learned that Hood's wagon train, bound for Columbus, Mississippi, had passed through Leighton two days earlier. Palmer promptly gave chase and caught Hood's pontoon train near Russellville the next day, destroying 200 wagons and 78 boats. On the night of January 1, 1865, Palmer further destroyed a large supply train consisting of 110 wagons and 500 mules en route to Tuscaloosa. Considering his mission accomplished, Palmer turned back. After successfully eluding Confederate forces sent in pursuit, he finally reached Decatur on January 6, having covered some 250 miles with a loss of only one killed and two wounded.[53]

Palmer's effort was the final touch. The campaign that had begun with threatening possibilities and that had seemed to unnerve Grant more than any other in the war had finally wound up producing one of the most significant Federal victories. Whatever dreams or schemes Hood may have entertained in October were shattered on the fields of Franklin and Nashville and in the ignominious retreat that followed. For all intents and purposes, the Army of Tennessee had been destroyed and though it would survive to fight another day its spirit would never be the same.

The Franklin-Nashville campaign had been significant in another way, in that the Federal cavalry had played a vital role (not simply a supportive or cooperative role) in a major offensive; it had been an integral part of the main effort. Wilson had been embarrassed by Forrest during the retreat to Nashville, but all things considered, he had done a superb job of putting together the kind of mounted force that played such a decisive part in the Battle of Nashville.

During the period November 30 to December 31, 1864, the cavalry corps took 3,232 prisoners, four stands of colors, 32 pieces of artillery, 2,386 stands of small arms, 184 wagons, 1,348 mules, 11 caissons, 3 locomotives, 2 hand-cars, 8 ambulances, 125 pontoon wagons, and 4 sabers. By contrast, the corps lost one field piece, 122 officers and men killed, 521 wounded, and 259 missing. It had been a particularly strenuous campaign for both horses and men.[54] Wilson wrote:

> It had lasted nearly six weeks through untold hardship of advance, battle and retreat. Men and horses suffered all the rigors of winter, snow, rain, frost, mud and exposure. During the nights, the

temperature would fall so as to make ice from half an inch to an inch thick, and this was far too thin to carry horses without breaking through. As a consequence, the roads were worked up into a continuous quagmire. The horses' legs were covered with mud, and this, in turn, was frozen, so that great numbers of the poor animals were entirely disabled, their hoofs softened and the hair of their legs so rubbed off that it was impossible for them to travel. Hundreds lost their hoofs entirely, and in all my experience I have never seen so much suffering.... During the fortnight from Nashville to the Tennessee, over five thousand horses were so disabled and so worn down by fatigue, exposure and starvation that such of them as it was not merciful to kill had to be gathered up and sent back for treatment.[55]

In summarizing the campaign, Wilson pointed out that he knew of

no battles in the war where the influence of cavalry was more potent, nor of any pursuit sustained so long and well. The results of the campaign, added to those following the same policy in the Army of the Potomac, clearly demonstrate the wisdom of massing the cavalry of an army, and it is to be hoped will obtain from the War Department a recognition of the corps already organized.[56]

Ahead of Wilson and his cavalry corps lay nearly three months of intensive training and reorganization, the net result of which would produce the largest mounted force ever assembled on the North American continent. Beyond that was the Selma campaign, the defeat of Forrest, and the capture of President Jefferson Davis.

Eleven
"Lyon Was an Illusive Cuss"

Lyon crossed the Cumberland yesterday below Clarksville, and is supposed to be moving toward Hopkinsville, Russellville, and Bowling Green; his force is estimated at 2,000 men. The greatest celerity is necessary. — Wilson to McCook, December 11, 1864[1]

In December 1864, with attention in Middle Tennessee focused on Nashville and the impending confrontation between Thomas and Hood, 28-year-old Confederate Brigadier General Hylan Benton Lyon prepared to launch a daring diversionary effort on Hood's behalf. This offstage episode of the Tennessee campaign was not unlike that executed by General Grierson during Grant's Vicksburg campaign.

Hylan Lyon, whom Wilson referred to as an "illusive cuss," was Kentucky-born and West Point–trained, having graduated from the academy in 1856 as a second lieutenant of artillery. At the outset of hostilities, he resigned his commission and joined the Confederacy as an artillery battery commander. Later, he was elected lieutenant colonel of the Eighth Kentucky Infantry, was captured at Fort Donelson, and exchanged. Lyon then went on to see action at Holly Springs and Vicksburg, escaping from the latter during Grant's siege. In June 1864, he was promoted to brigadier general and placed in command of a brigade of four Kentucky cavalry regiments under Forrest.[2]

On November 18 Lyon had received orders from Hood to cross the Tennessee and Cumberland rivers, move north, and take possession of Clarksville, an important Federal supply point some 40 air miles northwest of Nashville. Once he had accomplished this, Lyon was to put all mills on the north side of the Cumberland in operation for the Confederacy. He was, in addition, to "destroy the railroads between Nashville and Clarksville, and between Bowling Green and Nashville, taking care to keep all telegraphic communications between these places constantly destroyed."[3]

To carry out this rather formidable assignment, Lyon had 800 undisciplined, poorly organized troops, none of whom had more than four months' service. They were well supplied with small arms, but otherwise poorly equipped. One hundred were without shoes and few had blankets or overcoats. Many lacked clothing "sufficient to make a respectable appearance." To support this rag-tag force, Lyon could call on two 12-pounder howitzers.[4] After nearly four years of war, Confederate commanders were accustomed to operating with threadbare commands and Lyon was no exception. He promptly organized his troops into two brigades of 400 each. The first was commanded by Colonel J. J. Turner of the Thirtieth Tennessee Infantry, the second by Colonel J. Q. Chenoweth.[5]

On December 6, Lyon left Paris, Tennessee, 80 miles west of Nashville, crossed the Tennessee River at Danville two days later, and on December 9 took possession of Cumberland City, 30 miles below Clarksville. Here Lyon captured the Federal steamer *Thomas E. Tutt*, loaded with forage and provisions. The vessel itself was used to ferry men and horses across the Cumberland. Later that same evening, Lyon reported capturing two more steamers and four barges, which he then anchored in the middle of the river and set ablaze. In all, Lyon estimated he had destroyed $100,000 worth of Federal property.[6]

By that time reports were beginning to filter into Thomas's headquarters; as usual they were both conflicting and highly exaggerated. One, for example, had Lyon crossing the Tennessee with 3,000–4,000 men and several pieces of artillery. Another claimed 900–2,000 men, while a third reported 2,000 men and six pieces of artillery. No one seemed to know for certain precisely what Lyon's objective was but the consensus seemed to favor the Green River bridge and the railroad around Bowling Green, Kentucky.[7]

The Louisville and Nashville Railroad, a primary supply line for the Tennessee capital, crossed the Green River at Munfordville, Kentucky, and continued south through Bowling Green to Memphis Junction, where the line divided—the main branch went directly to Nashville, while the other went on to Memphis via Clarksville. Just across the Tennessee line, a branch of the Memphis-Clarksville division looped back to the southeast through Springfield, Tennessee, and rejoined the Louisville and Nashville line at Edgefield Junction. This last branch joined Clarksville to Nashville by rail.[8]

Troops and supplies reached Nashville either by rail or by steamers coming up the Cumberland River. There was little Lyon could do interfere with river traffic, but he could disrupt rail service. That, the Federals reasoned, could most effectively be accomplished by striking the key points of Bowling Green and the Green River bridge at Munfordville.

Whatever his objective, Lyon was moving quickly. Thomas had ordered local garrisons to be on the alert, but it would take a strong mounted column to catch Lyon. However, all of Wilson's cavalry at Nashville were needed for the upcoming battle with Hood. Still, Lyon had to be stopped. Accordingly, on December 10, Wilson advised General Eli Long, who was still in Louisville completing his remount, of these new developments and directed him to be prepared to intercept Lyon.[9] The next day, however, Wilson countermanded his order to Long, whose remount was not yet complete. Instead he directed McCook to proceed to Bowling Green by rail immediately and move against Lyon with the second and third brigades of his division.[10]

Back in October when Wilson initiated the reorganization of his cavalry corps, both McCook and Long had turned over their serviceable horses to Kilpatrick's division and sent their regiments by rail to Louisville for remounting. By early December, McCook's third brigade under Brigadier General Louis D. Watkins had completed its remount and returned to Nashville, while the second brigade, commanded by Colonel Oscar H. LaGrange, left Louisville on December 4.[11]

McCook himself left Nashville by train on the morning of December 12 and at the same time, Watkins marched north from Edgefield with his Third Brigade, consisting of the Fourth, Sixth, and Seventh Kentucky Cavalry and the Eighteenth Indiana Battery. From Bowling Green on December 13, McCook ordered LaGrange, then en route to Nashville, to concentrate at Franklin, Kentucky, some 15 miles south of Bowling Green, by that night if possible.[12]

Meanwhile, Lyon had gotten off to a good start. Finding Clarksville too strongly fortified to attack, he sent Lieutenant Colonel Cunningham to destroy the railroad and telegraph between the Red River bridge, four miles from Clarksville, to the junction of the Nashville-Clarksville's line at Russellville, Kentucky.[13] While Cunningham was off on his mission, Lyon moved with the rest of his command toward Hopkinsville, Kentucky. If nothing else, the maneuver confused the Federals, who were now uncertain as to the Confederate raider's objective. Green River Bridge and Bowling Green remained strong candidates, but now Springfield, Tennessee, and or Hopkinsville, Kentucky, could be added to the list.

In the meantime, McCook reached Bowling Green on December 12. At 11 P.M. that night he received a dispatch from Wilson saying that Lyon was moving toward Springfield. "Get your forces together as soon as possible and go for him," Wilson ordered. At 10 A.M. on December 13, McCook advised Wilson that LaGrange was already moving toward Franklin to join Watkins and that he (McCook) would be there that afternoon. From Franklin, McCook understood that he was to march for Springfield. However, having just received a dispatch from Thomas's headquarters to the effect that Lyon now appeared to be avoiding Springfield, McCook requested a confirmation of his orders of December 12. In view of this, Wilson directed him to head for Hopkinsville.[14]

On December 14, Watkins joined McCook and LaGrange at Franklin, where the First Division (now missing only Croxton's brigade) headed for Russellville, where McCook sent all of his excess baggage and wagons. At Russellville, the division was also reinforced by the arrival of the Seventeenth Kentucky Cavalry, which was assigned to Watkins's brigade.[15]

The next morning, McCook struck out on the road to Hopkinsville with Watkins in the lead. As the column approached Fairview (the birthplace of President Jefferson Davis), nine miles from Hopkinsville, Watkins's advance encountered Confederate pickets and promptly drove them back through town, capturing an officer and eight men. After halting for several hours to rest and feed his horses, McCook resumed his march at 1 A.M., intending to reach Hopkinsville at daylight. McCook reasoned that if Lyon was indeed at Hopkinsville and planned to make a fight of it, he would likely occupy the bluffs east of town that offered the strongest defensive position in the area. McCook planned his strategy accordingly.[16]

Meanwhile, when Lyon reached Hopkinsville, he discovered that the Federal garrison had withdrawn to Russellville. Lyon wasted no time taking advantage of an opportunity to obtain shoes and clothing for half of his command. Leaving Colonel Chenoweth with 400 men and one of their two 12-pounders at Hopkinsville, Lyon then headed west to Cadiz, before turning northwest toward Eddyville and Princeton.[17] Lyon's course of action at this juncture was a complete departure from what had been specified in Hood's orders of November 18. Lyon explained that his purpose was to capture garrisons, destroy barracks, and obtain clothing and supplies for his troops. With this in mind, he destroyed courthouses in Hopkinsville, Cadiz, and Princeton, claiming they were used as barracks. At Eddyville, Lyon also destroyed what he called a "corral" used as a rendezvous for Negroes.[18]

In the pre-dawn hours of December 16, as Wilson was preparing to assault Hood's attenuated line at Nashville, McCook was approaching Hopkinsville. Four companies of the Seventh Kentucky Cavalry under Lieutenant Colonel William Bradley had the lead and encountered a Confederate scouting party, which they drove back through town. Watkins immediately followed with the rest of his brigade as far as the local asylum, where he established a skirmish line.[19] Shortly, McCook himself arrived on the scene and issued orders for an attack. The plan called for Watkins to circle around to the right, deploying his brigade behind the Confederate position while LaGrange made a frontal assault. Watkins was further

Brigadier General Edward M. McCook (U.S. Signal Corps photograph no. 11-B-1846 [Brady Collection] in the National Archives).

directed to cover all roads the Confederates might use as an avenue of escape. The attack would get under way at daylight.[20]

And so it did. Promptly at first light, Watkins and LaGrange advanced according to plan. As McCook suspected, the Confederates were posted on the high bluffs. When the Federals advanced, Chenoweth opened up with his single 12-pounder and all the musketry at his disposal, but it was not enough to stop LaGrange's troopers who pressed steadily forward. In the face of the determined Yankee advance, Chenoweth's undisciplined troops broke and fled, abandoning their single piece of artillery. Many of the men threw away their weapons.[21]

McCook had figured to bag the entire Confederate force. He might have done so, too, had it not been for a miscue in Watkins's brigade stemming from a case of mistaken identity. Colonel J. K. Faulkner, commanding the Seventh Kentucky Cavalry described the incident:

> Moving within sight of Hopkinsville, I saw a portion of the Third Brigade [Watkins] formed near the seminary; at the same time I discovered a column of cavalry moving on my left, which I estimated at about 300, and which I mistook for one of our regiments, they being dressed differently from rebels I had formerly seen. Their movements were in every way calculated to deceive. I passed on toward the seminary, at which place General Watkins and staff were stationed. The portion of the Third Brigade at the seminary did not fire on the rebels, they being in close range, and thus increasing my belief that it was a body of Federal cavalry. When within 800 yards of the seminary, Captain [James] O'Donnell, of General Watkins' staff, ordered me to turn to the right and move in the direction taken by the advance of the brigade. Very soon after receiving this order General Watkins' bugler sounded the "halt;" next the "forward" was sounded, then the "left turn," then the "charge;" all of which was repeated by my bugler and promptly obeyed. After charging about 300 yards, General Watkins rode toward my regiment, informing me that the cavalry on my left was a body of rebels, who were then moving rapidly and almost parallel with my regiment. I was then ordered to throw the fence on my right and form a line of battle, which was executed as quick as possible; but before my line of battle was formed I was ordered to follow the general with my regiment, who moved rapidly out on the Nashville pike some distance, then turning to the left moved up on Seminary Hill, where we met the skirmishers of the Second Brigade.[22]

McCook, who was somewhat chagrined, reported that "Watkins had succeeded in getting in their rear before the attack was made in front, but through some unaccountable mistake the Greenville road had been left open by him." In any case, virtually all of Chenoweth's command escaped. The Federals captured only four officers and 57 men.[23]

McCook did not offer immediate pursuit. Instead, he bivouacked his command while Watkins sent out a reconnaissance party of 60 men from the Sixth Kentucky under Lieutenant E. R. Phillips. Phillips overtook the detachment guarding Lyon's wagon train some three miles out of Hopkinsville on the Princeton road. A running fight ensued for about five miles, with Phillips charging several times in an effort to capture the train.[24]

Lyon, meanwhile, returning from his Cadiz-Princeton-Eddysville mission, attacked Phillips and drove the outnumbered Federals back into Hopkinsville. Lyon, however, quickly discerned that a larger Union force was close at hand. In view of this, he prudently withdrew 16 miles and camped. Later that night, Chenoweth reported in, giving Lyon very nearly a full force with which to resume his mission. Accordingly, on December 17, Lyon moved northward through Charleston and Madisonville, to Ashbysburg on the Green River some 50 miles from Hopkinsville. Along the way, Lyon continued to burn courthouses, for which he seems to have developed a deep passion.[25]

McCook, meanwhile, had not been idle. He had his two brigades in the saddle and moving at daylight on the seventeenth as well. Approaching Princeton, he learned that Chenoweth had rejoined Lyon and the reunited Rebel force had turned east at Grubb's Crossroads. They had burned the bridge over the Tradewater River en route to Madisonville.[26]

At this point McCook concluded that his heavier column, encumbered with artillery as it was, could never hope to catch the fast-moving Confederate raiders. Moreover, he feared that by pursuing with both brigades, it would afford Lyon an opportunity to swing back and reach the Cumberland River via Hopkinsville. Accordingly, McCook decided to split his command. LaGrange would continue the direct pursuit, while Watkins and McCook, with the artillery, returned to Hopkinsville.[27]

So the pursuit now belonged to Colonel Oscar H. LaGrange, who had formerly commanded the First Wisconsin Cavalry of his present brigade. Wilson described LaGrange as a man of imposing physical stature who

> had risen through hard knocks and experience to command a
> brigade. He looked like a berserker and was full of enterprise and
> daring. His fixed rule was to let no man get deeper into the battle
> than himself.... Without being a martinet, he was one of the best
> all-round soldiers I ever met and had the war lasted he must have
> risen to much higher rank and more important command.[28]

LaGrange's brigade consisted of the Fourth Indiana, a battalion of the Second Indiana, and the First Wisconsin. With only two regiments and a battalion, the brigade probably did not exceed 1,200. In any case LaGrange easily outnumbered Lyon, and the quality of his veteran troops was superior to that of the Confederate raider.[29]

After being detached, LaGrange pursued as far as White's Mill on the Tradewater River, where he found a bridge that Lyon had burned and learned that his quarry was about 16 hours ahead of him. LaGrange did not rest his command but immediately put the troops to work building a makeshift bridge that allowed the brigade to cross the river the following day, December 18. Once across, LaGrange pushed on another ten miles before finally halting for the night between Madisonville and Charleston.[30]

The same weather front that was making such a grueling episode out of Wilson's pursuit south of Nashville was also plaguing LaGrange. Swollen by the heavy rains and snow, countless small streams in the area retarded the Federal pursuit and gave Lyon an edge.[31]

From captured prisoners, LaGrange learned that Lyon's rear guard was moving through Slaughterville and he pressed his pursuit accordingly, hoping to overtake the elusive raider and force a fight. At Madisonville, La-Grange sent a dispatch to McCook and pushed on. Reaching Slaughterville, he found that Lyon's trail turned north. Fearing that the Confederate would get across the Green River before he caught him, LaGrange ordered Captain Roswell S. Hills's 100-man battalion of the Second Indiana to move forward at a "trot," leaving orders for the rest of the brigade to follow as quickly as possible. As was his custom, LaGrange accompanied the advance element.[32]

Late on the afternoon of December 19, LaGrange and Hill sighted the Confederates about three miles from Green River. In the ensuing chase, the Federals suddenly found themselves in the middle of a two-mile-long causeway flanked on either side by swampland. LaGrange, fearing that he might be up against Lyon's entire force and realizing that Hill's battalion was quite vulnerable, sent forward a flag of truce, demanding that Lyon surrender all Confederates on the south side of the river.

Lyon, however, was not deceived. Upon reaching Green River he had crossed the entire command save for himself and 50 men, who remained on the south side to delay the Yankee pursuit. Thus, when LaGrange issued his ultimatum, Lyon recognized the ruse for what it was and promptly declined.[33] Fortunately for LaGrange, however, his main column arrived on the scene about this time and Lyon's rear guard scattered, some disappearing into the woods, while others crossed the Green River on ferry boats that were then destroyed. A handful of Confederates were forced into the river by the Federals and drowned attempting to swim to safety. LaGrange reported killing one and capturing seven. Reportedly, Lyon was forced to abandon four wagons and an ambulance that contained medical supplies and small arms.[34]

At any rate, having eluded his pursuers once again, Lyon now headed southeast to Hartford where he captured and paroled the Federal garrison of two officers and 46 men. Again, the courthouse was burned. From Hartford, Lyon turned due east, passed through Litchfield, and aimed for the Louisville Nashville Railroad at Elizabethtown.[35]

Meanwhile, on December 20, McCook received LaGrange's dispatch

Colonel Oscar H. LaGrange (reproduced from the Collections of the Library of Congress).

from Madisonville, advising him that Lyon was crossing the Green River at Ashbysburg. Based on this information, McCook correctly surmised that Lyon would try to cut the railroad at Elizabethtown. McCook reasoned that it would be impossible for Watkins to reach Elizabethtown from Hopkinsville before the Confederates got there. The Federal garrison at Louisville was close enough, so McCook wired the commanding officer asking him to be on the alert for Lyon's column. If a force from Louisville was able to intercept Lyon, it could drive the Confederates back on LaGrange's column ... or so it was hoped.[36]

LaGrange spent two days and nights getting his command across Green River. Sheds along the river bank were fired to provide light for working parties. The steamer *D.B. Campbell* was stopped on her way downriver and used to help ferry the troops across. Still, it was not until 1 A.M. on December 22 that LaGrange was able to resume his pursuit, albeit minus two companies. As the result of an orderly's blunder, two companies of the Fourth Indiana were left on the south bank of the Green River and were subsequently ordered back to Bowling Green by way of Greenville.[37]

When LaGrange reached Hartford, he found that Lyon had destroyed the bridges over Rough Creek, forcing the Federals to "pass a ford half a mile in length where the water reached the middle of the horses' sides." At Hartford, LaGrange sent his ambulances and all led horses on to Bowling Green by way of Wilson's Ferry, then pushed on after Lyon.[38]

The Confederates continued to remain far enough out of reach to destroy bridges, depots, and the like. Beyond Hartford, Lyon burned a bridge over Caney Creek, but this time LaGrange's advance party was able to repair the damage before the main column arrived. For once, the Federals incurred no delay. At Elizabethtown, Lyon left a detachment to torch the depot, trestle, stockade, and, of course, the courthouse while he moved on to Nolin Station with his main body.[39]

McCook's hope that Lyon would be caught between LaGrange and a Federal force from Louisville failed to materialize, however, when no force was sent from Louisville. LaGrange managed to reach Elizabethtown in time to save the trestle, but he was too late to save the bridge and the depots at Nolin Station and Glendale. At Nolin, Lyon had also captured a trainload of Federal troops as well as a blockhouse commanding the bridge over the Nolin River. The Confederates received the first word of Hood's defeat at Nashville and Lyon reported that it had a very demoralizing effect on his men. Indeed, that may have been the understatement of the war, because within 48 hours some 500 soldiers had deserted.[40]

From Nolin Station, Lyon turned east toward Hodgensville, but LaGrange did not follow due to the condition of his horses. Since leaving Green River on December 22, LaGrange had permitted no halt in excess of three hours until the column reached Elizabethtown on the morning of the twenty-fourth, having traveled 115 miles in two days "over terrible roads." LaGrange reported that his troops were well behaved as contrasted to Lyon's stragglers who "burned houses and forage, ravished women, and plundered indiscriminately on their line of march."[41]

With the cessation of LaGrange's effort, Wilson's horsemen were officially removed from the pursuit, even though Lyon was still very much at large. From Nolin Station the Confederate raider, with only a fraction of his original force, moved southeast to Columbia and Burkesville where he crossed the Cumberland River and continued south through Livingston, Sparta, McMinniville, and Winchester to Gunter's Landing on the Tennessee River.[42] Owing to Federal gunboat activity on the river and the presence of Union patrols, Lyon was forced to cross the Tennessee at night in canoes. The one remaining 12-pounder was dismantled and taken across in pieces. From Gunter's Landing, Lyon moved on to Red Hill, Alabama, where his camp was attacked on the morning of January 14 by Colonel William J. Palmer, who had just recently returned from his successful foray against Hood's wagon train.[43]

No doubt believing they were safe out of harm's way, Lyon and his men relaxed their vigil and as a result were taken completely by surprise. Lyon himself was quartered in the residence of one Tom Noble. When Palmer's advance reached the Noble house, one of the noncommissioned officers, Sergeant Arthur P. Lyon, ironically enough, encountered General Hylan B. Lyon at the front door, clad only in his nightclothes. He promptly arrested the Confederate general. The general asked for permission to dress and the request was granted. However, as the Union sergeant followed the captured Confederate into the bedroom, the general suddenly produced a pistol and shot his captor, afterward making his escape in the darkness. Palmer's men captured most of what remained of Lyon's command, including arms and horses. Lyon and the few who did manage to escape made their way through Blountsville to Tuscaloosa, where Lyon felt safe enough to establish new headquarters and begin recruiting.[44]

While Lyon was snaking his way through Kentucky and Tennessee, McCook, with scant information about the situation, concluded by December 23 that Lyon no longer represented a threat to the area. Reasoning that his horsemen could be put to better use elsewhere, he and Watkins started back to Nashville. En route they stopped for the night at the loyalist plantation of one Colonel Sebree near Trenton, Kentucky. That evening there was a rather heavy poker game in progress, which saw the host enjoying considerable success. Upon being advised by his black overseer that McCook's troops were using fence rails to build fires, the colonel waved him off. But the overseer persisted until, finally, Colonel Sebree, out of patience, rebuked him, saying, "Go away from here, you black rascal; don't you see I'm making fence rails a heap faster than those soldiers can burn them?"[45]

McCook and Watkins reached Edgefield on December 28, followed by LaGrange on January 5. McCook then departed on sick leave and Watkins assumed temporary command of the division, marching it south to the Tennessee River cantonments, arriving at Waterloo, Alabama, on January 24.[46]

McCook and Lyon each felt that he had accomplished the assignment given him. Lyon admitted later that McCook had prevented him from carrying out Hood's orders to the letter, but at the same time he declared, "When all things are considered pertaining to this expedition, it was a success beyond my most sanguine expectations."[47] McCook, on the other hand, felt that the damage inflicted on the Confederate raiders had not been all that he had hoped for. However, in view of the fact that so many were local guerrillas, he felt everything possible had been done to thwart their aims. "The primary object of the expedition," McCook wrote, "was accomplished, however, when the force of General Lyon was dispersed and rendered powerless for further harm."[48] McCook further suggested that to avoid this sort of incident in the future, western Kentucky should be occupied "with a small but active force of cavalry, whose duty it shall be to arrest and dispose of every man who is not known to be a bona fide resident of the neighborhood where found."[49]

Lyon had caused some anxious moments for the Federals, though hardly enough to really help Hood. He had destroyed a fair amount of government property, raised havoc in the towns through which he passed, and made life miserable for LaGrange and his men. But in truth, Lyon's raid could scarcely be considered the kind of successful enterprise its commander maintained. In the early days of the war, his escapade might have had some significance, but at this late stage it was nothing more than an annoyance to the Federals. If Lyon's raid accomplished anything of significance, it was the diversion of two brigades of Wilson's cavalry at a critical hour. However, in view of what happened at Nashville, even that would appear to have been of minimal value.

Twelve
Winter Quarters

When you arrive here we will have a splendid force with which to begin the next campaign. —Wilson to Upton, January 26, 1865[1]

The two principal sites along the Tennessee River selected as points of concentration for Wilson's cavalry were Waterloo and Gravelly Springs, Alabama, both situated along the north bank. Eastport, Mississippi, and Chickasaw, Alabama, on the south bank served as boat landings for incoming troops and supplies. Wilson reported, "The mild climate, rocky soil, and rolling surface of the country rendered this altogether the best locality that could have been found for recuperating and preparing both men and horses for an early spring campaign."[2]

Wilson reached Gravelly Springs about mid–January and established his headquarters in Wildwood, the home of Alabama Governor Houston's sister. "In a few days," wrote Wilson, "the word went out that although Northerners we were civilized and humane, in consequence of which the mansion soon became the social as well as the military center for the neighboring planters and their families."[3] Hatch, Croxton, and Hammond arrived shortly after Wilson, followed by Watkins and LaGrange on January 23 and Eli Long's Second Division on the twenty-fifth. Owing to the fact that a large part of the Fourth Division was absent with Grierson on a raid against the Mobile and Ohio Railroad, Upton's command did not reach the Tennessee River assembly area until mid–February.[4]

One of Wilson's first directives was to have suitable cantonments constructed: log cabins for the men and lean-to shelters for the horses. A sergeant in one of Long's Indiana regiments recalled that this was no simple task because there was no saw mill. All the work had to be done by hand using "axe, cross-cut saw and froe." Even with the hard work involved, the cantonments proved their worth, particularly during the prolonged rains that fell in March. "The final victory over Forrest and the Rebel cavalry," Wilson later declared, "was won by patient industry and instruction while in the cantonments at Gravelly Springs and Waterloo."[5]

As the incoming units settled into their assigned locations, changes in the corps organization were initiated. At his own request, Louis Watkins was relieved of the command of McCook's third brigade and ordered to report to R. W. Johnson in Nashville for a comparable command in the Sixth Division. McCook's third brigade was then disbanded and its regiments redistributed among the first and second brigades. In McCook's absence, Croxton was temporarily placed in command of all units in the Waterloo-Eastport sector.[6] Another departure was that of John Hammond. Plagued by ill health he was relieved of command and sent back to Nashville for treatment.[7]

Several regiments were moved from one division to another. Since R. W. Johnson's Sixth Division was composed largely of Tennessee troops, the Sixth Tennessee was transferred out of Upton's Fourth Division and sent back to join Johnson in Nashville. In return, the Fifth Iowa and Seventh Ohio were moved from Johnson's command to Upton's. Wilson was also forced to advise Upton that General Dana would probably retain the Second New Jersey, Seventh Indiana, and Fourth Missouri regiments in Memphis due to the recent directive calling for all troops in the Memphis area to be sent to Canby.[8]

Thomas, meanwhile, had begun to feel a resurgence of the pressure that nearly led to his removal at Nashville. On December 31 Halleck directed him to collect his forces along the Tennessee River and prepare to resume the campaign. He reminded Thomas that Grant did not intend for his command to go into winter quarters.[9] Thomas explained that he was keeping a close watch on Hood's line of retreat and that his scattered command was being assembled along the Tennessee as directed. However, the past few weeks had taken a heavy toll on the horses. Wilson's cavalry needed time to shoe up and recuperate. Thomas feared that an immediate continuance of the campaign would only result in "heavy losses from disease and exhaustion." It would be much better, Thomas urged, to be "well prepared before starting on an important campaign."[10]

Thomas's seeming reluctance to get started continued to exasperate Grant. In mid–January, Grant wrote to Halleck, pointing out that since the remnants of Hood's army had moved east to oppose Sherman, he wanted Canby to launch a winter campaign from the Gulf. Thomas must either undertake a similar effort or spare his surplus troops. If nothing else worked, perhaps the thought of being stripped of his command would make Thomas move.[11]

Accordingly, on January 19, Halleck wrote to Thomas advising him to be prepared to cooperate with Canby on a movement to Selma and that if he did not plan on a winter campaign, how many troops could he send to

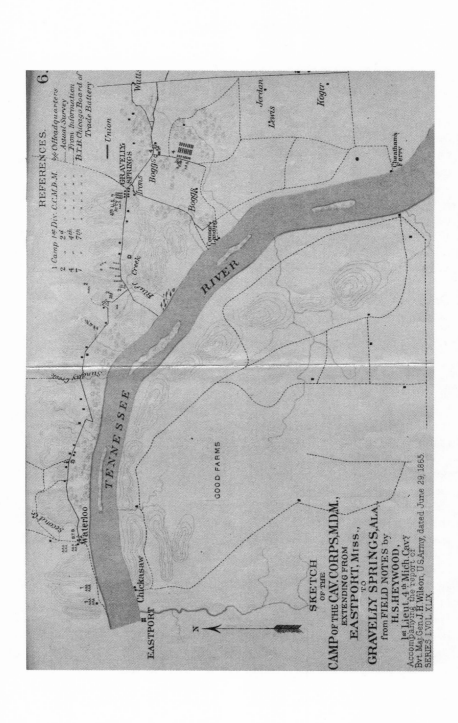

6.

REFERENCES.

1 Camp 1st Div. C.C.M.D.M.   ✸ O.Headquarters
2 "   " 2d "   "   "   —— Actual Survey
4 "   " 4th "   "   "   ········ From Information
7 "   " 7th "   "   "   B.T.B. Chicago Board of
                                    Trade Battery
—— Union

SKETCH
OF THE
CAMP OF THE CAV.CORPS,M.D.M.,
EXTENDING FROM
EASTPORT, MISS.,
TO
GRAVELLY SPRINGS,ALA.,
from FIELD NOTES by
H.S.HEYWOOD,
1st Lieut. 4th Mich Cavy
Accompanying the report of
Bvt.Maj.Gen.J.H.Wilson, U.S.Army dated June 29, 1865
SERIES I.VOL.XLIX.

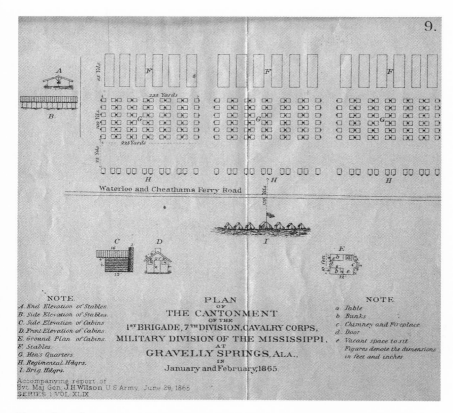

9.

Typical cavalry corps cantonment on the Tennessee River, 1865 (National Archives, Record Group 94, Plate LXVIII, No. 9; Civil War Atlas).

Canby? With customary patience, Thomas replied that he was organizing as quickly as possible and again urged that he not be ordered to take the field until this was completed. It had been Thomas's plan to move against Selma in the spring, as he told Halleck, but right now the roads were in no position to support a campaign. However, if Grant insisted, A. J. Smith's infantry and all the cavalry save for two divisions could be sent to Canby.[12]

Sherman, too, was prodding Thomas. He suggested that a small cavalry force operate from Knoxville down into North Carolina, while Thomas, with 25,000 infantry and all of Wilson's cavalry, should move south. Thomas should concentrate near Columbus, Mississippi, then march on Tuscaloosa

Opposite: Sketch map of Wilson's cantonments along the Tennessee River, 1865 (National Archives, Record Group 94, Plate LXXII, No. 6; Civil War Atlas).

and Selma, possibly even to Montgomery if conditions permitted it. "I would like to have Forrest hunted down and killed," Sherman added, "but doubt if we can do that yet."[13]

But as February approached with no sign of an Alabama campaign from Thomas, Grant finally directed Halleck to have Thomas send A. J. Smith's infantry and a division of Wilson's cavalry to Canby. On February 3, Wilson selected Knipe's division for transfer. Horses to complete Knipe's remount were taken from Hatch because the Fifth Division contained more dismounted men than any division in the corps. Additionally, the Nineteenth Pennsylvania and Tenth Tennessee regiments were transferred from the Fourth and Fifth divisions, respectively, to bring Knipe up to full strength.[14]

Meanwhile, even as Grant, Halleck, and Sherman tried to get Thomas to move, Wilson was pressing for more horses and Spencer carbines. In addition, many of his regiments were still woefully understrength. As of January 10, the corps numbered 796 officers and 18,922 men present for duty. However, when absentees were counted, the total nearly doubled, which meant that half the corps was either sick, on furlough, or on some form of detached duty. This latter category really disturbed Wilson; he requested Thomas to secure a peremptory order from Grant to have these men returned to their respective regiments.[15]

Shortly after arriving at Gravelly Springs, Wilson received a request from A. J. Smith for cavalry troops to perform picket duty. In the past, cavalry had been parceled out for such duty with no one giving the matter a second thought. This was a perfect illustration of how the cavalry was sapped of its strength. Wilson fumed. He was determined to put an end to it. He told Smith:

> You can't have a man. If you are going to move against the enemy & need me I'll go with my whole force. If you simply insist me to do picket duty for you I shall not do it, for I was sent here to rest, operate and prepare my cavalry for active service and I intend to do both. This habit of calling upon cavalry to protect infantry must be broken up or we shall have no cavalry.[16]

Wilson also had a similar request from Brigadier General Robert Granger who wanted to retain some Tennessee and Indiana Cavalry regiments for his District of Northern Alabama and, like Smith before him, was refused in no uncertain terms.[17]

Ironically, if the corps had been up to full strength it would have created an additional problem for Wilson, who was having no end of difficulty finding enough animals to mount all of his units, let alone twice that number. The campaign against Hood had been very costly in terms of both human casualties and horseflesh. Often careless handling on the part of indifferent or inexperienced troops contributed to the condition. On January 8, Wilson issued General Order Number 3, in which he pointed to the careless and injurious manner of feeding horses, an area particularly in need of attention. Feeding should be regular and forage ought never to be placed on the ground, as the horse was liable to injure its digestive tract by picking up sand and gravel.[18]

The Cavalry Bureau estimated that between October 31 and December 31, 1864, Wilson's cavalry corps had been issued 18,326 horses. Yet on January 2, 1865, Wilson advised Captain John Green, one of the special inspectors of cavalry in Nashville, that "not less than 10,000 [horses would be required] to completely mount us."[19] On January 3, Wilson wrote to Brigadier General Whipple, chief of staff for the Department of the Cumberland, requesting "that immediate steps be taken to secure 10,000 horses and all the Spencer carbines to be had." If the Cavalry Bureau was unable to supply the necessary number of animals, authority ought to be granted to impress horses in Ohio, Indiana, and Illinois. "The magnitude of the interests at stake would warrant it," Wilson declared.[20]

Two days later, Wilson wrote again, this time to Major William R. Price, chief inspector of cavalry in Washington, and to Major William P. Chambliss, special inspector of cavalry, Military Division of the Mississippi. Again Wilson pointed out the necessity of securing authorization from the secretary of war for filling the quota of horses from the country north of the Ohio River. To Price, Wilson further suggested that since R. W. Johnson's division had been tabbed for duty in Middle Tennessee, it might be dismounted and the horses turned over to the other divisions in his corps. Grease heel and hoof rot were again making an appearance among his horses, said Wilson.[21]

In response to Wilson's memorandum, Chambliss replied that the Cavalry Bureau had "ample means for the supply of any number of remounts you may require." As Chambliss saw it, the problem was not getting horses *for* Wilson it was getting them *to* him. He suggested that the dismounted regiments be sent back to Louisville to be mounted, saying that this would be no different than sending the same units north of the Ohio River.[22]

Wilson, however, was diametrically opposed to sending his regiments back to Louisville, or north of the Ohio River for that matter. He believed the function of the Cavalry Bureau was to come to the combat units, not the other way around. He wrote:

> The true policy of the bureau is to establish its depots for recuperation at such points, which being safe, are most easily accessible, so that broken-down stock may be easily got to it, and the proper supplies for the recuperation be readily obtained. The

remounts after being assembled at these points and properly prepared for the service, should be sent to the troops, if possible, instead
of sending troops for them.[23]

Chambliss finally agreed to forward remounts by steamer down the
Tennessee River to Eastport. The problem was that with Schofield's corps
having recently been transferred east and because of other priorities, steamers were not always available. As a result, resupplying Wilson's command
with horses continued to be a problem, although the Cavalry Bureau was
doing its best to fill his requisitions. In January Wilson had stated that 10,000
animals would be needed, but by mid–February he advised Whipple that
5,893 horses would now complete the remount of his entire corps.[24]

Despite this progress, however, by the end of February Chambliss was
forced to admit that he simply could not supply everyone. The picture had
changed in the past 60 days. Since Chambliss had written to Wilson in
January, Major General General George Stoneman had been ordered to prepare for a raid from East Tennessee down into South Carolina to destroy
rail lines and such other military resources Sherman might miss on his march
north. In Stoneman's absence, Brigadier General Alvin C. Gillem would
command in East Tennessee. Both Stoneman and Gillem needed horses, too,
so Thomas directed that the supply of remounts would have to be divided
between Stoneman, Gillem, and Wilson. Wilson did not agree with the priorities, but there was little he could do about it. The impressment of horses
from north of the Ohio River would have greatly alleviated the situation,
but Wilson's request was emphatically vetoed. "The places to impress horses,"
said Halleck, "are Mississippi, Alabama and Georgia."[25]

It was also proving difficult to obtain Spencer carbines. Fortunately,
many of the regiments were already equipped with Spencers, but others were
still armed with a potpourri of weapons, including Colts, Burnsides, Halls,
Sharps, and Maynards. Replying to Brigadier General A. B. Dyer, chief of
ordnance, Wilson declared that "all carbines are bad by comparison with the
Spencer, and that the troops of this army will receive no other without
protest." Indeed, back in November, McCook had written to Beaumont saying that his division would be ready for the field shortly, but would probably have to go without carbines. There were no carbines at Louisville, said
McCook, who preferred having his command "go into the field without
[carbines] to taking such inferior arms as they have had heretofore."[26]

Wilson requested that the cavalry depot in Nashville be furnished with
at least 10,000 and preferably 15,000 Spencer carbines as soon as possible.
However, the army's demand for Spencers was beyond the factory's capacity. Consequently, a competitor, the Burnside Arms Company, was contracted to furnish 3,000 Spencers monthly. Reinforced by this additional

source of supply, Chambliss advised Wilson that the cavalry corps could expect to receive its due proportion.[27]

While Wilson was of the opinion that the Tennessee River assembly area offered excellent facilities for the type of training he had in mind, the troops were somewhat less enthusiastic about their new home. Short rations, lousy weather, constant drills, and strict discipline together with the remoteness of the area contributed to the rank and file's disenchantment with these cantonments. Wilson seemed to put the needs of the horses ahead of his men, which meant that forage, for example, had a priority over rations. This policy earned for Wilson the dubious sobriquet of "General Starvation."[28] A Pennsylvania trooper in Long's division remembered that "one week we subsisted on parched corn—one quart only allowed per day for a man and a horse. Half rations of bread, and two days in five some beef bones and blue gristle constituted the average supply for the winter."[29]

Meat was the scarcest item on the menu and some troopers would go to great lengths to obtain it. On one occasion a group from the Seventy-second Indiana appropriated what they thought was a barrel of meat from the commissary, only to discover that their prize was not meat but coal tar. The chagrined troopers spent the remainder of the night trying to wash it off.[30] On another occasion, as Wilson was riding through the camp of Long's second brigade, some of the Fourth Ohio cried out "Hard tack! Hard tack!" Angered by the outburst, Wilson ordered the entire brigade under arms and into line, where they were forced to remain for nearly eight hours.[31]

As far as the cantonments themselves were concerned, one man described Gravelly Springs as a place "where nothing ever grew for man or beast."[32] Another trooper called it "one of the outsidest places I was ever in."[33] A large cavalry camp such as the ones at Waterloo and Gravelly Springs presented an unusual sight, too. An Iowan recalled that it "looked strange to see an army of 25,000 encamped, and see no long lines of infantry white tents, and hear no beat of drums," the customary method by which orders were communicated to infantry units.[34]

In addition to short rations and a desolate location, the men were also subjected to a rigorous training regimen. Every man was constantly on some kind of duty. One soldier described a typical day in camp as consisting of the same old routine of "wash, iron, scrub, bake."[35] But it did not end there. Drills, both mounted and dismounted, with and without saber, were conducted daily, regardless of the weather. Inspections were held frequently and every man was expected to show a weapon in perfect condition at any time. All duties other than drills were performed dismounted and guards were posted to prevent the men from leaving camp without proper authorization.[36]

A typical day in the cantonments commenced with the musician or bugler's call at 5 A.M. (in summer, 4 A.M.). The schedule that followed was an active one:

Orderly call	Squad drill
Roll call	Dinner call
Feed call	Company drill
Breakfast	Battalion call
Curry horses	Water call
Police quarters	Feed horses
Sick call	Supper
Guard mount	Evening roll (sundown)
Fatigue duty	Tattoo
Water horses	Taps

There were individual buglers for each unit. One trooper remembered that 300 bugles blowing at the same time created about as much noise as anyone would care to hear.[37]

Wilson, like most professional soldiers, thought the volunteer system was badly flawed. One of the most grievous shortcomings, he felt, was the system by which the men elected their own officers, a practice he eliminated during the cantonment period. Officers were selected by Wilson and his staff on the basis of past performance.[38]

In all, it was a tiresome and annoying time for the cavalry corps. Most of them were midwesterners completely unaccustomed to the strict brand of discipline and soldiering initiated by Wilson. The adjutant of the Fourth Iowa wrote:

> It was hard work, and so much more strictly required than before that many found it irksome. But all must have appreciated its good results. They saw that it would have been far better for the regiment if it had had such schooling during the earlier period of its service.[39]

If the days seemed long, dreary, and filled with the tiresome duties of camp life, there were also diversions. Occasionally, the sun managed to poke its way through the leaden sky. Periodically, a scouting party sortied out to skirmish with local guerrillas. At night, around brightly burning pine-knot campfires, the men would sing and often be serenaded by one of the regimental bands.[40]

The transfer of Knipe's division to Canby prompted additional changes in the corps organization. Hatch was directed to move his dismounted troops into the area formerly occupied by A. J. Smith's infantry. The third battalion, Twelfth Missouri Cavalry, Major J. M. Hubbard commanding, was designated as the pontonier unit of the corps. They would receive professional instruction from Major James R. Willett of Thomas's staff. Finally, the First Ohio was transferred from Long's Second Division to Upton's Fourth, which by now was finally beginning to take shape. It would shortly be the equal of any in Wilson's corps, due primarily to Upton's driving determination.[41]

Although training, refitting, and reorganization remained Wilson's top priorities, there were other matters that also required attention. Confederate deserters and roving bands of guerrillas roamed through the countryside, preying on the local citizens. In addition, legitimate Confederate raiding parties were attempting to disrupt river traffic, while spies tried to penetrate Federal lines to determine troop strength and objectives. Wilson countered by sending out his own patrols, which, together with local citizens, deserters, and Federal spies, provided sufficient intelligence to determine that Hood was no longer in command of the Army of Tennessee. What remained of that proud force had been sent east to oppose Sherman.[42]

Early in February, Wilson received a message from Forrest, delivered under a flag of truce, requesting protection for the civilians using the railroads in northern Mississippi. Wilson, however, saw it for what it was: a ruse on Forrest's behalf to obtain information on Yankee troop strength and location. The Confederate leader also suggested a meeting between the two of them to discuss a prisoner exchange. But two could play that game; Wilson responded by sending two members of his staff to advise Forrest that there could be no prisoner exchange without authority from Washington. Forrest's request was forwarded to Thomas, who in turn passed it on to Grant.[43]

Meanwhile, Wilson's two representatives, captains Lewis M. Hosea and James P. Metcalf, met with Colonel M. C. Galloway of Forrest's staff at Burnsville, Mississippi, 15 miles west of Eastport. Galloway conveyed his chief's concern over some 7,000 Federal prisoners in Alabama and Mississippi who were being badly treated. It was Forrest's hope that supplies might be sent to these prisoners and that arrangements for an exchange might be effected. Forrest further hoped that the citizens of northern Alabama and Mississippi might be permitted to trade cotton for the necessities of life.[44]

Later, Forrest invited Hosea to his headquarters for a personal meeting. On the dark, stormy night of February 23, in a scene reminiscent of *Wuthering Heights*, the two men met in an old country house where they discussed matters by flickering candlelight. For the young Hosea, it was a night to remember. He was impressed with the power of Forrest's personality. When Hosea told Forrest that Wilson was a West Point graduate with training in tactics, the Confederate leader replied, "I never rubbed my back up agin a college, an' I don't profess to know much about tactics, but I'd give more for fifteen minutes of the 'bulge' on you than for three days of tactics."[45]

Grant subsequently approved Forrest's request for supplies for Union prisoners and also authorized an exchange of prisoners, but ruled out the commercial trade for civilians. Back in 1862, he had taken similar action against wartime profiteering and gotten in hot water, but in 1865 his decisions were seldom overturned.[46]

On February 14, Grant wrote to Thomas advising him that Canby was preparing to move against Mobile and interior Alabama. Knipe's cavalry would disembark at Vicksburg and, together with the cavalry units already in that area, would move eastward to cooperate with Canby's offensive. Grant reminded Thomas that Hood's army had been greatly reduced by the "severe beating" it had taken in Tennessee. Since the remnants had been sent east, it was the ideal time to launch a cavalry strike south of the Tennessee River. The objective, said Grant, "would be three-fold":

> First. To attack as much of the enemy's force as possible to insure success to Canby. Second. To destroy the enemy's line of communications and military resources. Third. To destroy or capture their forces brought into the field. Tuscaloosa and Selma probably would be the points to direct the expedition against. This, however, would not be so important as the mere fact of penetrating deep into Alabama. Discretion should be left with the officer commanding the expedition to go where, according to the information he may receive, he will best secure the objects named above. Now that your force has been much depleted I do not know what number of men you can put into the field. If not more than 5,000 men, however, all cavalry, I think it will be sufficient. [47]

Grant suggested that it would be best not to start the expedition until the Vicksburg column was at least three or four days en route. Grant also thought the expedition should travel as lightly as possible. Thomas replied the same day, saying that he could send about 10,000 fully equipped men with a four-gun battery to each division. He asked to be notified three or four days in advance of the date Grant wished the expedition to get under way, as it took that long to get a message to Wilson. In the meantime, however, Thomas alerted Wilson to have 10,000 men or two divisions ready to move upon the receipt of Grant's order.[48]

Twenty-four hours later, on February 15, Grant decided that the time to launch the expedition had come. He telegraphed Thomas to get it started "as soon after the 20th instant as it can get off." Thomas replied immediately that the column would be ready to move by the designated time.[49]

Thus far there had been no indication that Wilson would personally lead the expedition. However, on February 22, Thomas traveled to Eastport to confer with his cavalry chief. It is not clear whether Thomas planned to name

Wilson or whether the latter requested the assignment. In any event, a week later, Thomas wrote to Canby advising him that Wilson would command the expedition from Eastport and would get under way about March 5 with 10,000 cavalry. Wilson's objectives would be to threaten the Mobile and Ohio Railroad as far south as Columbus, Mississippi. He was also to inflict maximum damage on Confederate military resources. Then, while engaging the enemy he would suddenly shift the axis of his attack toward Selma and Montgomery.[50]

Wilson, however, said that Thomas came down to Eastport on the twenty-third, with orders for him to prepare a cavalry force of 5,000–6,000 "'for the purpose of making a demonstration upon Tuscaloosa and Selma' in favor of General Canby's operation against Mobile and Central Alabama." According to Wilson, he convinced Thomas that it would be worthwhile to move with his entire mounted force, capture these places, and use them as a base of operations.[51] Wilson later wrote:

> in passing seventeen thousand troopers in review before Thomas, I convinced him that a "demonstration" in any direction would be a useless waste of strength and, if permitted to go with my whole available force into Central Alabama, I would not only defeat Forrest and such other troops as I might encounter, but would capture Tuscaloosa, Selma, Montgomery, and Columbus, and destroy the Confederacy's last depots of manufacture and supply and break up its last interior line of railway communications.[52]

Thomas reportedly gave his blessing and authorized Wilson "to pursue such a course as I might see proper, keeping in view the general objects of the impending campaign." Wilson added that the "instructions of Lieutenant General Grant, transmitted to me by General Thomas,... allowed me the amplest discretion as an independent commander."[53]

Wilson seemed to suggest that the strategy of the forthcoming campaign had been his idea, when, in fact, it was an idea that had been percolating for some time. Moreover, it was Grant, not Thomas, who suggested sending 5,000 cavalry. After receiving Grant's directive, Thomas advised both Grant and Wilson that it would be possible to field a force of 10,000. Wilson undoubtedly urged an aggressive campaign and probably convinced Thomas that if they were going to send 10,000 men, why not the entire cavalry corps. Of course if the entire corps went, Wilson would be the appropriate commander. The logic was sound, so Thomas approved.[54]

The assignment of Johnson's division to patrol Middle Tennessee with the transfer of Knipe's command to Canby left Wilson with only four divisions. Furthermore, since Hatch's division was now almost entirely dismounted and since it was apparently beyond the capacity of the Cavalry Bureau to fully supply everyone, the few remaining horses in the Fifth Division were turned over to Upton's Fourth Division. Thus, Hatch's splendid division would not play a part in the forthcoming campaign, but would remain behind in the cantonments and continue training. Wilson hoped that the division could be remounted in time to rejoin the rest of the corps in the field. With the approval of Hatch and Wilson, Coon voluntarily turned over all the Spencer carbines in his brigade to Croxton's command. As a result, all but a few hundred troopers were now equipped with the seven-shot Spencer breech-loading carbines. Those who did not have Spencers had weapons that fired metallic cartridges.[55]

Thus, the three divisions slated to participate in the campaign were McCook's First, Long's Second, and Upton's Fourth, a total of 13,480 men, of which approximately 11,980 were mounted. Some 1,500 dismounted troop from each of the three divisions would accompany on foot as a guard for the wagon train. Of the three, Long's Second Division was the largest by far, containing 5,127 men, compared with 4,096 for the First Division and 3,923 for the Fourth Division. Wilson's escort, the Fourth U.S. Regulars commanded by Lieutenant William O'Connell, numbered 334 men.[56]

Each division was composed of two brigades, supported by a battery of artillery. McCook's two brigades were commanded by Croxton and LaGrange. Long's brigade commanders were colonels Abraham O. Miller and Robert Horatio George Minty. Upton's two brigades were led by Brevet Brigadier General Andrew J. Alexander and Colonel Edward F. Winslow.[57]

The three divisions would be accompanied by a supply train of 250 wagons, 50 of which carried a light canvas pontoon train of 30 boats. There was also a mule pack train carrying additional supplies that would offer the column a faster-moving supply train if needed, as it eventually was. Captain W. E. Brown, acting chief quartermaster, was charged with the responsibility of the train itself, while the 1,500-man escort was divided into battalions under the overall command of Major Martin Archer.[58]

Wilson planned on a 60-day campaign, allowing that additional supplies could be garnered from the countryside as needed. He wrote:

> Division commanders were directed to see that every trooper was provided with five days' light rations in haversacks, twenty-four pounds of grain, one hundred rounds of ammunition, and one pair of extra shoes for his horse; that the pack animals were loaded with five days' of hard bread, ten of sugar, coffee, and salt, and the wagons with forty-five days' of coffee, twenty of sugar, fifteen of salt and eighty rounds of ammunition.[59]

Wilson's personal staff had grown from 15 to 20 members since December.

Beaumont continued to be the pivotal figure of this group, as he had been since the inception of the corps. The chief medical officer of the expedition was surgeon Francis Salter, assisted by chief division surgeons Benjamin McClure, Francis Green, and Frederick Corfe. In all, 50 medical officers accompanied the expedition.[60]

The expedition that Wilson was preparing to take south of the Tennessee River was the equal of any mounted command to be found in either army. They were veteran troops, well-trained, well-equipped, and well-led at virtually every command level. The senior unit leaders in particular were experienced and able. Wilson had managed to instill pride in his corps, a spirit that was perhaps best expressed by Long, who remarked that he was "sorry the war did not last just six weeks longer, for that would have brought us to Virginia, alongside of Sheridan's 'gayoso cavalry,' and I am sure we should have fanned the wind out of their sails, and shown them how cavalry should both march and fight."[61]

Grant had hoped that Canby, Stoneman, and Wilson would all get started early, but this was not to be. On February 27, Grant told Thomas to have Stoneman repeat his raid of the previous fall, destroying the railroad as far as Lynchburg, because Sherman was already out of South Carolina and moving north.[62] On the same day, Thomas advised Grant that Wilson's expedition would be late; the departure date was set for early March. The villain was the weather. Rains, the heaviest in 40 years, had forced the Tennessee River over its banks. Steamboats were unable to even reach the landings "except by working their way through the woods and fields until the river subsided to its natural banks."[63]

On February 28 Wilson informed Whipple that the river had risen 30 feet in four days and was impossible to cross. There was three feet of water between the river and the headquarters of Hatch's first brigade. Some 500,000 bushels of oats, enough to supply the horses of the entire corps for two months, were destroyed by flood waters at Chickasaw Landing.[64]

On March 1, Grant again wrote to Thomas, suggesting that it would probably be best for Wilson to start before the Vicksburg column, as the latter might not be able to cross the Pearl River until Wilson had created a diversion. However, as he had before the fight at Nashville, Grant appeared not to have appreciated the conditions facing Thomas and Wilson. As Wilson later put it, neither Grant nor the War Department seemed to understand "that although the weather was generally milder in the country south of the Tennessee [River] than farther north, the streams would be swollen and the roads impassable till the winter rains were over and the roads had measurably dried out."[65] It wasn't just Thomas and Wilson. On March 1, Canby advised Thomas that the projected cavalry raid from Vicksburg had to be canceled because of the heavy rains and that Knipe's division had been ordered on to New Orleans as a result.[66]

At any rate, before Wilson could really get under way, he first had to get his three divisions across the rain-swollen Tennessee and the way things looked as March arrived, that was going to take some doing. Lieutenant Colonel A. J. Mackay, chief quartermaster of the Department of the Cumberland, told Wilson that troops could be landed at Chickasaw with no real difficulty. The problem was in getting the troops from their camps down to the landing and aboard the steamers.[67]

On March 4, Wilson advised Thomas, "The rain storm just ended was the most violent of the season. The Tennessee is now higher than for many years and rising rapidly. It will be utterly impossible to get off tomorrow, though I shall use every possible effort to expedite the movement."[68] By the following day, an improvement in the weather seemed to be at hand. Wilson reported that the river was beginning to subside, but it would still be several days before he could begin crossing. On March 7 Wilson told Thomas that the rains had started again and that the river was still over its banks.[69] However, by the eleventh, McCook's division had gotten to the south side, followed by Long on the twelfth and thirteenth, and finally Upton's Fourth Division. The rains continued. On March 13, Wilson wrote to Sherman, bringing him up to date on plans for the forthcoming campaign, adding, "The unheard-of rains in this region within the last two weeks have covered the entire country as a sea."[70]

Nevertheless, by March 17 the entire corps was across the Tennessee River. Wilson advised Thomas that final arrangements would be completed by the following day and, roads permitting, they would at last get started on the nineteenth. However, when that date arrived, the movement had to be postponed another 24 hours. This was followed by yet a another postponement on March 20 when an expected shipment of rations failed to arrive. Accordingly, new marching orders were issued for 5:30 A.M. on March 21 and this time they would stand. The Selma campaign was under way at long last.[71]

Thirteen
In the Confederate Camp

[J]ist tell Gin'ral Wilson that I know the nicest little place down below here, in the world, and whenever he is ready, I will fight him with any number from one to ten thousand cavalry and abide the issue. — Forrest to Hosea, February 1865[1]

T hanks to a brilliant rear guard action by Forrest, Hood's shattered army managed to escape the relentless Federal pursuit. By January 10, the army had reached Tupelo, Mississippi, where Hood, dejected by the failure of his campaign, submitted his resignation which was accepted by President Davis. On January 23, John Bell Hood was officially relieved of command of the Army of Tennessee.[2] The command of the army, or what remained of it, passed now to Lieutenant General Richard "Dick" Taylor, the literary-minded son of former U.S. president, Zachary Taylor. Taylor's command jurisdiction embraced the departments of Mississippi, Alabama, and east Louisiana. Sherman was creating havoc along the eastern seaboard with virtually no force to oppose him, so Taylor was ordered to refit the Army of Tennessee and hurry east as quickly as possible.[3]

The order did not, however, include Forrest's cavalry, which would remain in the area and ready itself to repel the Yankee thrust that was certain to come. If the retreat from Nashville had been an ordeal for Wilson's cavalry, it was no less so for the Confederates; a complete rest and refitting was imperative. On December 27, with the Tennessee River safely between Hood's army and Wilson's horsemen, Forrest obtained permission to move his frazzled brigades into camp near Corinth, Mississippi. Brigadier General Philip Roddey's brigade alone was left to patrol the Tennessee River line between Decatur and Waterloo and provide an escort for Hood's pontoon trains.[4]

Upon reaching Corinth, Forrest immediately furloughed all men who had homes in the area. The men were given 20 days to see their families, procure fresh horses and supplies, and annoy the Federals in any way possible. As an added bonus, Forrest promised that any man who returned with a mounted recruit would be given an extra 20-day furlough sometime during the coming year. Like soldiers everywhere, Forrest's men were jubilant at the prospect of seeing home again and lost little time in departing. Some even recalled riding through a blinding snowstorm in order to make every minute count.[5]

Forrest doubted, however, that his men would really have an opportunity to take advantage of the extra bonus. Privately, he believed that the days of the Confederacy were numbered. Even so, he was a soldier and as such would continue to expend every effort on behalf of the cause until such time as he was directed otherwise.[6]

Like all Confederate commanders, Forrest was faced with the ever increasing problem of desertion. Those who did desert and were unlucky enough to be caught were shown no mercy. Ross's Texans, too far from home to be furloughed, were put on picket duty guarding the approaches to Corinth in an effort to halt the increasing number of desertions from Hood's army.[7] In one instance, two deserters were caught and tried by drumhead court-martial, which subsequently found the pair guilty and executed them. The bodies were later placed by the roadside where they would be in plain view of passing troops and serve as a reminder. Nailed to a nearby tree was a sign emphasizing the consequences of their act: "Shot for Desertion."[8]

Following Colonel William Palmer's surprise attack and destruction of Hood's pontoon train early in January, Beauregard wired Richmond suggesting that all of the cavalry in Taylor's command be placed under Forrest to ensure against further mishaps. Up to that point, independent cavalry commands such as Roddey's had been subject only to the orders of the department commander. Now, in accordance with Richmond's directive of January 24, Forrest assumed command of all mounted troops in east Louisiana, Mississippi, and Alabama.[9] Four days later, on January 28, Forrest issued a general order stating that he would require strict obedience to orders. The rights of citizens would be respected and protected and "the illegal organizations of cavalry, prowling through the country, must be placed regularly and properly in the service or driven from the country."[10]

On March 1 Forrest moved his headquarters to West Point, Mississippi, where he immediately initiated a reorganization of his command. The Tennessee troops of generals Tyree H. Bell and Edmund Rucker, along with Ross's Texans, were placed in one division under General William H. Jackson. The Mississippians of generals Frank Armstrong, Wirt Adams, and Peter B. Starke comprised a second division led by General James R. Chalmers. Finally, Abraham Buford's Kentucky brigade was assigned to serve under

General Dan W. Adams in the District of Alabama. Forrest retained as his escort, Colonel Robert "Black Bob" McCulloch and his Second Missouri regiment. At best, the strength of the entire command did not exceed 10,000 men. Like Wilson, Forrest was fortunate in having an able group of subordinates. Unlike his opponent, however, Forrest lacked the men and resources with which to supply his subordinates.[11]

While Forrest was tireless in his efforts to refit his command, it appears that the rank and file were not subjected to anything like the rigorous training program being carried out in the Federal cantonments. Some Confederate troops recalled that they had a lot of spare time, which was often devoted to such pastimes as playing checkers and shooting marbles. Forrest apparently did not object to these amusements, but he severely punished any man involved in horse racing or the aimless firing of weapons; these activities wasted precious horseflesh and ammunition. Indeed, Forrest's own son was punished for becoming involved in some horse-racing enterprises by carrying rails on his shoulders.[12]

In addition to desertion and resupply, a third problem also confronted Forrest. In some areas of the Confederacy, influential citizens were receiving permission to organize resistance behind Federal lines. A few of these operations proved beneficial, but for the most part they hindered rather than aided the Confederate cause. Acting under the guise of the military, these groups (which in most instances were little more than outlaw bands) were robbing local citizens of food, horses, and anything else they wished to plunder. In addition, this was a resourceful way to dodge legitimate military service. The whole business angered Forrest, who vowed to destroy these groups using any means at his disposal.[13]

On February 9, Robert E. Lee was named commander of all Confederate forces, a directive that might have had a most significant influence on the outcome of the war had it happened earlier. Two days after receiving his appointment, Lee issued an amnesty to all deserters who returned to the army within 30 days. Communication within the Confederacy was poor, however, and many never learned of the proclamation until long after the deadline had passed. In the west, General Taylor extended the time in his department until April 15, by which time, of course, the whole thing was academic.[14]

Three weeks after Lee's appointment, Forrest was promoted to the rank of lieutenant general, marking the zenith of a remarkable military career. At the outbreak of the Civil War and only a month shy of his fortieth birthday, wealthy plantation owner Nathan Bedford Forrest enlisted in the Confederate army as a private. By October 1861 he had raised and mounted a battalion of cavalry on his own and was commissioned lieutenant colonel. He covered the Confederate rear guard action during the retreat from Shiloh

General Nathan Bedford Forrest (reproduced from the Collections of the Library of Congress).

and was promoted to brigadier general for his performance. After conducting a series of raids that began to build his reputation, he was promoted to major general in December 1863. During the Atlanta campaign, a frustrated William Tecumseh Sherman declared, "That Devil Forrest ... must be hunted down and killed if it costs ten thousand lives and bankrupts the Federal treasury."[15]

During January and February 1865, Forrest's scouts reported heavy concentrations of Federal troops, both in the gulf region and along the Tennessee River. It was evident that the Yankees were priming for a strike at interior Alabama, undoubtedly at the arsenals and machine shops of Selma and Tuscaloosa as well as the port city of Mobile. From which direction the Federals would strike first and which effort would pose the greatest threat were the questions that Forrest and Taylor had to address.

After his conference with Captain Hosea, Forrest may have concluded that Wilson posed the most immediate threat. In any event, he now began shifting his forces to cover Selma from the north. Scouts were out constantly, courier lines were set up, and a series of identifying marks were blazed on trees and sign boards, pointing the way to both Selma and Tuscaloosa. Forrest wanted no miscues if a quick movement became necessary.[16]

Late in March, Chalmers was moved east to Pickensville, just inside the Alabama line, then almost immediately was ordered on to Selma. General Taylor had learned that a Federal column from the gulf was apparently headed toward either Mobile or perhaps central Alabama.[17]

On March 25, Forrest, having belatedly learned that Wilson was already three days under way and coming fast, sent William Jackson's division to Tuscaloosa with orders to strike the flank of the Federal column as quickly as possible.[18] The uncertainty of the situation that now involved the distinct possibility of two Federal columns converging on Selma caused General Taylor to make a choice. The most imminent threat, Taylor concluded, was posed by the column from the Gulf. Wilson was a secondary threat and would be the easier of the two Federal columns to repel. Taylor wrote to Forrest on March 26:

> In view of the movements from Russellville and Moulton, your order for Jackson to move via Tuscaloosa is right. Jackson with his own and Lyon's command, should meet, whip, and get rid of that column of the enemy as soon as possible.[19]

In this instance at least, Forrest's intelligence network failed to provide an accurate picture of the cantonments along the Tennessee River. Neither Taylor nor Forrest seem to have appreciated the size of Wilson's force. Moreover, Forrest's failure to learn of Wilson's departure for three days proved a critical blow to the Confederate defensive capabilities, limited as they were. Had Forrest been able to move promptly and intercept Wilson early on, he might well have delayed or possibly even turned back the Federal column.

Fourteen
South to Selma

My corps took this place [Selma] *by assault late on the evening of the 2d.* —Wilson to Thomas, April 4, 1865[1]

T here was something about the Civil War, even after nearly four years of bloody conflict, that continued to bring out the romantic and the poet in some men who marched off on a new campaign. To be sure, the naïveté of 1861 had long since disappeared, but even as late as the spring of 1865, some men could still look on a new campaign as a glorious adventure. Lieutenant William L. Curry of the Fourth Ohio Cavalry, Long's division, was one who viewed the Selma campaign in just that fashion, likening Wilson's horsemen to the conquistadores of Hernando Cortés.

> It was one of those bright, sunshiny spring days, succeeding a long enterval of sombre gloom, when the first welcome green, so long hid in the wintry earth, was "climbing to a soul in grass and flowers."
> Never can I forget the brilliant scene, as regiment after regiment filed gaily out of camp, decked in all the paraphernalia of war, with gleaming arms and guidons given to wanton breeze. Stirring bugle songs woke the slumbering echoes of the woods. Cheer upon cheer went up from joyful lips, and brave hearts beat high with anticipation. But all knew, that like the Conquistadores of Cortez [*sic*] they burned their ships behind them when they left the Tennessee, staking all upon success.[2]

The opening phase of the campaign was critical for Wilson. Forrest, he well knew, would waste no time making his considerable presence felt once he learned the Yankees were coming. In an effort to confuse Forrest as to the Federal objective, Wilson divided his command into three separate columns. The strategy was risky because the broken, hilly terrain of northern Alabama would make it extremely difficult for the three columns to support each other in the event Forrest attacked.[3] Wilson's decision to divide the expedition was also predicated on a logistical need. In addition to the threat posed by Forrest, the expedition was going to have to live off the land to a large extent. The wagons would be able to haul only a fraction of what was needed to support them. This was especially true where forage for the horses was concerned. The valley of the Tennessee River had been hit hard by the war and was literally drained of supplies. "In all directions for 120 miles," wrote Wilson, "there was almost absolute destitution."[4]

Selma, Wilson's principal objective, lay nearly 300 miles to the south. The latest reports put the main body of Forrest's command at West Point, Mississippi, 150 miles southwest of Eastport and a little more than that northwest of Selma. Roddey was thought to be in the vicinity of Montevallo, 35 miles north of Selma, but his small command was not perceived as a major threat.[5]

In addition to negotiating the rugged terrain of northern and central Alabama, the expedition would also have to cross three major waterways and several smaller streams en route to Selma. The first two, the Mulberry and Locust forks of the Black Warrior River were between Jasper and Elyton (now Birmingham), while the Cahaba River was south of Elyton.

A wide, swift river under normal conditions, the Black Warrior was then running bank full from the recent rains. It represented a formidable barrier to the expedition's southward passage. Moreover, the Mulberry Fork ran through a gorge-like setting, between hills several hundred feet high, posing an additional hazard. Some waterways, such as the Sipsey Fork of the Black Warrior, were not as dangerous as they were disagreeable. An Indiana trooper in Long's division recalled crossing the Sipsey Fork at night and that it made him shiver just to remember the incident:

> The night was very dark and the swamp itself just like all the other swamps on the low lands of the South, a vast sea of mud, growing full of trees, vines and thick underbrush, with a large quantity of water sluggishly making its way through; a paradise for miasma, bullfrogs, serpents and alligators.[6]

Although Wilson had gotten a three-day head start on Forrest, time was still of the essence. If Forrest was able to intercept them before they got south of the Cahaba, he could, at the very least, cause a great deal of trouble. Indeed, the adjutant of the Fourth Iowa thought it was a "grave mistake on the part of the enemy, that they did not resist Wilson in this mountainous region."[7]

At any rate, against this backdrop, the cavalry corps drove south along three separate, parallel routes. Upton's Fourth Division took the most easterly route, moving through Barton's Station, Throckmorton's Mills, Russellville,

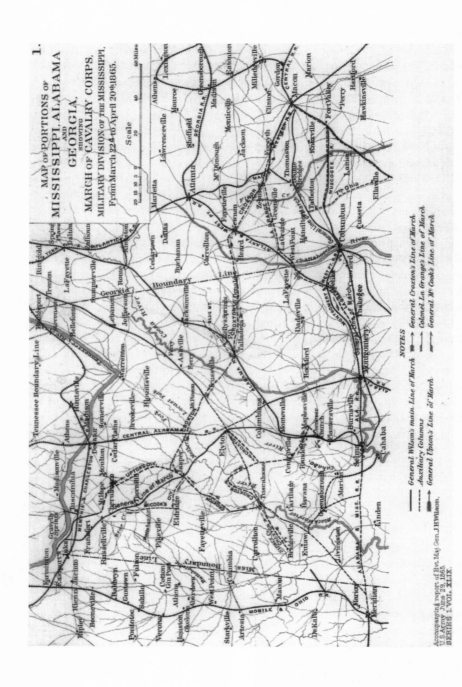

1.

MAP OF PORTIONS OF
MISSISSIPPI, ALABAMA
AND
GEORGIA,
SHOWING
MARCH OF CAVALRY CORPS,
MILITARY DIVISION OF THE MISSISSIPPI,
From March 22d to April 20th 1865.

Scale

20 15 10 5 0   20   40   60 Miles

NOTES

⟶ General Wilson's main Line of March
---- Auxiliary Columns
⟶ General Upton's Line of March.

⟶ General Croxton's Line of March.
⟶ Colonel. La Grange's Line of March.
⟶ General McCook's Line of March.

Accompanying report of Bvt. Maj. Gen. J.H.Wilson,
U.S. Army, June 29, 1865.
SERIES 1 VOL. XLIX.

and Jasper to Saunders' Ferry on the west or Mulberry Fork. Long's Second Division marched by way of Cherokee Station and Frankfort to Russellville, then south on the Tuscaloosa Road and east through Thorn Hill and Jasper to Saunders' Ferry. Finally, McCook's First Division followed Long's route as far as Bear Creek on the Tuscaloosa Road, then continued south to Eldridge before turning east to Jasper and Saunders' Ferry.[8]

Though blessed with favorable weather during the first few days, the heavy rains had turned the roads into a mass of ruts. Although Chief Surgeon Salter described the roads as being "rough but firm and passable," the unit commanders were somewhat less euphemistic.[9] Long had been given the responsibility of convoying the pontoon train; as a result, his division moved more slowly than the other two. Long, however, charged that part of the delay was simply the "excessive badness of the roads we were forced to travel."[10] After reaching Elyton on March 30, McCook declared that it had been a nine-day march over "the worst roads I ever saw."[11] John Croxton agreed, later calling March 27 one of the toughest days of the campaign. "The roads were in terrible condition," Croxton wrote, "and I was compelled to cut new roads, corduroy old ones, build bridges over swamps, and use my command to carry wagons and ambulances along."[12] Wilson wrote:

> It was throughout a hilly, gravelly, and barren region, covered with dense stands of pine and oak, broken here and there by the small clearings of poor white folks. The valleys are deep and narrow and the roads which threaded them much of the way were often almost impassable for lack of bridges and from the presence of quicksand and quagmire. While both men and horses could pick their way and make fair progress, especially along the ridges, it was frequently necessary to construct corduroy roads in order to get the artillery and wagons forward at all.[13]

A headquarters clerk in Upton's division described it as a

> country of rivers. The little wriggles of ink down the page of our military map are mountain streams flowing by stately pine woods, through hemlock-bordered ravines; some clear and colorless, others shaded blue and green that when falling in sunlit cascades are very beautiful.[14]

Progress with the wagons was maddeningly slow. The men were frequently called on to lift a wagon out of the mud. Sometimes it took eight mules

Opposite: **Route of Wilson's Cavalry through Alabama and Georgia, March–April 1865 (National Archives).**

to move a single wagon. The mules were small and evidently not as strong and healthy as they might have been, which compounded the problem. As early as March 28, six days out, Major Hubbard reported that due to heavy loads, he was forced to abandon about one-fourth of all the lumber he was carrying if it was of a type that could be procured in the region.[15]

When Wilson reached Jasper on March 27, he learned that part of Chalmers's division was reported to be marching via Tuscaloosa toward Selma. If true, it meant that Forrest was moving to counter them. It now became imperative to get across the Black Warrior and Cahaba Rivers as quickly as possible.

As soon as the Black Warrior was reached, Wilson ordered the columns stripped to their lightest marching order. Division commanders were instructed to have the men replenish their haversacks and see that the pack mules were fully loaded. Captain Brown's wagon train would follow the three divisions under the protection of Major Archer's dismounted troops. Archer and Brown were directed to push on to Elyton as rapidly as circumstances allowed. At Elyton, they would find additional orders waiting for them. Wilson's decision to leave the wagon train behind was based on his belief that at this point Forrest was primarily interested in the main Federal column.[16]

If crossing the Sipsey had been a disagreeable proposition, the Mulberry and Locust forks were different breeds. Both were deep, fast-flowing waterways, and crossing them was made more difficult by the threat of rain. Upton's fast-moving Fourth Division was the first to reach the Mulberry Fork. The pontoon train was still far to the rear, however, so the resourceful Upton offered a Confederate prisoner his freedom if he would test the ford. The prisoner agreed, was put on a good mount, and successfully navigated a crossing, winning his freedom. Upton then promptly ordered his division to commence crossing.[17]

An Iowa trooper remembered that during the crossing "many had fallen into the river, some swimming, others clinging to the rocks, and some plunging far down where the channel ran between precipitous banks at the mercy of the foaming waters."[18] The crossing of the Black Warrior River was marred by the loss of one trooper. A number of horses were also swept away in the process.[19]

On the morning of March 28, Upton advised Wilson that he would complete his crossing of the Black Warrior within three hours. He also called Wilson's attention to the fact that 700 Confederates had earlier been reported at Montevallo, but had since been ordered to a point 80 miles south of Selma. Wilson acknowledged the report and directed Upton to push on through Elyton to Montevallo. If Montevallo was undefended, Upton was to move toward Tuscaloosa unless he learned that Selma was undefended, in which case that was to become the objective.[20] By mid-morning on March 28, Upton was across the Locust Fork of the Black Warrior and advancing on Elyton. The Fifth Iowa of Alexander's brigade skirmished lightly with the Fifth Alabama virtually all the way into town. Aside from that, the Confederates offered little in the way of resistance.[21]

Alexander's brigade bivouacked that night in Elyton, while Winslow's brigade took over the plantation of one William Hawkins two miles to the west. Some of Winslow's troops discovered that the war had somehow managed to bypass the Hawkins larder. A headquarters clerk in the Third Iowa recalled that among other things, they found a wine cellar

> where rows of casks and dust-covered bottles were flanked by baskets and portly demijohns. "And monks might deem their time was come again, if ancient tales say true." Rolled the barrels of peach and apple brandy from among the musty cobwebs into the light of day, and those who were fortunate enough not to have taken the pledge were seen to smack their lips even before the bungs were started! On one point my recollection is quite distinct: An ancient barrel of apple—or was it peach?—brandy, the delightful odor of which pervaded the air as its contents flowed into our cups like syrup, was confiscated without delay, lest it might give aid and comfort to the enemy.[22]

Reports gleaned from newspapers and civilian informants continued to provide a fragmented picture of developing events. From Elyton, Upton reported that Confederate deserters were claiming that Roddey had been ordered to Greenville to oppose a raid from Pensacola and that Chalmers had been due at Tuscaloosa on the twenty-second. Upton further advised Wilson that he planned to push on to Montevallo immediately and expected to be there by noon on March 30. It was Upton's belief that the Confederates would concentrate either at Montevallo or somewhere east of the Cahaba. There was "an abundance of forage here for McCook and Long," Upton added.[23]

Wilson responded promptly, instructing Upton to watch for Chalmers, who was now reported to be moving toward Montevallo. Wilson concurred with Upton's assessment of the situation, but had "not yet determined to send to Tuscaloosa till we fully try the fortunes of war toward Selma."[24]

Although Elyton's future as a great industrial center known as Birmingham was as yet unrealized, it was nevertheless an important source of pig iron for the foundries at Selma during the Civil War. Accordingly, before continuing his drive south, the Third and Fourth Iowa of Winslow's brigade destroyed the Red Mountain and McIlvain Iron Works, as well as several collieries.[25] Long's Second Division reached Elyton about dark on the thirtieth, not long after Upton's men had put the torch to the iron works. "The sky was read for miles around," remembered Sergeant Benjamin McGee of the Seventy-second Indiana, "caused by fires burning cotton gins, mills, factories, &c., by our scouts and the 4th division which were just ahead of us."[26]

Although Wilson had issued strict orders against pillaging, the expedition was expected to sustain itself off the countryside and destroy anything of military value. Often, however, the distinction between the needs and objectives of the expedition vis-à-vis personal property was fairly vague and sometimes totally ignored.[27]

Pushing on to Montevallo, Upton discovered that the Confederates had felled logs and placed obstructions in the ford across the Cahaba River. Alexander managed to get a regiment across, but it was a slow and dangerous process. When Winslow arrived with his second brigade and saw the problem, he immediately dispatched scouts up and down the river. They discovered that the Tennessee and Alabama Railroad that ran between Selma and Elyton crossed the river near Hillsborough on a trestle that was still standing.

Though only 28, Winslow already had considerable experience as a railroad builder. With a keen engineering eye, he quickly discerned that the trestle could be converted to a foot bridge. By now it was dark and raining, but with the first available light, Winslow put his troops to work planking over the trestle. The adjutant of the Fourth Iowa set the scene:

> It was in the dull, slaty light of early morning in a driving rain— the swollen rushing river, the high narrow bridge, the surrounding dark forest, the two thousand horses and the unemployed men standing in silence while the men employed pushed their work with nervous energy, the sharp orders of officers, with anxious outlook in fear that the enemy would appear on the opposite bank before the last ties were laid—the scene is one that must still be distinct in the memory of all who were there. Within a few hours the bridge was finished with a floor eight feet wide and three hundred yards long, and the advance companies, in single file, were carefully leading over their trembling horses.[28]

The crossing proved a somewhat perilous undertaking as Sergeant McGee of the Seventy-second Indiana discovered when his regiment reached the river. He wrote:

> This by all odds was the most dangerous feat we had ever undertaken, or that we ever heard of. Allow three feet for the width occupied by each horse, and you see the men had to walk on the ends of the ties and also on the outside of the stringers under them. Now suppose the column had got started across all right and was being kept closed up just as well as it could be, and then suppose a horse should drop a leg through a crack and stick fast. In his effort to free himself he would either tumble off himself and carry his rider

with him, or push the horse by side off the other way, make a balk in the column and play smash generally. Or suppose that both horses should at the same time "shy" a little, how easy it would be to push a man off! We want to tell you that there were times while crossing that bridge when we drew our breath very short and thanked God when we were over.[29]

At Elyton on the night of March 30, Wilson assessed the situation. He concluded that with Chalmers reportedly moving toward Tuscaloosa, 60 miles to the southwest, his right flank was vulnerable. Accordingly, McCook was directed to detach Croxton's brigade and send it on to Tuscaloosa. The maneuver was intended to counter any Confederate movement from that quarter and destroy the military value of Tuscaloosa, which had been specified in Grant's February 14 letter to Thomas.[30] Croxton's orders were to "destroy the bridge [over the Cahaba], factories, mills, university (military school), and whatever else may be of benefit to the rebel cause." Croxton was also warned to watch for Lyon, "who was expected at Tuscaloosa yesterday with a small force marching toward Montevallo." In the event that the bridge at Centerville was destroyed, Croxton was instructed to cross the Cahaba wherever he could and eventually rejoin the main column at Selma. The way it worked out, Croxton's assignment turned out to be an odyssey all its own.[31]

Wilson reached Montevallo at 1 P.M. on March 31 and immediately ordered Upton to resume the advance. With Alexander's brigade in the lead, the Fourth Division pused out on the road toward Randolph. The Fifth Iowa, which had extricated itself in such singular fashion from the predicament at Duck River back in November, was in the forefront of Alexander's advance.[32] Resistance was encountered almost immediately in the form of Roddey's command and some of Colonel Edward Crossland's Kentuckians. The Confederates had taken up a position along a small creek about four miles south of Montevallo. Sixty troopers of the Fifth Iowa, still commanded by Colonel Young (he had been a major back at Duck River), promptly charged the Confederate line and drove it back for a mile and a half, at which point they dismounted and continued to advance on foot.

After Battery I, Fourth U.S. Artillery shelled the enemy position, Winslow's mounted brigade passed to the front and picked up the attack. The Tenth Missouri, then the Third and Fourth Iowa each contributed to an overpowering rout of the badly outnumbered Confederates, who were driven all the way to Randolph. Darkness ended further pursuit. Upton's command bivouacked for the night 14 miles south of Montevallo.[33] The advance was resumed on the morning of April 1. At Randolph, pursuant to Wilson's orders, Upton turned east through Maplesville to the old Selma road, while the rest of the corps continued south along the new road.

In addition to his superiority in men and resources, Wilson's Selma campaign was blessed with three strokes of good fortune. At the outset, he had gotten a three-day jump on Forrest, whose attention had been diverted by the threat of a Federal column from the Gulf region. The second stroke of luck came at Randolph. Nearing the town, Upton's men captured a Confederate courier carrying dispatches to General William Jackson. The dispatches provided Wilson with a complete picture of the disposition of the Confederate forces. Forrest, himself, with a portion of his command was in front of them. Jackson's division with wagons and artillery was marching from Tuscaloosa (via Trion and Centerville) to join Forrest, and Chalmers had reached Marion, 25 miles northwest of Selma. The dispatches further revealed that Croxton had apparently attacked Jackson's rear guard near Trion in an effort to delay the Confederate column from that quarter before moving on to Tuscaloosa as ordered. Shortly after intercepting the Confederate dispatches, a courier arrived from Croxton, confirming his position as detailed in the captured documents.[34]

A key spot in this unfolding picture was the bridge that spanned the Cahaba at Centerville, ten miles west of Randolph. The bridge was the only crossing point over the Cahaba north of Selma. Forrest, recognizing its value, had placed a detachment there with orders to keep it out of Federal hands. Wilson, too, had seen the importance of the bridge and had ordered McCook to send a battalion to secure it. However, the contents of the captured dispatches, together with Croxton's report, caused him to reevaluate his thinking. A single battalion might not be strong enough to do the job and by that time, Croxton might also need help. With this in mind, McCook was directed to take LaGrange's entire second brigade, march rapidly to Centerville, secure the bridge, effect a junction with Croxton, then rejoin the corps.[35]

Meanwhile, Long and Upton were ordered to give Forrest "no rest, but push him toward Selma with the utmost spirit and rapidity."[36] Both divisions commenced skirmishing almost immediately. Long, with elements of the Seventy-second Indiana in the lead, drove the enemy pickets back to a place called Ebenezer Church, six miles north of Plantersville. Forrest had chosen to make a stand there and had selected a strong position along the north bank of Bolger's Creek. His right flank rested on Mulberry Creek, his left along a high, wooded ridge where four pieces of artillery were positioned to sweep the road from Randolph, along which Long's troops were advancing. In addition, a pair of field pieces covered Upton's line of advance along the old Maplesville Road. Finally, a portion of the Confederate front was protected by a slashing of pine trees and rail barricades.[37]

Despite the natural strength of the position, it was woefully undermanned and, at best, incapable of doing anything more than slowing the powerful

Federal advance. Forrest had a mixed bag of troops that included Roddey's division, Crossland's Kentuckians, Armstrong's brigade of Chalmers's division, plus a detachment of militia up from Selma and Forrest's own personal escort. In all, about 2,000 Confederates opposed nearly five times that many Yankees.[38]

Approaching the Confederate position, Long brought rest of the Seventy-second Indiana forward and into line. Dismounting the regiment on the left side of the road, Long ordered them forward. As they advanced and began to break through the outer Confederate defense, Long reinforced the effort with a mounted charge of four companies of the Seventeenth Indiana. They were led by Lieutenant Colonel Frank White, whom Wilson characterized as a "berserker of the Norseman breed, broad-shouldered, deep-chested, long-limbed, over six feet tall, and 'bearded like a pard.'"[39] Sabers swinging, White's troops passed through their dismounted comrades and drove the Confederates back on their main line, disabling one field piece in the process. Then, finding themselves cut off, the Indianans proceeded to cut their way out. In the melee, Captain James D. Taylor of the Seventeenth had a running duel of sorts with Forrest, who finally shot the young captain and managed to escape. Later, in a meeting with Wilson after the fall of Selma, Forrest remarked to Wilson that if Taylor had used the point of his saber rather than the edge, "I should not have been here to tell you about it."[40]

While Long's troops were thus engaged, Upton, with A. J. Alexander's brigade in the lead, heard the sounds of battle and responded. Ordering his brigade forward at a trot, Alexander came up against the Confederate right flank held by the militia from Selma. Pushing ahead, Alexander's advance, composed of a detachment of the Seventh Ohio, received a surprisingly stiff fire from those militia troops, sustaining several casualties in the process. Reforming his line, Alexander advanced again. After a stubborn fight that lasted nearly an hour, he finally succeeded in driving the defenders back, capturing two pieces of artillery and 200 prisoners. Winslow's brigade quickly took up the pursuit, but was unable to catch the fleeing Confederates. The cavalry corps bivouacked that night at Plantersville, only 19 miles from Selma.[41]

The Federal troopers were exuberant with their victory over Forrest. Wilson wrote:

> The foraging parties brought in plenty of provisions that night and a more joyful bivouac was never made by hungry and tired soldiers. All were full of hope for the morrow. No command ever worked more harmoniously. The *élan* was perfect and the cooperation all that could be desired.... The weather was fine and the landscape beginning to show the first approach of spring.[42]

Though Wilson could not help but be pleased with the progress of the campaign thus far, Selma remained a concern. He was well aware that the city was heavily fortified, but otherwise had little precise information on which to base an attack plan. At this juncture, Wilson's third stroke of good fortune arrived in the form of an Englishman named Millington who surrendered himself to Upton at Plantersville. A civil engineer, Millington, had been employed on the Selma fortifications. He had become disenchanted with the Confederate cause and volunteered to tell the Federals all he knew, even going so far as to prepare pencil sketches in detail. It was an unbelievable break.[43]

After a thorough reconnaissance confirmed the accuracy of Millington's sketches, Wilson, in council with Long and Upton, formulated his plan of attack. Despite the advantage of having an accurate picture of Selma's defenses, Wilson was concerned about the challenge facing them. With the exception of Upton, none of his unit commanders had had any experience assaulting a fortified position. Wilson, accordingly, drew heavily on Upton's knowledge.

The attack would come under cover of darkness. Long's division, the heavier by two regiments, would attack from the northwest, diagonally across the main or Summerfield Road. Meanwhile, Upton's assault would come from the north along the Range Line Road and pass partially through a swampy area east of the city. Upton was also directed to send a squadron to cover the Burnsville Road, which entered the city from the east. As a part of the overall plan, Lieutenant Joseph Rendlebrock with a battalion of Wilson's escort the Fourth Regulars was directed to follow the Alabama and Mississippi Railroad as far as Burnsville, burning stations, bridges, and trestles. The signal for the assault was to be a single cannon shot from Lieutenant George B. Rodney's Battery I, Fourth U.S. Artillery, fired as soon as Upton was in position.[44]

Wilson resumed the advance at daylight on April 2 with Long's division in the lead, followed closely by Upton. En route to Selma, Wilson conferred with Long and his two brigade commanders, colonels Robert H. G. Minty and Abraham O. Miller. Just as he had prior to the Battle of Nashville, Wilson wanted to make certain that the key commanders understood their role in the overall scheme of the attack. Upton, he knew, understood perfectly because of his experience at Marye's Heights and Spottsylvania, but Long and his brigade commanders did not have that experience to guide them.[45]

About six miles from Selma, Long was directed to shift his advance to the right to approach the city along the Summerville Road in accordance with the plan, while Upton advanced along the Range Line Road. As they approached Selma, there was light skirmishing but nothing that really checked the advance. By 4 P.M. the Federal horsemen were facing the city's outer line of defense.[46]

Situated on the north bank of the Alabama River, Selma featured an irregular, horseshoe-shaped outer line of defenses, both ends of which were anchored at the river. At its farthest point, this outer line extended about one and a half miles from the center of the city. A second, unfinished inner line of defense extended across the breadth of the outer line, approximately one-half mile from the center of the city. The outer defense line was composed of eight-foot-high earthworks, 15 feet thick at the base. In front of this was a four-foot-wide ditch, five feet deep, filled with water, and fronted by a sharpened, five-foot-high stockade. Four forts, each with artillery, were located to cover the approaches from the north and west.[47]

Forrest was charged with the responsibility of defending Selma which, despite its rather formidable line of defenses remained a vulnerable city due to a shortage of defenders. Thus, Forrest's task was not an enviable one. Although every able-bodied male had been pressed into service, Forrest had only a portion of the manpower he needed to effectively man the defenses. Still, Forrest was nothing if not a commander who could get the most out of the least, as he had proved time and again over the past four years. Accordingly, Armstrong's brigade was placed on the left flank, Roddey's troops on the right flank, and the militia in the center. Backing up the militia were Forrest and his escort with Crossland's Kentuckians. In all, the Confederate defenders probably did not exceed 3,000–4,000.[48]

Meanwhile, as Wilson and the main body of the corps advanced toward Selma, McCook and LaGrange moved out from Randolph on April 1, secured the bridge at Centerville, then pushed on to Scottsville where they unsuccessfully attempted to open communications with Croxton. From prisoners, however, McCook learned that Jackson's division, estimated to be 3,000 strong, was between his two brigades. The prisoners also reported that Croxton had turned back toward Elyton on March 31.

At daylight on April 2, as Long and Upton were driving on to Selma, McCook sent a detachment of the Second and Fourth Indiana regiments out to probe the road to Trion to see if Jackson's division might be located, as indeed he was and spoiling for a fight, too. After a brief but sharp skirmish, the Indianans withdrew. Concluding that he was outnumbered and unable to really assist Croxton if he could even find him, McCook recrossed the Cahaba at Centerville, then burned the bridge as well as any boats his troops could find. Having thus ensured that Jackson was now isolated west of the Cahaba and unable to reinforce Forrest, McCook moved to rejoin Wilson at Selma.[49]

Even as McCook and LaGrange were attempting to link up with Croxton, Chalmers's division, bound for Selma, had passed through Marion, about 20 miles southwest of Centerville and an equal distance northwest of

Colonel Robert H. G. Minty (reproduced from the Collections of the Library of Congress).

Selma. By the time Long and Upton reached the outskirts of Selma, Chalmers was close at hand. As it played out, he was too late to join Forrest in defending the city, but managed to jump on Long's mule pack train and led horses guarded by the Seventy-second Indiana. Long, fearing that this might upset the timing of the assault, decided to attack at once rather than wait for the prearranged signal.[50]

The order was given and 1,500 dismounted troops of the Second Division advanced toward Selma's outer defense line, drawing a savage fire from both artillery and muskets. Approximately a half-mile separated the troops from the city's outer defense line. As the men closed the gap, they opened up with their Spencer carbines. Reaching the stockade, they scaled it and then forced their way over the outer works. Despite fierce resistance by the defenders, many of whom used their muskets as clubs, Long's troops were not to be denied. The Confederates were soon forced to fall back.[51] Captain Owen Wiley of the 123rd Illinois Mounted Infantry described the moment:

> at General Long's "forward" the entire line started up with a bound, yelling, shooting, and all pushing forward under a most terrific cannonade and through a perfect storm of bullets, losing officers and men at every step, until we cleared the high picket fence, crossed the ditch, and scaled the high earth-works, and planted our regimental standard first of any in the command on the works of Selma.[52]

It took the Second Division 25 minutes to breech the outer line, but not without cost. Long sustained a serious head wound that resulted in a severe concussion and paralysis that would keep him out of action for the remainder of the campaign. Three senior colonels and 300 enlisted men were also casualties—20 percent of the attacking force, a tribute to the tenacity of the defenders.[53]

With Long out of action, command of the Second Division devolved to Colonel Minty, the colorful, Irish-born commander of the second brigade and a former ensign in the British army. Lieutenant Colonel Horace Howland, Third Ohio, assumed command of Minty's brigade. Colonel Miller, the tall, former country doctor commanding Long's first brigade, was also wounded and was replaced by Colonel Joseph G. Vail.[54]

When Long launched his attack, Upton's division with Winslow's brigade in the lead was in the process of forming along the Range Line Road. They heard the sounds of battle to their right and sensed that Long had, for some reason unknown to them, commenced his attack prematurely. The dismounted units of the Fourth Division promptly moved forward on their own volition, led by a battalion of the Fourth Iowa under Major William W. Woods.[55] Displaying the same brand of enthusiasm that characterized Long's assault, Upton's troops struck the works in their front and, like their second division counterparts, quickly broke through and drove the defenders back to the second line of defense.[56]

Both divisions were now caught up in the whirlwind of battle. Wilson

himself proved no exception. Climbing aboard a fresh horse—his gray gelding "Sheridan"—Wilson directed his escort to follow him in a charge right
down the middle. He later wrote:

> Straight down the turnpike, through the first line of works we all
> rode together, every man with saber drawn and nerves strained to
> the utmost, as though his personal example was essential to victory,
> and while Long, to the right, swept over stockade, ditch, and para-
> pet, driving Forrest and Armstrong from their outer entrenchments
> back upon the inner line, I found myself abreast of our dismounted
> men, close enough to the enemy's second line of entrenchments to
> hear an officer call out: "Shoot that man on the white horse." My
> horse fell instantly with a bullet in the breast. As he sank to the
> ground I threw myself from the saddle, but had hardly touched the
> ground before he was on his feet with his head high in the air and
> his eyes blazing as though they were balls of fire.[57]

As the outer defenses were breached, the Federal batteries rushed forward to pour a deadly barrage of canister and shrapnel into the retreating
Confederates. Forced back to their second line by Long's onslaught, Forrest's
defenders continued to offer stiff resistance. Pressure was now being applied
both from Upton on the left and from the right where Minty had regrouped
the Second Division and sent the Fourth Michigan, Fourth Ohio, and
Seventeenth Indiana against the city's inner line of defense. Under the force
of the two divisions, the line began to crumble and give way.[58]

As the interior line ruptured, the Federals poured through, driving the
defenders back into the city. Many cried out that they were conscripts and
begged not to be butchered.[59] "The troops," wrote Wilson, "inspired by the
wildest enthusiasm, swept everything before them and penetrated the city
in all directions."[60] In the gathering darkness and tumult of battle, Forrest
and Armstrong, with the remnants of their command, escaped west along
the Burnsville Road.[61]

The men of the cavalry corps were ecstatic. "We never saw our boys so
wrought up with the excitement of battle and the unrestrained joy of victory. They laughed, they shouted, they clapped their hands for joy! Comrades
met clasped hands, wept, and blessed God that so many of us were safe."[62]
Pandemonium reigned in the fallen city. Fires broke out and vandals plundered businesses and homes. Wilson set up headquarters in the Gee Hotel
and promptly established a provost guard. The staff was directed to assist
local citizenry in restoring order and bringing the fires under control.[63]

It is difficult to determine how much plundering was done by the
Federals, but certainly they were not guiltless. Wilson, in fact, admitted that
some of his troops were undoubtedly guilty, and one report described how

"The Union Army became a perfect mob, breaking open the saloons and stores, taking anything they wanted, and then setting the city on fire, burning the entire waterfront and nearly all of one side of Broad Street, including the Episcopal Church."[64] On the other hand, there is evidence that the fleeing Confederates fired a storehouse filled with cotton, which in turn spread to barracks and warehouses containing ammunition. Local vandals also took advantage of the situation to pillage at will.[65] By midnight the fires were largely under control and the provost guard had managed to restore a semblance of order. If it had been a disastrous day for the city of Selma, it had been a glorious hour for the men of the cavalry corps. Both shared the utter exhaustion of the moment. An Iowa soldier described the scene:

> The soldiers overpowered by weariness, wrapped in their blankets, sunk to rest about the streets; the citizens exhausted by excitement and fear, the cries of their children hushed at last, snatching a troubled sleep; the wounded, lulled by opiates into forgetfulness of their amputated legs and arms; the dead in their last sleep, with white faces upturned to the sky; for the passion, cruelty, bitterness and anguish of war, this Sunday night now nearly gone, will be remembered. If there is a merciful God in the heavens, He must be looking down upon this scene in pity.[66]

For Wilson, the day's success represented an achievement of the first magnitude and demonstrated once again, the value of using cavalry en masse. For the first time in the war, a fortified city had been captured by cavalry alone; there had been no infantry support. Wilson personally felt that the "capture of Selma [was the] most remarkable achievement in the history of modern cavalry."[67] (Ironically, Richmond had fallen on that same April Sunday, although Wilson's troops did not become aware of that coincidence for another three weeks.) Wilson wrote:

> Sunday, April 2, 1865, was the greatest day in the history of the Cavalry Corps M.D.M., for on that day it had not only captured the most complete set of fortifications in the South, covering the most important Confederate depots of manufacturing and supply, but it had by the same act planted itself firmly across the central line of railway connecting Richmond with the southwestern states. It had practically turned the Confederacy's left flank, captured its last and most valuable stronghold, put itself in position to occupy and roll up its last line of interior defense and communication, and finally made it certain that the cavalry army which had done these things could in a month more join Sherman and Grant in Virginia. But it was not till three weeks later that we knew Richmond, at the other end of the line, had fallen on the same day with Selma, and that these simultaneous events were practically the end of the War for the Union.[68]

The Yankee horse had taken Selma. The Civil War was finally drawing to a close. Another week would find Lee surrendering to Grant at Appomattox. Yet Wilson, unaware of the situation in the east, would shortly point his divisions toward the east: Montgomery, Columbus, and Macon.

Fifteen
Selma to Montgomery

*My command took possession of this place yesterday morning after slight
skirmishing. Buford and Adams have fled with their forces in the direction
of Columbus.... There are no forces in Alabama that can resist you, or even
stand before my corps.* —Wilson to Canby, April 13, 1865[1]

With Selma in Federal hands, Wilson was faced with the task of
administering a captured city and regrouping his command in
preparation for the next stage of the campaign. Edward
Winslow was placed in command of the city and charged with the responsibility of destroying everything of value to the Confederate war effort. Next
to Richmond, perhaps no other city in the Confederacy had stockpiled as
much war matériel as Selma. During the next few days, Winslow's men
destroyed more than 50 buildings from the huge Selma arsenal and ironworks, naval foundry, niter works, powder mill, and magazine. The latter
was filled with artillery pieces, caissons, and siege guns, together with more
than 60,000 rounds of artillery ammunition and 1 million rounds of small
arms ammunition. The men were astonished at the size of the arsenal. One
recalled that the "shot and shell [were] piled up in great rows, through the
long shops."[2] Additionally, the Federals destroyed 3 million feet of lumber,
10,000 bushels of coal, and railroad engines, boilers, cars, and machine shops.
A horseshoe-manufacturing plant was also destroyed, but not before the
Federals appropriated 8,000 pounds of horseshoes for their own use.[3]

The naval foundry was fired on the evening of April 4 in a dazzling
display of pyrotechnics. An observer described the scene:

> The large foundry was fired just at dark; shells are exploding one
> after another, then by platoons and squadrons, then back to one,
> and up and away again, never stopping, a bright light flashing and
> wavering, throwing shadows over the housetops, trees, church
> spires, and in among the columns that support the balcony over our

heads. A few of us are sitting together, our chairs tipped back against
the pillars listening to the war music and chanting.[4]

A large number of horses and mules had also been captured. After
replacing all of the unserviceable mounts in his command, Wilson ordered
the surplus of 500 animals penned in the quartermaster's yard, shot, and
thrown in the Alabama River. It was a drastic measure, but Wilson feared
the animals might be put to use by Confederate forces still in the area.[5] The
river also became the repository for artillery pieces and other equipment that
had been left in the entrenchments.[6]

In addition to the vast stockpile of supplies, munitions, and other war
matériel, Selma also had a prisoner-of-war stockade, holding a number of
soldiers who had been imprisoned since the battles of Chickamauga and
Missionary Ridge.[7]

Some of Wilson's troops observed that the general populace of Selma
held more hatred for the Union army than any place they had been. One
lady diarist, Sarah Ellen Phillips, recorded the horrors of those days immediately following the fall of Selma as justification for that hatred:

> Every day that week the Yankees went out depredating for miles
> around Selma—gathering up watches, jewelry and silverware as
> well as all the money possible. In this matter they were no respec-
> tors of persons—taking from one of the colored men, "For whom
> they were so sorry," a silver watch, his own personal property, ten
> dollars, in gold from another and jewelry from others.
>
> Many ladies concealed valuables on their persons, but would
> invariably give them up rather than submit to search, which was
> often attempted. No souvenir was too sacred to restrain their van-
> dalism.[8]

Though there was some looting and vandalism on the part of the
Federal horsemen, Wilson made every effort to see that offenders were
caught and punished. After the war, Confederate General Richard Taylor
remarked, "I have never met this General Wilson, whose soldierly qualities
are entitled to respect; for of all the Federal expeditions of which I have any
knowledge, his was the best conducted."[9]

At least two cavalrymen, however, found Selma a delightful place and
illustrated how romance can still bloom in a captured city in the midst of
war. Having made the acquaintance of a local family, the two were invited
to supper and an evening with the family, which had two lovely daughters.
Supper was followed by a little vocalizing of the popular songs of the day
and some lighthearted conversation, after which the two men returned to
camp. The following day, one of the troopers received a parcel from his lady

companion of the previous evening. The parcel turned out to be the lyrics to a popular song, with the words "hoping we meet again" underscored. With soaring heart, the trooper reported that he was "unfit for duty all the rest of the day."[10]

Several days later, when the corps was on its way to Montgomery, a skirmish with a detachment of Confederate cavalry resulted in the mortal wounding of a young Confederate officer who proved to be the brother of the Union trooper's girlfriend. Ironically, the officer's last words were whispered to this Yankee soldier who had been smitten by the dying Confederate's sister. The trooper saw to it that the young man's final words were delivered to the family. Later, in Macon, Georgia, the Union cavalryman received a letter from the young lady that continued to fan the flame of love. The trooper confided to his diary that "if sweet Kate be willing, I shall do my part toward that happy reunion."[11]

After the city had been secured, one of Wilson's first responsibilities was to notify General Edward Canby that Selma had fallen and of the future plans for the cavalry corps. The primary function of the expedition, he told Canby, had been to make a demonstration toward Selma and Tuscaloosa in support of Canby's Mobile campaign, after which he was to exercise his own discretion as to a future course of action. The fall of Selma, Wilson concluded, ensured the success of Canby's operation and thus freed Wilson from further responsibility in that direction. Exercising his latitude as an independent commander, Wilson decided to head east, through Montgomery and on into Georgia. His eventual goal was uniting with Sherman somewhere in Virginia.[12]

Meanwhile, Emory Upton had been sent north by Wilson early on the morning of April 3. Upton's assignment was to clear the area of any lingering detachments of Forrest's command, particularly Chalmers's division, and open communications with McCook. Upton was also directed to see that the wagon train that was still en route reached Selma safely.[13]

That night, Wilson sent a separate dispatch to McCook, expressing his concern over Croxton and the whereabouts of the wagon train. McCook was ordered to wait at Plantersville and hold his command in readiness to operate under Upton, who had been ordered into the area. Upton himself sent a message to McCook on the morning of April 4, directing him to send two companies back along the corps's recent line of advance until the wagon train was located. McCook was then to escort the train to Selma.[14]

Having attended to this, Upton then moved with Winslow's brigade, (temporarily commanded by Colonel John Noble, Third Iowa, since Winslow had been placed in command of Selma) to the vicinity of Summerfield, hoping to locate Chalmers. Failing to do so, he sent a battalion to Johnson's Ferry on the Cahaba. There, he learned that General Peter Starke's brigade of Chalmers's division had crossed to the west side of the river the day before, taking the pontoon bridge with them. Upton concluded that no Confederate force of any size remained east of the Cahaba River.[15]

Meanwhile, Brevet Brigadier General A. J. Alexander's brigade of Upton's division had taken the Plantersville Road; through him, McCook received Upton's directive. McCook responded that afternoon, saying he would reach Randolph that night, April 4, but expressed concern that the Confederates were on both of his flanks and urged Alexander to come on quickly in support.[16]

On April 5, McCook reported to Wilson that he had located the wagon train near Randolph. Mostly, McCook said, his peregrinations had been uneventful, but his horses were worn out. Most disturbingly, he had heard nothing from Croxton himself, although stragglers from his brigade had joined up with the wagon train near Elyton. They reported that Croxton had turned his extra horses loose and was making a run for it. McCook said he would check out the report.[17] As for the wagon train, it had been attacked just south of Montevallo by a mixed force of militia and guerrillas on April 4, but had repulsed the attack without loss. McCook's fear that the train might be subject to more attacks proved unfounded, however. It reached Selma without further incident on April 6, followed 48 hours later by Upton's division.[18]

Along with the capture of Selma and its stores, Wilson also acquired a large number of Confederate prisoners—2,700 in all. The management of these prisoners posed something of a problem. A number of his own men were still missing, so Wilson arranged for a meeting with Forrest to effect a mutually beneficial prisoner exchange. He hoped, as well, to learn something of Croxton's whereabouts.

Wilson left Selma on the morning of April 7, but found the nearby streams so swollen that he was forced to turn back. Starting out again the following day, he managed to reach the town of Cahawba, where he met with Forrest at the home of one Colonel Matthews, a wealthy planter who had remained loyal to the Union. This first meeting between Wilson and the nearly legendary Forrest was a memorable experience for the young Federal cavalry commander. Although impressed with Forrest's mien generally, Wilson was somewhat disappointed in his physical appearance. He recalled:

> I found him loosely put together, if not somewhat stooping and slouching in appearance, and he appeared rather under than over six feet. His frame was large and his body full, and I guessed his weight at one hundred and seventy-five pounds. His countenance was serious, his conduct diffident, but self-possessed, and his bearing free

from military affectations. It took but a glance to discover that life and its duties were all-important to him, and that whatever engaged his attention would receive most careful consideration.[19]

After a pleasant dinner, Wilson and Forrest retired to the parlor to discuss business. Forrest pointed out that he had no authority to conduct a prisoner exchange, but agreed to pass Wilson's offer on to higher authorities. He also indicated that Croxton had suffered some losses but was still at large. Having thus settled the matter of a prisoner exchange for the moment and having learned something of Croxton, Wilson returned to Selma to make preparations for the resumption of his campaign.[20]

Once more, the Yankee horsemen would be confronted with the job of fording a river swollen by recent rains. The current in the Alabama River was swift and filled with floating debris. Spanning these waters would not be easy. Amazingly, within 48 hours after beginning work on April 7, Major Hubbard's pontoniers had completed an 870-foot bridge composed of barges plus 30 canvas and 16 wooden pontoons.[21] Transferring the cavalry corps to the opposite shore commenced almost immediately. By 4:30 P.M. on the eighth, Oscar LaGrange had his brigade in motion, followed by Eli Long's first brigade, both of which had completed crossing by 7:30 P.M. However, before Long's second brigade could get started, the swift current snapped the bridge and several men drowned. The pontoniers, already exhausted by two grueling days of labor, were reinforced by a large working party. Repairs went forward immediately.[22]

By noon on Palm Sunday, April 9 (the day marked by Lee's surrender at Appomattox), the balance of Long's Second Division was safely across the turbulent waters. As Upton's troops started over, however, the bridge began to sag in the middle. This, coupled with the pressure of the current and constant impact from floating chunks of driftwood, resulted in yet another break. General Alexander was thrown into the water and nearly drowned while attempting to guide a floating log around the bridge. Once more, the rupture was repaired and crossing continued.[23]

The Fourth Iowa, bringing up the rear of Upton's division, was still in transit when a third break occurred. It was dark and several buildings along the river bank were set on fire to provide light for the repair crew. Adjutant William Forse Scott of the Fourth Iowa painted a picture of the scene:

> The big river rushing full between its banks, the many busy men at work about the bridge under the sharp orders of the officers, the endless stream of soldiers coming down out of the darkness on one side into the glaring light, leading their horses, splashing through the water on the sunken planks, and disappearing into the darkness beyond, the crowds of wondering and excited negroes looking

on, the great flames of the costly torches, throwing every object into high relief against the dense blackness surrounding all;—it would be, perhaps, as difficult to paint it with a brush as to describe it with a pen.[24]

By midnight the entire corps was finally across, except for Edward Winslow and a small detachment who remained in Selma and crossed the river on the morning of the tenth. Once across, however, Winslow had barely ridden two miles when he discovered that he had left his watch back in the Gee house. One of his aides, Lieutenant Hugh Pickel, accompanied by an orderly, galloped back across the bridge, retrieved the watch, and returned.[25] The pontoniers withheld destruction of the bridge until Pickel and his orderly returned from their mission. Once the pair were back across, Hubbard's men proceeded to dismantle the project they had labored so hard to complete. All of the barges, wooden pontoons, and canvas boats were scuttled. Also destroyed were 30 wagons from the corps's train; the mules that had previously pulled those wagons were used to mount the pontoniers.[26]

Wilson left 68 casualties behind in the Selma hospital, along with rations for 40 days and an adequate supply of medicines. Surgeon John Larkin of the Seventeenth Indiana and Assistant Surgeon John Raley of the Tenth Missouri remained behind with the wounded.[27]

Since Forrest had been unable to exchange prisoners, Wilson decided to bring his prisoners along and release them in small groups under parole.[28] In addition to the Confederate prisoners, a large number of fugitive slaves attached themselves to the column and threatened to slow progress to a crawl. Wilson solved this problem by taking the able-bodied men of military age and organizing them into regiments commanded by one of his officers. All other fugitives were forbidden to remain with the column unless they were employed in some specific capacity.[29] Wilson felt this was a successful tactic. He wrote:

> No matter what distance the white troops covered, the negroes always got into camp at a reasonable hour the same night. Upon one occasion many of them marched forty miles on foot without stopping.... During our march to the eastward a number were also used as teamsters, train guards, and road makers, in all of which work they soon became experts and found their highest utility.[30]

The eastward movement commenced in earnest on April 10. The next objective was Montgomery, capital of the moribund Confederacy. LaGrange's brigade had the advance, followed by Upton, then Long's division in charge of the wagons.[31] Almost from the outset, LaGrange was engaged in a running fight with General James Clanton's brigade of Buford's cavalry. Near the town of Benton, a battalion of the Second Indiana under Captain Roswell S. Hill moved up in support of the Seventh Kentucky, which had borne the brunt of the fighting that day. The Indianans took the wrong road, however, and ran into a swampy creek, where an officer drowned. That night, two companies of the First Wisconsin under Captain Edward Town relieved the Seventh Kentucky and pursued the Confederates to Lowndesborough, where Town finally abandoned the pursuit due to exhausted horses.[32]

On April 11, the long column of horsemen entered an area known locally as the "Big Swamp," between Church Hill and Lowndesborough. The road, which was muddy from recent rains, had been turned into a quagmire by LaGrange's earlier pursuit. It had to be corduroyed in order to make it passable. Progress was slow and as darkness descended the column was still winding its way through the gloom of the swamp. Adjutant Scott wrote:

> The march of the afternoon had been over low, wet lands, in damp, heavy air, under a cloudy sky. The swamp was dark and dismal, in its mysterious impenetrable depths of dense forest and tangled breaks standing ever motionless in the black water and slime.

Presently, the column emerged from the swamp to find a scene of quiet beauty in marked contrast to the dank region from which they had just emerged. Adjutant Scott of the gifted pen continued:

> As the horses dragged themselves out on the eastern side, covered with mire, their riders, surprised and pleased, found that they rose abruptly to high, dry land. Radiant gleams shone through the trees ahead and then suddenly they emerged from the forest upon an open prairie, flooded with the silver light of a glorious full moon shining from a clear sky. Night was never so beautiful. An enchanting scene of splendor after the hideous swamp! The very air was new and delightfully sweet. The soiled and tired troopers were suddenly in another world. Soon the road ran between fields bordered by hedges of Cherokee roses, now in their early bloom and spreading their rich fragrance abroad. An hour later came the village of Lowndesborough, long noted as the home of wealthy planters. The way led through its principal street, a long, wide avenue bordered by great live-oaks. It was past midnight. No living creature appeared in the town, not a light was seen, not a sound heard except the subdued rattle of arms in the column. Even the horses' feet were hardly heard as they trod the sandy way. The broad white houses stood back from the avenue, surrounded by trees and shrubbery in ample grounds, brilliant with broad patches of the wonderful moonlight. Roses and jasmines gleamed in white stars against their dark foliage, and filled the soft air with delicate colors. It was a dream world, through which the war-torn soldiers marched silently in the deep shadows of the oaks.[33]

Earlier that same evening, while the main column was struggling through Big Swamp, Colonel Wickliffe Cooper, commanding the Fourth Kentucky Cavalry of LaGrange's brigade, had captured the Pensacola Railroad bridge five miles from Montgomery. At daylight on April 12, Cooper crossed Catoma Creek and entered Montgomery, planting the regimental standard of the Fourth Kentucky in front of the capitol building. Additionally, he laid claim to 23 prisoners, three field pieces, one siege gun, and a considerable supply of commissary and medical stores. There was no resistance.[34]

The Confederates apparently had created no plan to defend the city, which surprised Wilson. He was nonetheless pleased when the mayor and several principal citizens rode out with a flag of truce to surrender the city unconditionally. The offer was readily accepted and Wilson promptly notified his superiors that Montgomery had surrendered.[35]

Wilson described the triumphant entry of his command, as it passed through a captured city with all the pomp and precision of a Roman legion:

> With perfect order in column of platoons, every man in his place, division and brigade flags unfurled, guidons flying, sabers and spurs jingling, bands playing patriotic airs, and the bugles now and then sounding the calls, the war-begrimed Union troopers, batteries, ambulances, and wagons passed proudly through the city. Not a man left the ranks, not a loud word was uttered, and not an incident happened to hurt the feelings of the misguided people. It was an example of discipline, order and power lasting nearly all day and constituting a far more impressive spectacle than a bloody battle would have been.[36]

So, with this display of power, Wilson's Cavalry Corps entered Montgomery. Of all the cities in the Confederacy, it was ironic that this, the first capital, should have surrendered without a shot being fired in its defense. Like Selma, the citizens of Montgomery had dreaded the arrival of the Yankee cavalry. Tales of horror had preceded the Federals. Some locals, hoping to avoid trouble, emptied their wine cellars, breaking bottles on the curbstones. Wilson recalled that when he arrived in the city, "gutters were red with running wine."[37]

As he had done in Selma, Wilson took immediate steps to safeguard private property. The Fourth Regulars, which had been the first unit to arrive in the city, functioned as the temporary provost guard. They were later replaced by a mixed force from the Third Iowa and First Wisconsin. Edward McCook was placed in command of the city and Colonel Cooper was charged with the responsibility of destroying any equipment or facilities that might aid the Confederacy.[38]

In evacuating Montgomery, the Confederates torched some 85,000 bales of cotton, valued at $40 million in gold, thereby arousing the anger of local citizens.[39] In addition, Wilson learned that a large quantity of supplies had been loaded on a fleet of steamers and moved 12–15 miles up the Coosa River near Wetumpka. Accordingly, a detachment of the Fourth Kentucky under Major John F. Weston was dispatched to retrieve the steamers and their cargo. After locating the steamers and finding them under guard, Weston and three of his men swam the river. They returned with several skiffs that Weston used to ferry his detachment to the opposite shore. From there, the enterprising Federals managed to sneak up on the guard detachment, which quickly surrendered, allowing Weston and his detachment to bring the steamers triumphantly back to Montgomery. After unloading the cargo and appropriating some for themselves, the Federals burned the boats, "making a brilliant bonfire for the multitude which lined the shore."[40]

As in Selma, the destruction of property deemed useful to the Confederate war effort was brutally thorough. Colonel Cooper's detachments destroyed the arsenal, containing some 20,000 stands of small arms; one foundry and moulding shop; a car wheel-foundry; niter works; the Pensacola and West Point Railroad depot, along with a locomotive, 20 rail cars, and a machine shop containing a number of unfinished cars.[41]

On April 13, Wilson wrote to Thomas, advising him that Montgomery had fallen. He had decided to continue his eastward movement, convinced that by doing so he would "best accomplish what is expected of me by you and Grant." He pointed out that his command was in excellent condition, but he did want Hatch and Croxton to join him as quickly as possible. Though he had heard nothing from Canby, Wilson told Thomas, he felt certain that Mobile would pose no problem for the Federal effort in that quarter.[42]

Perhaps suspecting that Thomas might just have it in mind to attach him to Canby's command, or perhaps even send him back to Middle Tennessee, Wilson closed his report by pointing out that to return would involve a long march "without any object. Campaign in this quarter here is terminated, and everything ought to be pressed toward the Atlantic slope," he concluded. Wilson's suspicions were well founded; on April 17, Thomas advised Halleck that he would order Wilson to "hold Selma and operate west of the Alabama River against Taylor's forces, with a view of aiding General Canby as much as possible." By that time, however, the Federal horsemen had already taken Columbus.[43] On the same day he wrote to Thomas, Wilson prepared a second communiqué for Canby, entrusting it to Sergeant Bailey, Fourth Michigan. "There are no forces in Alabama that can resist you, or even stand before my corps," Wilson assured Canby, adding that he had "only to move into the interior, occupy Selma and Montgomery, and restore the State to the Union."[44]

Since leaving the Tennessee River, Wilson had operated in a virtual vacuum of information. There were rumors aplenty, but no official word as to the status of the war. Back on the eleventh, Wilson learned from Montgomery papers that Grant had broken the stalemate at Petersburg and that Richmond had fallen on the same day the cavalry corps had taken Selma. The news posed something of a quandary for Wilson. On one hand, the reports seemed believable, but on the other, "I could get no detailed confirmation of them," Wilson later recalled.[45] News of Lee's surrender had not yet filtered down; so far as Wilson was concerned, it was business as usual and he felt obliged to "continue 'breaking things' along the main line of Confederate communications through central Alabama, Georgia and the Carolinas." The next objective was Columbus, gateway to central Georgia.[46]

Sixteen
Montgomery to Columbus

*My forces captured this place [Columbus] by a most gallant attack 10
o'clock last night, losing 25 men killed and wounded, and captured about
1,500 prisoners, 24 field guns, and 1 gun-boat carrying six 7-inch rifled
pieces.* —Wilson to Canby, April 17, 1865[1]

Wilson did not linger long in Montgomery, resuming his eastward thrust on April 14. Upton was ordered to head directly
for Columbus, 80 miles distant. The Second Division with
Minty in command (Long was still recovering from his Selma wound) followed Upton.[2] With the Fourth Kentucky and a detachment of the First
Wisconsin, McCook remained in Montgomery under orders to complete the
destruction of military facilities. Also left behind in Montgomery were an
additional 144 wounded, left to the care of Assistant Surgeon David Dome
of the Seventeenth Indiana.[3]

Although there was little to seriously contest the Federal advance, skirmishing was frequent and often brisk. LaGrange clashed again with Buford's
cavalry, surprising his camp a dozen miles east of Montgomery and scattering his command. Otherwise, the Yankee horsemen could move about
with impunity. By midday on April 15, Wilson had reached the handsome
little community of Tuskegee, future home of Booker T. Washington and
the Tuskegee Institute. Once again he was greeted by a delegation of the
town's principal citizens and his cavalry corps entered the town with guidons
flying and the strains of martial airs filling the spring day.[4] Elswehere, a pall
would descend on a nation, rejoicing over General Lee's surrender only to
be devastated by the news of Lincoln's assassination.

Just as he had at Montgomery, Wilson took steps to protect private
property. While he had no qualms about destroying anything of military

value, Wilson proved to be fair, reasonable, and ready to countermand a destruct order if sufficient cause for its revocation could be demonstrated. In one instance, orders had been issued to destroy a printing press used in the publication of a Confederate newspaper. The owner—an irate woman—called on Wilson to vent her anger, protesting that her press had been used to print Bibles and schoolbooks. Wilson told her that he had been unaware that her press had been used to print these things. He then advised her that if she were willing to post a bond for $5,000 with the mayor and two principal citizens guaranteeing that she would not print anything against the Union or the Constitution and would confine her publishing activities to Bibles and schoolbooks, he would suspend the order to destroy her press. Surprised but pleased at this turn of events, the woman promptly accepted the offer and returned to her endeavors.[5]

From Tuskegee, McCook was ordered to send LaGrange's brigade on to West Point, 40 miles above Columbus, to secure a crossing over the Chattahoochee River. Additionally, LaGrange carried instructions to destroy all rail bridges along his line of march. Wilson wanted to leave nothing to chance here. Like other rivers the cavalry corps had come up against during this campaign, the Chattahoochee was running high and fast, swollen by spring rains. Beyond the river lay the prize of central Georgia, but first came the challenge of getting across this considerable waterway. Columbus offered a pair of bridges, but in the event the Confederates managed to destroy these crossings, the corps would have an alternate at West Point 40 miles to the north.[6]

About 2 P.M. on April 16—Easter Sunday—the advance of Alexander's brigade (six companies of the First Ohio, commanded by Colonel Beroth B. Eggleston) encountered enemy pickets near Crawford, 12 miles west of Columbus. Eggleston and his Ohioans struck fast, driving the Confederate pickets back six miles to Wetumpka Creek. The Confederates put up a brief stand before burning the bridge and continuing their retreat. Only briefly delayed, Eggleston's troops quickly repaired the bridge and resumed their pursuit as far as Girard, Alabama, just across the river from Columbus.[7]

The last major manufacturing center and storehouse of the Confederacy—Columbus, Georgia—was situated on the east side of the Chattahoochee River. As a river city, Columbus specialized in building and repairing river craft and featured an important naval ironworks. On the west side of the river, the suburb of Girard straddled Mill Creek, a sizable stream flowing into the Chattahoochee from the northwest. Like Selma, Columbus was well fortified. In this case, however, the Federals did not have the advantage of knowing the details of the city's defensive setup. Columbus was ideally suited to repel an attack from the west. Around Girard, steep hills ranging in height from 100 to 500 feet and separated by narrow valleys, presented a problem for an attacking force.

Traffic across the river was carried by two wagon/foot bridges, each about 1,000 feet in length. The upper bridge entered Columbus from the northwest and provided access to the city from Opelika and Salem. The southernmost bridge passed through Girard and entered Columbus from the west on the Crawford Road, along which Upton's division was marching. There was also a third bridge at Clapp's Factory, three miles north of the city. Two companies of the Tenth Missouri under Captain Jeremiah Young had been detached at Crawford to move ahead and secure this bridge. However, they found it partially destroyed on arrival. As a result it played no part in the forthcoming battle.

In addition to river steamers, Columbus was served by two railroads. The Muscogee crossed the Chattahoochee on a trestle and passed around the north end of the city. The Montgomery and West Point also spanned the river on a trestle, passing through the southern portion of the city about 500 yards south of the lower bridge.[8]

Charged with the defense of Columbus was Major General Howell Cobb, former secretary of the treasury under President James Buchanan and first president of the Confederate Congress. Cobb had at his disposal a system of defenses at least equal to, if not superior to those of Selma. Just as with Selma, however, the Confederates had neither sufficient guns nor manpower to take full advantage of their defensive works. What they did have was enough to give a good account of themselves.[9]

Four outlying forts capable of mounting 13 guns were strategically positioned to cover the northwest approach from Opelika, but owing to a shortage of guns and manpower, these forts were unoccupied when Wilson's forces arrived. The northern approach was covered by a line of rifle pits, one three-gun fort, and another with four guns. The main line, a bridgehead, was a fishook-shaped line of rifle pits, supported by 11 pieces of artillery extending from a point midway between the two wagon bridges north for about one mile before hooking around to the east. Finally, there were four guns at the east end of the lower bridge, two at the east end of the upper bridge, and four at the east end of the Muscogee Railroad trestle. In all, the Confederates could muster 27 guns and 3,000 men with which to defend Columbus.[10]

The citizens of Columbus were expecting the worst. For several days, rumors about the approach of a large Federal army had caused considerable alarm. Refugees poured into the city from Alabama, seeking safety. On Sunday morning, April 16, as Wilson's brigades were approaching, Episcopalians and Roman Catholics attended early Mass and communion, praying for victory.[11]

When Eggleston's Ohioans reached Girard about 2 P.M. on the six-teenth, they immediately moved to secure the lower bridge, but were dri-ven back by heavy artillery and musket fire. Simultaneously, the defenders, having made all the necessary preparations beforehand, set fire to the bridge. Temporarily stymied, Eggleston retired behind a nearby ridge.[12]

When General Alexander arrived with the rest of the brigade, he had Rodney's Battery I, Fourth U.S. Artillery, wheeled into position and fire a few rounds to develop the strength and position of the enemy's artillery.[13] Upton, meanwhile, had sent two companies of the Fifth Iowa under Captain John P. Lewis on a scout along the Opelika-Summerville Road. As Winslow arrived with his brigade, he was directed to march to a point on the Salem-Opelika Road and await further instructions.[14]

When it became clear that an attack from Alexander's position was likely to be repulsed due to the strength of the Confederate defenses, Upton directed him to occupy the crest of a ridge overlooking the city and hold his position there while Winslow attacked along the Opelika Road. The plan was relatively simple: A force of dismounted troops would strike the upper bridge and rupture the Confederate line, paving the way for a mounted charge to secure the bridge and enter Columbus.[15] Upton was acting on his own volition here, as Wilson had not yet arrived. Long's division had had the post of honor at Selma and Upton seemed determined that his Fourth Division would not be relegated to a secondary role at Columbus.

Wilson arrived on the scene about 4 P.M., reaching Winslow's brigade first. Shortly thereafter, he found Upton, who informed him that all was in readiness to attack except that he had been unable to locate Winslow.[16] When Wilson advised him that Winslow's brigade was concealed in a nearby valley, Upton remarked that it would be too dark by the time Winslow was in position to attack.[17] Satisfied that Upton's plan was sound and the corps now had some experience in night fighting, Wilson told Upton to go ahead as planned and prepare to attack at 8:30. Minty's division would stand ready to support the movement if needed. "Do you mean it?" Upton replied, "It will be dark as midnight by that hour and that will be a night attack, indeed!" Assured that this was exactly what Wilson had in mind, Upton exclaimed "By jingo, I'll do it; and I'll sweep everything before me!"[18]

By dark, Winslow was ready. Six companies of the Third Iowa (the remainder of the regiment was still in Montgomery), commanded by Colonel John Noble (future secretary of the interior in President Benjamin Harrison's Cabinet), faced a pair of outlying forts and a line of rifle pits. The left flank of the regiment rested on the Opelika Road. Behind Noble's regiment stood 11 mounted companies of the Fourth Iowa and eight of the Tenth Missouri.[19] About the time that Noble received his attack order—around 9 P.M.—

the Confederates opened up with a furious fire that lit up the entire area. Fortunately for the Federals, its effectiveness was not equal to its pyrotechnic display. In any event, the Iowans moved forward, working their way through the clutter of brush and downed timber, then on into the rifle pits, forcing the defenders back.[20]

Believing that the main Confederate line had been pierced, Winslow ordered Colonel Frederick Benteen, commanding the Tenth Missouri, to charge and secure the bridge.[21] Upton, however, perhaps sensing that the main line of defense still awaited them, revised the order and directed instead that only two of Benteen's eight companies be sent forward. Accordingly, these two, led by Captain Robert B. McGlasson, charged boldly down the road and quite suddenly found themselves confronting the main line of resistance. Surprised though he was, McGlasson nevertheless drove on through the enemy, some of whom mistook the Missourians for Confederates. Reaching the bridge, McGlasson captured 50 guards and prepared to hold his position. A detachment under Lieutenant Frederick Owen even managed to cross the bridge and capture the battery on the opposite side. The advantage proved short-lived. With no support forthcoming and the Confederates beginning to recover, McGlasson was forced to regroup and lead his command back through the Confederate lines at a full gallop.[22]

Realizing that there was another line of defense, the Third Iowa was called on once more. Scrambling down a wooded ravine, across a marshy stream and up through the same slashing of brush and trees the Missourians had passed earlier, Colonel Noble led his Iowans in their second assault of the evening. The Confederates were prepared, however, and responded to this second effort with all available firepower. Some of Noble's men managed to reach and temporarily take a portion of the line, but lacked the strength to hold on.

Anticipating the need for support, Winslow brought up two battalions of the Fourth Iowa, dismounted them and sent them forward to aid their sister regiment. Reinforced, the Iowans renewed their attack. Up to this point, Confederate resistance had been stout, and strong enough to repel the Federals. But when confronted by the weight of two additional battalions, the line began to crumble and eventually gave way altogether. Winslow's troops poured through the breaks, calling for the defenders to throw down their arms and surrender. Upton and Winslow, however, were after the bridge. Following close behind the troops, they directed the men not to bother with prisoners, exhorting them "to go for the bridge!"[23]

Captain Lot Abraham's battalion of the Fourth Iowa overwhelmed a four-gun battery at the west end of the bridge. But as they started across the structure they became entangled with Captain Newell Dana's battalion of their regiment. Driving on across the bridge, the two battalions became further intermingled with retreating Confederates. In the darkness it was impossible to distinguish friend from foe. The April night also reeked with the odor of turpentine. The Confederates had prepared to fire the bridge, but the Federal onslaught had been so swift that the opportunity evaporated. Once across, the Iowans had a brief but furious struggle to capture the battery at the east end of the bridge, suffering several casualties before the Confederate gunners were finally overwhelmed.[24]

Winslow, meanwhile, had ordered the rest of the Fourth Iowa, Major Edward Dee's mounted battalion, to charge across the bridge as soon as the dismounted units had secured the structure. Clattering across the bridge behind the last of their dismounted comrades, Dee's troopers galloped through the streets of Columbus, administering the coup de grâce to the last of the defenders, now in full retreat. Cobb and his staff with a few of the defenders managed to escape to Macon, where they surrendered to Wilson a few days later.[25]

As it had been in Selma, the night was lit by the burning buildings in Girard, which the defenders had torched to light their operations. The spectacle was witnessed by the noncombatants of Columbus, who remembered it being like a "sheet of flame on the Chattahoochee."[26]

Once the attack had gotten under way in earnest, it had only taken the Federals something like an hour to secure the gateway to Georgia. By midnight, Upton's division was across the Chattahoochee with Minty's command not far behind. In marked contrast to the riotous aftermath in Selma, the Union troops found that Columbus seemed "very quiet."[27]

While Upton's Fourth Division was approaching Columbus, LaGrange was readying his brigade for an assault on Fort Tyler, a strong redoubt covering the approach to West Point. Departing from Montgomery on April 14, LaGrange promptly got hooked up in a 38-mile running fight with Clanton's cavalry, killing a dozen Confederates and capturing another hundred, while suffering a dozen casualties himself.[28] On the fifteenth, the brigade turned off the main Columbus road and bivouacked for the night at Auburn. LaGrange had the men up and moving after only a few hours' rest. At 2 A.M. on the sixteenth, the Second and Fourth Indiana with a single gun from the Eighteenth Indiana Battery pushed on toward West Point. The Second Indiana, in the forefront of the advance, encountered Confederate pickets near Opelika and drove them through town, capturing 14 wagons in the process.[29]

By 10 A.M. both regiments had arrived within range of Fort Tyler's guns, taking up sheltered positions within carbine range. While they awaited the arrival of the rest of the brigade, the Eighteenth Indiana's single field piece dueled with Fort Tyler's artillery.[30]

Fort Tyler was a small but stoutly constructed earthwork redoubt, 35 yards square and surrounded by a ditch 12 feet wide and ten feet deep. The fort's heavy armament consisted of two 32-pounders and a pair of field guns. The defenders consisted of some 265 militia members, along with a few regulars temporarily diverted from returning to their regiments by the fort's commander, Brigadier General Robert Charles Tyler, a former soldier of fortune who had been with William Walker in Nicaragua but had escaped Walker's fate (a court-martial resulting in conviction and execution). Tyler, who had come up through the ranks of the Confederate army, had lost a leg at Missionary Ridge. He would perform his last duty as a Confederate officer in the hopeless, stubborn defense of this small earthwork built under his direction and named after him.[31]

When LaGrange arrived on the scene with the rest of the brigade about 1:30 P.M., he dismounted sections of the Second Indiana, First Wisconsin, and Seventh Kentucky, positioning them on three sides of the redoubt. When all was ready, the signal was given and the dismounted troops advanced. As they approached, the Confederates opened fire, but it was too high to be effective. The Eighteenth Indiana's counterbattery fire was more damaging, silencing both Confederate 32-pounders.[32]

Reaching the ditch that surrounded the fort, the attack bogged down. The resourceful LaGrange, however, quickly posted sharpshooters to provide a covering fire while the rest of the men were put to work building platforms to bridge the ditch. When the men were ready, the bugler sounded the charge. Then, placing their platforms across the crevice, the troops charged across amidst a murderous fire, scaled the parapets, and entered the fort. Sergeant Edwin Farel, First Wisconsin, was reportedly the first man inside Fort Tyler, while his comrade, Indian Steve Nichols, captured the Confederate flag.[33]

It had been a tough, costly little fight. LaGrange suffered seven killed and 29 wounded, including Lieutenant Colonel Henry Harnden of the First Wisconsin and Captain Roswell Hill of the Second Indiana. The defenders, for their part, had resisted stubbornly and suffered accordingly. Eighteen officers including General Tyler were killed; an additional 28 had been wounded, mostly in the head, a testament to the accuracy of LaGrange's sharpshooters.[34] The inside of Fort Tyler was something to behold. "No slaughterhouse could be bloodier than the inside of Fort Tyler, where the dead and dying were piled knee-deep," wrote one observer.[35] Another man described how the defenders "had chiefly been shot through the head, and the blood and shivered remains of dead men were too shocking for description."[36]

While most of the brigade was engaged in attacking Fort Tyler, the Fourth Indiana charged through West Point and secured both bridges across the

4.

SKETCH
OF
WEST POINT, GA.,
AND
LINE OF DEFENSES.
UNDER SUPERVISION OF
LIEUT. HEYWOOD,
Engineer in charge.

Scale:
1200 900 600 300 0   1200 Feet.

Note. a. Rifle-pits
b Circular Stockade
c Burned Warehouses and Bridges

———— Union
———— Confederate

CHATTAHOOCHEE RIVER

WEST POINT R.R.

Ferry

King's Gap Road

Fort Mc Road

WEST POINT AND MONTGOMERY R.R.

River Road

FORT TYLER

Fredonia Road

La Fayette Road

Opelika Road

Accompanying the report of
Bvt. Maj. Gen. J.H. Wilson, U.S.Army, dated June 29 1865
SERIES I VOL XLIX.

Portrait of Colonel Henry Harnden, First Wisconsin Cavalry, J. R. Stuart (State Historical Society of Wisconsin).

Chattahoochee, scattering a detachment of Confederate cavalry in the process. Additionally, the Indianans captured and destroyed five steam locomotives and a train of cars.[37]

The capture of West Point and Fort Tyler also netted LaGrange two field pieces, one 32-pounder, 500 stands of small arms, 19 engines, and 340 railroad cars loaded with quartermaster supplies, commissary stores, machinery, leather, and other war matériel. Fort Tyler itself was destroyed. Casualties

Opposite: **Sketch map of West Point, Georgia, and defenses (National Archives).**

from both sides were entrusted to the care of Confederate surgeons. Sugar, corn, and bacon were left in charge of the mayor of West Point to provide a food fund for the wounded.[38]

That same day, April 16, LaGrange advised Wilson and Upton of his success and requested further instructions. The response, however, came from McCook who, having completed his duties in Montgomery, had rejoined the corps. McCook directed LaGrange to push for Macon as quickly as possible because Wilson expected the First Division to handle the main effort against that city. Thus far, Long and Upton had gotten the plums and Macon figured to be McCook's last chance.[39]

Accordingly, on April 17, LaGrange marched his brigade for Macon, moving by way of LaGrange, Griffin, and Forsyth. Along the way he cut the Macon and Atlanta Railroad. He would have reached Macon at noon on the twentieth except that he was compelled by orders to wait for the detachment of the Fourth Kentucky under Colonel Cooper that was marching from Columbus. As a consequence, LaGrange did not reach Macon until April 21, by which time the city had already surrendered.[40]

Columbus and Fort Tyler proved to be the final battles of the campaign, although scattered, minor skirmishing continued for some time. Wilson wrote:

> The final performance of the cavalry, involving as it did not only the successful assault of strong entrenchments, but the capture of bridges spanning the Chattahoochee, was one of the most remarkable, not only of the war, but of modern times, and shows that American cavalry and mounted infantry when properly trained and led are equal to any enterprise that can fall to their lot by day or by night.[41]

Seventeen
Columbus to Macon

Unless otherwise ordered I shall "go ahead" in obedience to your last order, and by 9 a.m. enter Macon or be engaged with the enemy. —LaGrange to McCook, April 20, 1865[1]

E arly on the morning of April 17, the Federal cavalrymen once more turned to the systematic destruction of Confederate military resources. Winslow was placed in command of the city, his second such assignment of the campaign. Under the Iowan's direction, working parties proceeded to destroy six warehouses containing cotton, corn, tobacco, sugar, and commissary stores. In addition, the Federals destroyed locomotives, rolling stock, a naval armory, foundries, niter works, arsenal and powder magazines, an oil cloth factory, a paper mill, a pistol factory, and thousands of small arms, uniforms, shoes, and tools. The biggest prize, however, was the gunboat *Jackson*, mounting six heavy guns and ready to put to sea.[2] As Wilson put it, "The destruction of the last factories, depots and warehouses of the Confederacy was as complete as fire could make it, and of itself must have been the deathblow to the Confederacy, even if it had been able to keep its armed forces together for a further struggle."[3]

Wilson took particular satisfaction in the destruction of the printing facilities of three Columbus newspapers: *Enquirer, Sun*, and *Times*. Also put out of action—finally—was the *Memphis Appeal*, a notoriously pro–Confederate paper whose owner had somehow always managed to move his press out of town just ahead of the Federals. From Memphis he had moved to Grenada and Jackson, Mississippi, then to Atlanta, and finally to Columbus, where he was overtaken. Wilson later referred to the capture of the *Appeal* as "One of the most glorifying incidents" in the taking of Columbus.[4]

On Monday, April 17, Wilson wrote to Canby, advising him that Columbus had fallen, that his command was still "in magnificent condition" and he was about to resume his eastward movement. Wilson requested that Canby forward this news on to Thomas and Grant.[5]

Wilson did not tarry in Columbus. Long's division—with Minty still in charge—would have the point of honor when the corps struck out for Macon. On the evening of the seventeenth, Minty was ordered to send two regments on ahead to secure the twin bridges over the Flint River, yet another considerable waterway about halfway to Macon. Minty directed the Fourth Michigan and Third Ohio, both under the command of Lieutenant Colonel Benjamin D. Pritchard, Fourth Michigan, to make a rapid night march and secure the objective. The remainder of the division would follow within an hour.[6] Stripping his command to "light-marching trim," Pritchard moved out at 5:30 P.M. After the "mournful monotony" of a rapid night march, they arrived at a point about nine miles from the bridges at daylight on April 18.[7]

Through the next five miles, Pritchard encountered and captured several Confederates. At Pleasant Hill, four miles from the bridges, the Federals came upon a refugee train accompanied by a small party of Confederate soldiers who offered halfhearted resistance, but were quickly brushed aside by Pritchard's column.[8] Approaching the bridges, Pritchard ordered the charge sounded and a battalion of the Fourth Michigan under Captain Charles T. Hudson swept down on the bridges, striking so swiftly that the 50-man guard was taken completely by surprise. The guard detail had barely enough time to respond with a few scattered shots before beating a hasty retreat. Hudson's battalion pursued for four miles before finally turning back to rejoin the main column.[9]

Having secured his objective, Pritchard immediately positioned his command to repel any attempt to retake the bridges, then settled down to await the arrival of Minty and the main body of the division, which arrived later that morning. At that juncture, Minty elected to rest his command for the remainder of the day, having marched 63 miles in just over 24 hours.[10]

Other detachments were ranging about the area, foraging, burning railroad facilities, and destroying anything deemed valuable to the Confederates. In their zeal, however, one detachment fired a cotton factory that nearly burned a bridge across which their regiment was passing. Near Thomaston, the Federals seized a locomotive arriving from Macon carrying mail and an announcement that Lee had surrendered.[11]

On the nineteenth, Minty had his division on the move again. En route to Macon they destroyed three cotton factories, bivouacking that night near Thomaston. At 3 A.M. on April 20, the advance resumed. Near Spring Hill, 21 miles from Macon, Minty's advance, consisting of four companies of the Seventeenth Indiana, commanded by Major John J. Weiler, encountered a few Confederates at Society Hill but quickly dispersed them.[12] After a brief rest, Lieutenant Colonel Frank White, commanding the Seventeenth Indiana, brought the rest of the regiment forward to reinforce Weiler and the column then pushed on toward Macon. Near Montpelier Springs the Indianans found more Confederate defenders, this time positioned behind a barricade of rails and brush. Undeterred, White promptly ordered a charge that quickly dispersed these Confederates as well.[13]

Up ahead was a bridge over Tobesofkee Creek at Mimms Mills that needed to be secured. White moved the regiment forward at a fast trot. Approaching the bridge, they found a force estimated at several hundred Confederates in line on the east end of the bridge, which had been fired by the defenders before they pulled back. White's advance attempted to charge across, but discovered the planking had also been

Colonel Benjamin D. Pritchard, Fourth Michigan Cavalry (Michigan Historical Commission, negative no. 51291).

removed. After reinforcing his advance detachment with a pair of dismounted companies, the Indianans, after a "sharp fight of about five minutes, drove the enemy off in confusion" and double-quicked across the burning stringers.[14]

Pressing on, White was met about 13 miles from Macon by Confederate Brigadier General Felix Huston Robertson, an old West Point classmate of Wilson's, carrying a flag of truce and a dispatch announcing an armistice between Sherman and General Joe Johnston. White promptly sent the letter back to Minty, who read it and passed it on to Wilson, who received it about 6 P.M. The letter was from Howell Cobb and included an enclosure that Cobb had just received from General Beauregard.

> Headquarters Department of Tennessee and Georgia
> Macon, April 20, 1865

> Commanding General U.S. Forces:
> General: I have just received from General G.T. Beauregard, my immediate commander, a telegraphic dispatch of the following is a copy:

> Greensborough, April 19, 1865
> (Via Columbia 19th, via Augusta 20th)
> Maj. Gen. H. Cobb:
> Inform general commanding enemy's forces in your front that a truce for the purpose of final settlement was agreed upon yesterday between Generals Johnston and Sherman, applicable to all forces under their commands. A message to that effect from Sherman will be sent him as soon as practicable. The contending

forces are to occupy their present position, forty-eight hours' notice being given on the event of resumption of hostilities.

G.T. BEAUREGARD
General, Second in Command.[15]

Uncertain as to the authenticity of the letter, Wilson sent a staff officer on ahead to halt Minty's forward movement, then started for the front himself with a small escort. By the time Wilson reached the forward units, however, he discovered that Minty had already resumed his advance.[16]

Meanwhile, after he had read the letter and sent it to Wilson, Minty prepared a reply for General Robertson, advising him that General Cobb's dispatch had been sent to Wilson, but in the interim he would continue his forward movement until directed to do otherwise. Minty's reply was passed on to General Robertson through Colonel White, along with instructions to give the truce party five minutes to disperse, after which time White was to resume his march and secure the next bridge over Rocky Creek at Bailey's Mill.

HDQRS. SECOND DIV., CAVALRY CORPS,
MIL. DIV. OF THE MISSISSIPPI,
In the Field near Macon, Ga., April 20, 1865

GENERAL: I have received the dispatch from General Cobb and have sent it by special messenger to Major General Wilson, a few miles in my rear. As there may be some delay in receiving an answer, it will be necessary for you to return immediately to Macon, to which place General Wilson's reply will be forwarded. I have directed the officer commanding my advance to move forward five minutes after this is handed to you.

I am respectfully, your obedient servant,

ROBT. H.G. MINTY
Colonel, Commanding Division[17]

Once Minty's reply had been duly delivered and the truce party had dispersed, Colonel White sent Adjutant Lieutenant William E. Doyle on ahead with an advance party of 15 men, followed closely by the rest of the regiment. Doyle had proceeded barely two miles when he caught up with the truce party, which was moving slowly, apparently in an effort to mask the retreat of 250 Confederate troops. Doyle promptly charged, scattering the truce party and capturing three officers. Doyle, in the meantime, had sent back a request for reinforcements, which Colonel White honored by dispatching a company under Major Weiler.[18] Arriving at Rocky Creek in the April darkness, Weiler and Doyle drove off a detachment attempting to burn the bridge and pursued them as far as the palisades. Breaking through, they reached the Confederate lines and demanded the surrender of the defenders. The commanding officer was not present, but his subordinate, believing they were cut off, quickly complied with the demand.[19]

When White arrived and accepted the surrender of a brigade amounting to some 500 men, he left a detachment to guard the prisoners and pushed on to Macon itself. At the edge of the city he was met by a second truce party from General Cobb. The party inquired as to the terms of surrender, to which White reported, "My answer was unconditional surrender, and gave the flag five minutes to get out of the way."[20]

Inside the city, White was met by yet a third contingent from Cobb, who stated that he accepted the terms and was surrendering the city. White proceeded to Cobb's headquarters, took formal possession of Macon, and immediately placed guards on duty. Surrendering were generals Cobb, Gus W. Smith, William Mackall, and Hugh Mercer, together with 3,800 officers and enlisted men, five stands of colors, 60 pieces of artillery, and 3,000 stands of arms.[21]

Wilson arrived in Macon about 8:30 P.M. and immediately met with Howell Cobb. Cobb protested that Wilson had failed to acknowledge the armistice and insisted that the Federals should be withdrawn from the city to the point at which the news of the alleged armistice was first delivered to Colonel White. Wilson explained that while he did not doubt the existence of an armistice, he was not obliged to honor it as such until he received official notification from higher authority.[22] Wilson then reportedly inquired whether Lee had surrendered, but Cobb declined to comment. Thereupon, Wilson directed the same question to General Gus Smith, whom he had known while a cadet at West Point. Smith confirmed that Lee had in fact surrendered. This satisfied Wilson, who advised Cobb that he no longer held any doubt as to the existence of an armistice but still required official confirmation. He further advised Cobb that all hostilities would be suspended and the Macon garrison would be considered prisoners of war until such time as he received word from Sherman. "I shall conduct my operations hereafter on the theory that any man killed on either side is a man murdered," Wilson told Cobb.[23]

At 9 P.M., on April 20, Wilson sent the following dispatch to Sherman using a cipher code:

> HDQRS. CAVALRY CORPS, MILITARY
> DIVISION OF THE MISSISSIPPI,
> Macon, Ga., April 20, 1865—9 P.M.
>
> Maj. Gen. W.T. Sherman:
> (Through headquarters of General Beauregard, Greensborough, N.C.). My advance received the surrender of this city this evening. General Cobb had previously sent me under a flag of truce a copy of a telegram from General Beauregard declaring the existence of an armistice between all the troops under your command and those

under General Johnston. Without questioning the authenticity of this dispatch or its application to my command, I could not communicate orders to my advance in time to prevent the capture of the place. I shall therefore hold its garrison, including Major-Generals G.W. Smith and Cobb and Brigadier General MacKall, prisoners of war. Please send me orders. I shall remain here a reasonable length of time to hear from you.[24]

Sherman was also thinking about his young cavalry commander, because he sent a dispatch to Wilson on the same day, but Wilson did not receive it until 6 P.M. on April 21. At the time he wrote, Sherman had not yet seen Wilson's message. His dispatch, while clarifying the situation, did not specifically address all of Wilson's concerns:

HEADQUARTERS MILITARY DIVISION
OF THE MISSISSIPPI,
Raleigh, April 20, 1865

Major-General Wilson,
    Commanding Cavalry, U.S. Army in Georgia:

General Joseph E. Johnston has agreed with me for a universal suspension of hostilities looking to a peace over the whole surface of our country. You will therefore desist from further acts of war and devastation until you hear that hostilities are resumed. For the convenience of supplying your command you may either contract for supplies down about Fort Valley or the old Chattahoochee Arsenal, or if you are south of West Point, Ga., in the neighborhood of Rome and Kingston, opening up communication and a route of supplies with Chattanooga and Cleveland. Report to me your position through General Johnston, as also round by sea. You may also advise General Canby of your position and the substance of this, which I have also sent round by sea.

W.T. Sherman,
Major-General, Commanding[25]

By April 21, Sherman had received Wilson's communiqué and promptly fired off a response:

HDQRS. MILITARY DIVISION OF
THE MISSISSIPPI,
In the Field, Raleigh, NC., April 21, 1865

GENERAL JAMES H. WILSON
    Commanding Cavalry Division of the Mississippi, Macon, Ga.:
    (Through General J.E. Johnston.)
GENERAL: A suspension of hostilities was agreed on between General Johnston and myself on Tuesday, April 18, at 12 noon. I want that agreement religiously observed, and you may release the generals captured at Macon, occupy ground convenient, and contract

for supplies for your command, and forbear any act of hostility until you hear or have reason to believe hostilities are resumed. In the meantime, it is also agreed the position of the enemy's forces must not be altered to our predjudice. You know by this time that General Lee has surrendered to General Grant the rebel Army of Northern Virginia, and that I only await the sanction of the President to conclude terms of peace coextensive with the boundaries of the United States. You will shape your conduct on this knowledge unless you have overwhelming proof to the contrary.

> W.T. Sherman
> Major-General, Commanding[26]

Based on this directive, Wilson, on April 21, posted an official notice of the armistice to his command:

MACON, GA.,
April 21, 1865

SPECIAL FIELD ORDERS
No. 22

It is hereby announced to the Cavalry Corps of the Military Division of the Mississippi that an armistice has been agreed upon between General J.E. Johnston and Maj. Gen. W.T. Sherman with a view to a final peace. The troops of the Cavalry Corps are ordered to refrain from further acts of hostility and depredations. Supplies of all kinds are to be contracted for and foraging upon the country will be discontinued. The officers of the Cavalry Corps will enforce strictest discipline in the commands. Guards will be established, private and public property respected, and everything done to secure good order. The brevet major-general commanding again takes great pleasure in commending the officers and men of the corps for their galantry, steadiness, and endurance in battle and during the arduous marches to this place. He enjoins them to remember that people in whose midst they are now stationed are their countrymen, and should be treated with magnanimity and forbearance, in the hope that, although the war which has just ended has been long and bloody, it may secure a lasting peace to our beloved country.

By command of Brevet Major-General Wilson:
> E.B. Beaumont
> Major and Assistant Adjutant-General[27]

Some in Macon, however, refused to accept the fact that Lee had surrendered. One rumor even speculated that there had indeed been an armistice but that the Confederacy had been recognized by France, England, Spain, and Austria. As always under such conditions, the rumors were wild and absurd. On April 22, one Confederate officer wrote to another stating he had heard that President Lincoln, Secretary of State William Henry Seward,

Tennessee governor Andrew Johnson, and Secretary of War Edwin Stanton were all dead and Lee's surrender was in doubt.[28]

Whatever they chose to believe, the Confederate dream had ended. The original agreement between Sherman and Johnston was not ratified, but that issue was resolved with Johnston's surrender on April 26. Generals Richard Taylor and Edmund Kirby Smith surrendered within a month, making capitulation complete. Scattered shots continued to be exchanged and isolated pockets of Confederate troops remained in a quasi-active state for several weeks, but the war was over. Wilson's cavalry had conducted the last major campaign of the Civil War.

But if there was joy in the realization that the war had at long last come to an end, there was little time for the men of the cavalry corps to savor that feeling. On April 23 came the news of President Lincoln's assassination and a pall of disbelief, sadness, and anger pervaded the corps. It hit them "like a stunning blow," wrote a member of the Third Iowa. "The soldiers loved him, and grieve for him as though they had lost a father."[29] Another remembered how the men refused to believe it at first, but were nevertheless deeply affected, so much so that there was grave concern that a serious reaction might be felt:

> Their expressions and conduct were so plainly marked that the officers watched them for some days in much anxiety. They were now freely mixing with the citizens, and paroled rebel soldiers were passing daily by thousands on their way to their homes. Distressing results might have followed any indiscreet word or act on the part of a Southerner in those days.[30]

Fortunately, the close watch by Wilson's officers, coupled with news of the flight of former Confederate President Jefferson Davis, diverted the attention of the men and avoid an incident.

With hostilities over, Wilson set about enforcing the laws of the United States in Macon and seeing to the community's needs. The Cavalry Corps was able to devote time and energy to reorganizing and refitting. Upton's division reached the city shortly after Minty's, and on the April 23, LaGrange's brigade arrived from West Point, leaving only Croxton's command still outstanding. Within a week, he, too, was on hand.

Eighteen
Croxton's Odyssey

The admirable judgment and sagacity displayed by General Croxton throughout his march of over 650 miles in thirty days, as well as the good conduct and endurance of his command, are worthy of the highest commendation. —Wilson, Official Report, June 29, 1865[1]

R ecall that when Wilson reached Elyton on March 30, he directed McCook to detach one of his brigades and send it on an independent mission to Tuscaloosa, 50 air miles southwest of Elyton. McCook complied by sending Croxton's first brigade. (The independent movements of Croxton's brigade occurred simultaneously with those of Wilson's main body. Consequently, in order for a recounting of Croxton's movements to make sense within the larger context of the Selma campaign, it makes the most sense to first follow the main thrust of the Cavalry Corps to Macon, then jump back in time and retrace Croxton's movements.)

Croxton's specific orders were to destroy the bridge, factories, mills, the military school "and whatever else may be of benefit to the rebel cause."[2] If practical, Croxton was also to break up the railroad between Selma and Demopolis. He was to rejoin the main body of the corps along the Centerville Road or by whatever route proved most expeditious. Wilson's strategy was to not only destroy the military resources of Tuscaloosa and the surrounding area, but also to counter any Confederate movement designed to strike his main column in the flank.[3]

Local sources had advised Wilson that only a few militia and the cadets at the Alabama Military College would be available to oppose Croxton. Nevertheless, that "illusive cuss" Hylan Lyon was reported to be in the area. Croxton was also cautioned to be on the watch for a portion of Forrest's command reportedly moving toward Tuscaloosa.[4]

Croxton's brigade was composed of Colonel Joseph H. Dorr's Eighth Iowa, Lieutenant Colonel Thomas Johnston's Second Michigan, Major

William H. Fidler's Sixth Kentucky, and Croxton's old regiment, the Fourth Kentucky Mounted Infantry, now led by Lieutenant Colonel Josephus Tompkins. Normally, the brigade mustered 1,500 effectives, including the Fourth Kentucky, which had been marching in the rear with the corps's wagon train and had not reached Elyton when Croxton departed at 4 P.M. on March 30. The Kentuckians were directed to rejoin the brigade at least by the time it reached Tuscaloosa if not sooner.[5]

When Croxton pulled away from the column that afternoon, neither he nor any man in his command suspected that this particular assignment would turn out to be anything more than a brief diversion; they would carry out their mission and rejoin the corps in a day or two, perhaps three. They were soon to discover, however, that this mission spun a web of its own. Before it ended, this hard-riding brigade completed a 31-day odyssey of skirmishing, marching, and countermarching before finally rejoining their comrades in distant Macon, Georgia, on May 1.

After a short march, the brigade camped the first night eight miles south of Elyton and was on the move again at daylight. Along the way, Croxton sent detachments to destroy the stores at Jonesborough and the Saunders Iron Works. After completing their assignment, the two detachments rejoined the main column ten miles from Trion late on the afternoon of March 31. At that point a captured Confederate reported that Forrest's entire force was even then moving through Trion, bound for Centerville and Montevallo.[6]

In reality, it was not Forrest's entire force, but the division of Brigadier General William Hicks "Red" Jackson. Despite the report of the Confederate prisoner, Croxton was in the dark as to the size of the Confederate force. What he did know was that it posed a threat to Wilson. Although Tuscaloosa was the main objective, Croxton was also obliged to cover Wilson's right flank. Accordingly, the Federal brigadier decided to put Tuscaloosa on the back burner while he took time to bushwhack the Confederate column. He hoped to at least delay his opponent from interfering with Wilson's southward march.[7]

John Croxton was resourceful and imaginative. While the main body of the brigade took time to rest and feed their horses, an advance party was sent off in pursuit of the Confederate column. At the same time, Croxton prepared a written dispatch for Wilson. The dispatch was broken into three parts and one part was given to each of three scouts, along with a verbal message to supplement the written communiqué. In this fashion, should any one of the three couriers be captured, only a portion of Croxton's strategy would be revealed.[8]

In short order, the advance party reported back that the Confederates were in strong force and holding the party in check on the Centerville Road. Several attempts to outmaneuver the enemy proved unsuccessful. By midnight Croxton was convinced his position had become somewhat precarious and that at daylight he would be on the receiving end of a Confederate attack.[9]

By this time, the strategy, which was certainly still admirable in its design, was beginning to look a bit shaky, mainly because the size of the enemy force seemed to be larger than what he was capable of handling. Prudence suggested that he withdraw while there was still an opportunity to do so. Orders were given and the brigade withdrew ten miles west to Mud Creek Road, which ran parallel to the road on which they had been traveling. Two companies of the Sixth Kentucky under Captain Edmund Penn were left behind to further determine the enemy's strength and if possible, course of action. Scouts were also dispatched to guide the Fourth Kentucky to a safe reunion with the brigade.[10] What Croxton did not realize, and could not have known, was that his brigade had inadvertently gotten between Jackson's main body and his artillery and wagon train. Had the Federals taken the direct road on into Tuscaloosa, Croxton would have discovered Jackson's guns and train and, presumably, been able to destroy both.[11]

At any rate, the last of the brigade had barely left camp at daylight on April 1, when, true to Croxton's suspicion, the Confederates attacked. Captain Edmund Parrish's company of the Sixth Kentucky charged the attackers, but in the dim light of dawn, Parrish became confused. He mistook some of the enemy for his own troops and subsequently found himself surrounded and captured.[12] The impetus of the Confederate attack drove Captain Penn's command back on the main body of the brigade. Major Fidler's Sixth Kentucky was bringing up the rear of the column and Fidler promptly dispatched a battalion to assist his subordinate. The reinforcements enabled Penn to keep the attackers at arm's length, though the Federals suffered 32 casualties.[13]

The action, perhaps a tactical victory for the Confederates, proved to be a strategic victory for Croxton in that the delay cost Jackson the opportunity to carry out Forrest's plan of intercepting the Yankee column early on. About the same time that Jackson was giving battle to Croxton, Upton's men captured the Confederate courier carrying dispatches that outlined Forrest's plan of action.[14] Meanwhile, instead of pursuing Croxton, Jackson positioned part of his command between Croxton and Tuscaloosa, then marched with the rest of his division to join Forrest. Unaware of Jackson's move and unwilling to clash with a numerically superior force, Croxton, as he put it, was now "determined to effect by stratagem what I could not hope to accomplish directly." Turning north, Croxton marched ten miles along the Elyton road, then halted to feed the horses and wait for the Fourth Kentucky to join the column.[15]

Reinforced at last by the Kentuckians, the brigade resumed its march, turning west to Johnson's Ferry on the Black Warrior River, 40 miles above Tuscaloosa, which they reached at sundown on April 1. Croxton promptly ordered the Eighth Iowa to begin crossing; by sundown on April 2 the entire brigade was west of the river, the troops having all crossed on a single flat boat, while the horses swam.[16]

On April 3 the brigade continued its march toward Tuscaloosa, with the advance rounding up Confederate scouts, and civilians for that matter, to mask their approach. Some of those captured provided Croxton with a picture of the city's defenses, which, he learned, included 400 militia and 350 cadets from the military college.[17]

That night, the brigade reached the outskirts of Northport, a suburb of Tuscaloosa. Assembling his command in a cedar grove, Croxton detailed 150 picked men from the Second Michigan to move into position near the bridge over the Black Warrior River. Croxton's plan was to have this detachment seize the bridge by surprise at daybreak, then charge across with the main body and capture the city before the defenders could be assembled.[18]

As they approached the bridge, however, the Federals heard sounds that turned out to be troops removing the flooring of the structure. Quickly Croxton ordered the Michigan troops forward to secure the bridge while it was still intact. As Croxton's troops attacked, the Confederate rear guard fired the bridge, then fell back to take up positions behind bales of cotton. The Second Michigan shortly clattered across the bridge, routed the defenders, and put out the fire.[19] Once the bridge was repaired, the remainder of the brigade crossed over, dismounted, and prepared to repel an attack from the militia and cadets who were assembling nearby. Several unsuccessful efforts failed to dislodge the numerically superior Federal horsemen. Morning found Croxton largely in possession of the area, having taken 60 prisoners and captured three pieces of artillery.[20]

While Croxton's troops were fighting around the bridge, a wedding was taking place at a nearby church. The ceremony was interrupted by the Federals, who proceeded to round up all the men, including the groom (a Confederate officer, Captain James Carpenter). At his request, the captain was taken before Croxton; as it turned out, both men had known each other in Kentucky before the war. Carpenter then proceeded to explain to Croxton how his bride was dying of consumption and asked to be paroled to care for her rather than be sent to a northern prison. Croxton graciously agreed and returned the captain to his bride with an escort.[21]

On April 4, the brigade destroyed the local foundry, a factory, two niter works, and the military university along with all military stores and supplies, after first taking what was needed to replenish their own inventory.[22] Having accomplished his mission at Tuscaloosa, Croxton next addressed the question of how best to rejoin the Cavalry Corps. It was Croxton's understanding that Jackson's division, reinforced by a brigade from Chalmers, was then at Greensborough, due south of Tuscaloosa, and on the direct route to Centerville and Selma. If he tried to link up with the corps by moving southeast through Centerville (as per his instructions), he would be exposing the brigade to a superior Confederate force.

Confronted by this reality, Croxton decided to effect his junction with Wilson in a somewhat roundabout fashion. He would recross the Black Warrior River and move west, then turn south to destroy the Alabama and Mississippi Railroad between Demopolis, Alabama, and Meridian, Mississippi. From there, his future course would be determined by circumstances as he found them. If Forrest sent a smaller force after him, Croxton would dispose of it. If, however, Forrest should send a larger column than his own, he would have to deal with it as best he could, taking satisfaction in knowing that he had caused a sizable Confederate force to be diverted from opposing Wilson. Croxton was also concerned that the absence of his brigade might cause Wilson to jeopardize the movements of the main column. He prepared a coded message advising Wilson of his plans and sent it by courier. Unfortunately for Croxton, the messenger did not get through; for the moment, Wilson remained ignorant of Croxton's whereabouts.[23]

Having thus reformed his strategy, Croxton recrossed the Black Warrior River on April 5; after burning the bridge at Northport, he marched 25 miles on the road to Columbus, Mississippi. Along the way, Captain William A. Sutherland and a company of the Sixth Kentucky was ordered to cross the Sipsey River and feint toward Columbus before turning south to rejoin the brigade.[24]

On the sixth, Sutherland's command captured a few scouts belonging to Confederate General Wirt Adams at Carrollton. After burning the courthouse, they turned south toward Bridgeville, but turned and headed for King's Store after learning that Adams was at Bridgeville. While at King's Store, Sutherland received word that Croxton had had a fight with Adams but had managed to drive him off. Circumstances had compelled Croxton to cross the Sipsey without waiting for Sutherland. Isolated and unable to rejoin Croxton, Sutherland, after being attacked at King's Store and forced to release his prisoners, headed north for Decatur. He reached Decatur on April 10, the first of Wilson's expedition to return.[25]

Meanwhile, on April 6, Croxton had taken the Pleasant Ridge Road and marched a dozen miles to Lanier's Mills on the Sipsey, eight miles from Vienna.

There, word reached him that 3,000 of Forrest's men were en route from West Point, Mississippi, and were headed down the Tombigbee River. Forrest himself, Croxton further learned, was at Marion; Red Jackson was still in the vicinity of Tuscaloosa; most important, Wilson had taken Selma.[26] The fall of Selma changed Croxton's plans. As a result of Wilson's victory, Forrest's surviving command had been pushed back west of the Cahaba River and their presence there ruled out a prosecution of the strategy just formulated at Tuscaloosa. In view of the circumstances, Croxton decided to recross the Sipsey and head back toward Northport, burning mills in the area as he traveled.[27]

The column had just turned about and resumed the march following a brief halt when the rear guard was attacked near Romulus by Adams with a force of two brigades estimated at 2,800 men. Once again it was Major William Fidler's Sixth Kentucky performing the rear guard duties. They were promptly driven back in confusion. Croxton quickly sent in Colonel Johnston's Second Michigan to stem the tide and the Michiganders proved equal to the challenge, closing the door on the Confederates. The affair cost Croxton 34 casualties and forced him to leave two ambulances behind.[28]

Following the scrape with Adams, Croxton moved north along the Byler Road to a point 12 miles beyond Northport. Here the brigade remained until April 11, trying unsuccessfully to establish communications with Wilson, who by that time was en route to Montgomery. Croxton reasoned that if Wilson had left Selma, he had probably moved either south or east. Had he moved west, it would likely have driven Forrest out of the area and thus have made it a relatively easy matter to communicate with the corps. However, it did not seem possible to contact Wilson, so Croxton concluded that the corps had either continued south or turned east toward Montgomery. With all of this in mind, Croxton elected to recross the Black Warrior and move into the Elyton Valley where he hoped it would be possible to ascertain whether Wilson headed toward Mobile or Montgomery.[29]

On April 11, the brigade marched to Wyndham's Springs on the Black Warrior, only to discover that all boats had been destroyed, making it necessary to move farther north in search of a crossing. On the fourteenth, Croxton reached Calloway's and Lindsey's ferries on the Sipsey Fork of the Black Warrior River. Three days were consumed in rebuilding the bridge, but by April 17, the brigade was across and marching via Arkadelphia to Hanby's Mills on the Mulberry Fork of the Black Warrior.[30]

After fording the Mulberry Fork on April 18, the brigade pushed on to Menter's Ferry on the Little Warrior. Again, boats were not available and the troops were forced to use canoes. The operation took until sundown on the nineteenth. While there, word also reached Croxton that the Cavalry Corps had taken Montgomery and continued its eastward drive.[31]

At that juncture, Croxton had just about made a full circle. He had passed through this same area nearly a month earlier. One of the troopers jokingly suggested that perhaps Croxton had somehow gotten hold of one of the circus horses that Wilson had impressed during the Nashville campaign, as he seemed unable to avoid traveling in a circle.[32]

After destroying a foundry and niter works near Mount Pinson, Croxton moved on to Trussville and Cedar Grove, where he turned south toward Montevallo for a few miles to create the impression that it was his objective.[33] On April 21, Croxton turned east toward Talladega, sending the Fourth Kentucky on ahead to secure boats at Truss's and Collins' ferries on the Coosa River. This time, boats were available and by noon on April 22, the brigade was east of that river.[34]

On April 23, Croxton learned that Confederate General Benjamin J. Hill's brigade was between Talladega and Blue Mountain. Croxton headed in that direction. Hill's command, numbering 500 men supported by a single piece of artillery, was found in position at Munford's Station ten miles from Talladega. Promptly attacking, the brigade easily routed Hill's troops, capturing a number of prisoners and the lone artillery piece.[35] Having disposed of Hill's command, Croxton turned his attention to the destruction of the Oxford and Blue Mountain Iron Works, together with railroad bridges and depots. This accomplished, the brigade moved on to Blue Mountain, where they destroyed the depot, some rolling stock, and a quantity of ordnance stores.[36]

On April 24, the Eighth Iowa marched by way of Jacksonville, while the rest of the brigade moved via Oxford and Davison, where it was rejoined by the Iowans. Pushing on, Croxton next burned a cotton factory and camped that night at Bell's Bridge on the Talapoosa River. On the twenty-fifth, the brigade marched through Arbacoochee Bowdon to Carrollton, Georgia, then on to Moore's and Reese's ferries on the Chattahoochee, where they executed another successful river crossing on April 27.[37]

Between Newnan and Flat Shoals, Georgia, Croxton encountered the commander of the Newnan garrison carrying a flag of truce. The Confederate commander informed Croxton of an armistice and claimed protection under its terms. Croxton advised him that while he could not officially recognize the armistice, he would nevertheless presume it to be true and promised not to bother anyone who stayed out of his way. Croxton also promised to respect the armistice insofar as foraging was concerned, but refused to halt his march.[38]

On April 28, the brigade crossed the Flint River at Flat Shoals and marched through Barnesville, then to Forsyth. From Forsyth Croxton dispatched Captain Madison M. Walden and Lieutenant Thomas B. Prather of his staff to inform Wilson of the brigade's approach.[39]

On the last day of April 1865, the brigade passed through Forsyth to Crawford's Station. On May 1, they finally rejoined the Cavalry Corps after a 31-day separation. During that time, Croxton's brigade had marched a total of 653 miles, crossed four major rivers, destroyed five large iron works and three factories, not to mention numerous mills and large quantities of supplies. In addition, they captured four pieces of artillery, several hundred small arms, and collected 300 prisoners. Croxton's own loss was four officers and 168 men, about half of whom had been captured while straggling in from foraging parties.[40]

At the outset, Croxton's raid created a diversion in support of Wilson's main effort against Selma. Beyond that, however, the 31-day odyssey contributed nothing to a war that had already ended. Croxton, of course, had no knowledge of those events, being less informed than Wilson. He'd had no real choice but to conduct his movements as he did. Still, the raid was certainly a tribute to Croxton's imagination and resourcefulness.

Nineteen
The Pursuit and Capture
of Jefferson Davis

I have the honor to report that at daylight of the 10th instant Colonel Pritchard, commanding Fourth Michigan Cavalry, captured Jeff. Davis and family. —Wilson to E. M. Stanton, May 12, 1865[1]

On Sunday morning, April 2, 1865, with Wilson's cavalry only hours away from victory at Selma, President Jefferson Davis attended services at St. Paul's Church in Richmond. In the midst of the services, a messenger entered and quietly approached Davis. Moments later, the president was en route to his office to consider the implications of the dispatch that had just been given to him. The communiqué was from General Robert E. Lee who advised his commander-in-chief that it was no longer possible to maintain the Richmond-Petersburg defensive line.[2]

Summoning his officials (the president's wife and children had gone south some time ago), Davis made the necessary preparations for moving the seat of government and by 11 P.M. he and those officials of state who could be assembled were on board a special train for Danville.[3] For Davis, the days that followed were hectic and filled with the hope that somehow, something of this desperate, four-year conflict might yet be salvaged from the shadow of defeat. Then on Sunday, April 9, General Lee surrendered the Army of Northern Virginia, ushering in the final act of the tragedy that had begun on such a bright note for both Davis and the Confederate States of America.

Though Lee had surrendered, the armies of Joe Johnston, Richard Taylor, and Edmund Kirby Smith remained active. Despite the fact that these forces possessed little capacity for perpetuating the struggle, Davis refused to concede total defeat. Until the time of his capture a month later, he persisted in clinging to the hope that the means could be found to keep

211

going. The immediate strategy was to get west of the Mississippi River and, once on the other side, muster whatever forces were available. If that could be managed, Davis reasoned, the war might be prosecuted long enough for the Confederacy to achieve at least some of its original objectives.[4]

On April 10 Davis and his party left Danville and proceeded to Greensboro, North Carolina, where they remained until the fifteenth. After meeting with and authorizing Johnston to negotiate terms with Sherman, the Davis party headed south with a cavalry escort, arriving at Salisbury, North Carolina, on the seventeenth.

News of Lincoln's assassination added to the confusion and tragedy of the hour. On April 18 Sherman and Johnston concluded an agreement that terminated hostilities and called for the surrender of all remaining Confederate forces in the field. The agreement, however, was rejected by authorities in Washington—only unconditional surrender was acceptable. On the twenty-sixth Johnston surrendered, accepting the federal government's terms, despite his agreement with Davis to continue the struggle. Now there remained only the armies of Taylor and Smith.[5]

Meanwhile, continuing their southward flight, the Davis party reached Abbeville, Georgia, on May 2. The cavalry escort, having grown restless and its officers feeling that further resistance was futile, was paid from the contents of the Confederate treasury and released from further obligation. That night the party crossed the Savannah River and pushed on to Washington, Georgia. On May 9 they reached Dublin, where Davis was reunited with his wife and children.[6]

Meanwhile, Federal authorities had been directed to take appropriate measures to capture the Confederate leader. Word of Davis's movements had actually reached Wilson as early as April 11 when he saw accounts in the Montgomery newspapers stating that Davis had moved the seat of the Confederate government to Danville.[7] On April 23 a citizen of Macon informed Wilson that he had seen Davis at Charlotte, North Carolina, only a few days before and that the Confederate leader was bound for the trans–Mississippi department. Four days later, on the twenty-seventh, Wilson received official word from Sherman regarding the surrender of Joe Johnston's army. Sherman's news officially ended the Selma campaign. Wilson immediately took steps to disperse his command to cover strategic points in Georgia, both for paroling returning Confederate soldiers and watching the various routes that Davis might follow in attempting to evade capture and get west of the Mississippi.[8]

Accordingly, on April 28, Upton, with a portion of his division, was shifted to Augusta while Winslow, with the balance of the Fourth Division, went north to Atlanta where detachments of the First Ohio scouted the country as far as Dalton and West Point. McCook and 700 of his First Division troopers were ordered to Tallahassee. When Croxton returned, he retained the balance of the First Division at Macon, with orders to cover the line of the Ocmulgee River from Macon to Yellow Creek. Croxton also sent a detachment back to Talladega.[9]

Minty's Second Division was directed to pick up coverage of the Ocmulgee River line from the right of Croxton's command as far as Abbeville. Detachments were also sent to Cuthbert and Eufaula. Minty was further directed to cover the Flint and Chattahoochee rivers as far as his resources permitted.[10]

Over and above Wilson's coverage, General William J. Palmer's cavalry command was at Athens, Georgia, and General George Stoneman had a force moving east from Tennessee into the Carolinas. Thus, in early May the network of Federal patrols reached from Kingston, Georgia, on the north to Tallahassee, Florida, on the south. In all, some 15,000 Union troops were on the lookout for the Davis party.[11]

One of the many small bodies covering points along this perimeter was a detachment of 20 troopers from Eggleston's First Ohio of Upton's division, under the command of Lieutenant Joseph D. Yoeman. Disguising themselves as Confederates, Yoeman and his men set out to see what they could learn about the Davis party. After a rapid march to the northeast, along an axis he believed might lead them to intercept their quarry, Yoeman and his men not only located the Davis party, but managed to join the escort and ride along for several days. After Davis parted company with his cavalry escort, however, Yoeman lost contact. Dividing his command into smaller parties, Yoeman dispatched them to try and relocate Davis, meanwhile sending couriers to his brigade commander, General Alexander, who in turn apprised Wilson of these developments.[12]

Wilson acted promptly on the receipt of Yoeman's report. Croxton was directed to send the best regiment in his division to Dublin on the Oconee River. The regiment was to move as rapidly as possible, scouting toward the north and leaving detachments to cover the main roads. To carry out this assignment, Croxton selected Lieutenant Colonel Henry Harnden and the First Wisconsin Cavalry, a veteran regiment under an experienced and able officer. Harnden, with 150 picked men from his regiment left Macon on the evening of May 6.[13]

Even as Harnden was leaving Macon, Wilson was about to unwittingly set in motion events that would subsequently lead to a tragic and embarrassing confrontation. Convinced that Davis was going to try to escape south into Florida, Wilson directed Minty to select his best regiment and send it without delay to the southeast along the north bank of the Ocmulgee River.

The regiment's assignment was to cover all crossings between Hawkinsville and the mouth of the Ohoopee River. Not surprisingly, Minty's choice was his own former regiment, the Fourth Michigan, commanded by Lieutenant Colonel Benjamin Pritchard.[14]

Upton had previously urged Wilson to offer a $100,000 reward for the capture of Davis. Such action, Upton declared, would surely be endorsed by the secretary of war. While Wilson was not about to assume a responsibility of that magnitude on his own volition, he did authorize Upton to issue a proclamation offering a reward in that amount to be paid out of such money as might be found in the possession of Davis or his party. In other words, no reward money would come out of the Federal treasury. In any case, Upton agreed to this and had copies of the notice printed and in circulation throughout the region by May 6.[15]

Harnden, meanwhile, left Macon on the sixth as per his instructions. That evening he reached Jeffersonville, where he detached Lieutenant Charles L. Hewitt and 30 troopers to watch the crossroads in that area. By 5 P.M. on the seventh, Harnden was at Dublin on the Oconee River, 55 miles southeast of Macon. Although citizens there claimed no knowledge of the Davis party, Harnden was informed by "some negroes that a wagon train and escort had crossed the river on the ferry that same day,… going on the Jacksonville Road." Later that night, Harnden learned "from another negro that Jeff. Davis and wife were with the train."[16]

Detaching Lieutenant Theron W. Lane and 45 men to guard the ferry and patrol local roads, Harnden pushed on at daylight with the balance of his command, now reduced to 75 troopers, moving in a southwesterly direction. At Turkey Creek, Harnden learned that the train had taken the road to Telfair. Moreover, a local woman described one of the occupants of the train as a man Harnden concluded was Davis.[17]

The trail led through a pine woods and was becoming increasingly difficult to follow. Harnden impressed as a guide a local man who also claimed to have some knowledge of the train's movements. At Alligator Creek, they found where the train had recently camped. After picking up a new guide and resting his horses, Harnden resumed the pursuit, believing they were now only four hours behind the train. The route continued southwest across Alligator and Gum Swamp creeks, where Harnden finally called a halt when the trail became too difficult to follow in the dark. The day's march had totaled 40 miles.[18]

In the saddle again at 3 A.M. on May 9, Harnden's column pushed on to Brown's Ferry on the Ocmulgee River, where a delay in crossing cost the Federal pursuers two precious hours. Finally reaching Abbeville, Harnden learned that the Davis party had left that place at 10 A.M. bound for Irwinville.[19]

Sending his command on in pursuit, Harnden himself went to meet with Colonel Pritchard, whose detachment was advancing along the Hawkinsville Road. When the two officers met, Harnden apprised Pritchard of the situation reporting that his command was even then closing in on the party that he was convinced included Jefferson Davis. Pritchard then advised Harnden that the Fourth Michigan had been ordered to Abbeville to watch for Davis. Pritchard offered Harnden some of his Michigan troopers, but the Wisconsin colonel declined on the grounds that he already had an adequate force for the work at hand. Moreover, the additional troops would only add to the already difficult problem of securing forage for his horses.[20]

The two officers then parted. Harnden, after catching up with his command and proceeding ten miles, found still-burning campfires belonging to the fleeing train. Pushing on toward Irwinville, Harnden halted about 9 P.M. to rest his horses, but was on the move again at 3 A.M. They had barely proceeded a mile, however, when the advance party under Sergeant George Hussey was halted by a party hiding among the trees. Assuming he had encountered a Confederate outpost, Hussey chose to fall back. As he did so, his detachment was fired on with three Wisconsin troopers being wounded.[21]

Harnden also concluded they had run into a Confederate outpost from the Davis train. He sent a ten-man detachment forward to probe the enemy's strength, but when they, too, seemed to encounter strong opposition, Harnden deployed his entire force and advanced. Fortunately, a prisoner was taken almost immediately who proved to be a member of Pritchard's Fourth Michigan.[22]

Once the mistake was discovered, the firing immediately ceased. Shortly Harnden learned that following his meeting with Pritchard, the latter had pushed on ahead along the river road with a select force, reaching the south end of Irwinville two hours before Harnden began his final approach. What really stung the Wisconsin troops was that while they were exchanging volleys with Pritchard's men, the rest of the Michigan regiment had moved into the Confederate camp and captured the Davis party.[23]

Harnden was angry and bitter about the turn of events, feeling that he had been preempted. Pritchard, on the other hand, felt that his actions were entirely justified and within the scope of his orders. Leaving Macon at 8 P.M. on May 7, Pritchard had marched with a force of 439 officers and men. They were under orders to patrol the south bank of the Ocmulgee River for 75–100 miles, securing all ferries below Hawkinsville, and generally watch the river line as far as his strength permitted.[24] By mid-afternoon of the ninth Pritchard was at Abbeville, where he first learned of the movements of the Davis train. His meeting with Harnden later that day brought him up to date on the Federal pursuit. Whether motivated by a desire to see Michigan at least share in the glory of capturing the Confederate president, or whether it was an honest feeling that Harnden might require support is not known. Pritchard later claimed that he came into possession of additional facts that forced him to conclude that the Davis party might be able to evade Harnden. In any event, Pritchard decided he ought to participate in the capture. Accordingly, selecting 135 of the best men in his regiment, he trotted off in pursuit.[25]

After following the river road for a dozen miles, Pritchard turned southwest through a pine forest for an additional 18 miles, reaching Irwinville at 1 A.M. on May 10. There, the Michigan colonel bluffed his way around locals, saying that his was a Confederate force looking for the Davis train. Pritchard was apparently convincing because he was advised that a train answering his description had camped for the night a mile and a half north on the Abbeville Road.[26]

Impressing a local guide, Pritchard advanced to within a half mile of the bivouacked train. From there, Lieutenant Alfred Purinton with a 25-man detachment was sent around to the north or rear of the train to prevent its escape in that direction. Purinton was cautioned to be on the lookout for Harnden's command.[27]

At this juncture it was 2 A.M. Pritchard decided to postpone his attack until dawn, fearing that some of the party might get away. "The moon was getting low," Pritchard reported, "and the deep shadows of the forest were falling heavily, rendering it easy for persons to escape undiscovered to the woods and swamps in the darkness."[28] With first light, Pritchard moved forward and surrounded the camp, taking it completely by surprise. Just then, however, firing broke out at the north end of the camp. Pritchard at first supposed it was Purinton tangling with a Confederate outpost. Detailing a guard to watch over the prisoners, he quickly moved to Purinton's support. Once he reached the scene of the firefight, however, Pritchard became suspicious that they might be shooting at Federals because of "the determination displayed on their part and the peculiar report of their fire-arms." Shortly the facts came to light, but not before two troopers of the Fourth Michigan had been killed and another wounded, so that with Harnden's three wounded, there were six Federal casualties.[29]

Pritchard felt that the Wisconsin unit bore responsibility for the fight and the whole affair could have been avoided if Sergeant Hussey had only answered the challenge of Purinton's pickets. In any case, it was a lamentable tragedy, one that tarnished the record of the Cavalry Corps in the just-concluded campaign.[30] Harnden's brigade commander, LaGrange, wrote a stinging rebuke of Pritchard's action, describing it as "unsoldierly selfishness." Minty responded by accusing LaGrange of casting a "slur upon the name and character of one of the most honorable and gallant officers in the service." Wilson tried to arbitrate the dispute by declaring that Harnden was in no way responsible for the unfortunate collision between the two regiments and that he and his men were entitled to a full share of credit. On other hand, Wilson also cited Pritchard for his aggressive action. Pritchard would "have been more culpable had he remained in camp," said Wilson.[31]

Once order was restored, Pritchard and Harnden returned to the captured train. The party did indeed include Davis, his wife Varina, and their four children, together with Mrs. Davis's sister, Miss Maggie Howell, and several servants. Davis's officials included Postmaster General John Reagan; Burton N. Harrison, the president's secretary; five military aides; a midshipman in the Confederate Navy; and 12 soldiers. The train itself consisted of five wagons, three ambulances, 15 horses and 25 to 30 mules.[32]

The most intriguing aspect surrounding the capture of Davis is the allegation that he was caught disguised as a woman while attempting to escape. The former Confederate president was reportedly wearing a waterproof cloak with a black shawl and carrying a small tin pail while walking between his wife and sister-in-law. The stories created sensational copy in the north. Although privately Wilson seems to have regarded the charge as a distortion of the truth, he may also have felt that such distortion brought national attention to his Cavalry Corps, whose accomplishments had been overshadowed by the end of the war and Lincoln's assassination.[33]

After allowing time for breakfast, Pritchard organized his column and began the return trip to Macon, preceded by Harnden's detachment. The party camped for the night near Abbeville, recalling the balance of the Fourth Michigan from its patrol duty along the river. The two men who had died in the unfortunate clash between the two regiments were buried there.[34]

Near Hawkinsville, Pritchard was met by the rest of the brigade which had come out from Macon bringing news of President Andrew Johnson's proclamation and Wilson's offer of a reward for the capture of Davis. At 3 P.M. on May 13, Pritchard arrived in Macon with the former Confederate president.[35]

After spending several hours with Wilson, who treated him with every courtesy, Davis and his party were sent north, escorted by Colonel Pritchard, whom Davis had requested. Eventually, Davis spent two years in prison at Fort Monroe, Virginia, before the freedom of civilian life was again his.[36]

Twenty
Epilogue

I regard this corps to-day as a model for modern cavalry in organiza-
tion, armament and discipline.... —Wilson to Sherman, May 8, 1865[1]

D espite the embarrassment surrounding the event, the apprehension of Jefferson Davis was a notable postscript to the final campaign of the war. For all practical purposes, the arrival at Macon signaled the end of the Cavalry Corps, Military Division of the Mississippi. The war was over and within days after reaching Macon, the various regiments and brigades were dispersed, never to be reassembled. The corps had more than fulfilled its mission. During their remaining weeks in the service, Wilson's troopers performed the various administrative and police functions of an army of occupation. The divisions of Hatch and Johnson, both of which had remained in Middle Tennessee during the Selma campaign, were largely involved in patroling the countryside, skirmishing with the many bands of out-laws that infested the area, and trying to prevent the smuggling of contraband.[2]

Early in May, Hatch received information that led him to suspect that Forrest might be planning a raid on Memphis. He reported his suspicions to Thomas, who directed him to send a summons to Forrest under a flag of truce, calling on the Confederate cavalry leader to surrender. In a most uncharacteristic show of feeling that sounded more like Sherman, Thomas further instructed Hatch to advise Forrest that if the rumors of a raid on Memphis were true, the Federals were prepared to deal with it and that Forrest would be "treated thereafter as an outlaw, and the States of Mississippi and Alabama will be so destroyed that they will not recover for fifty years."[3]

For a time it appeared that the Cavalry Corps might be assembled and sent to Texas along with other Federal forces to drive Austrian Archduke Maximilian out of Mexico where he proclaimed himself emperor. The oppor-tunity vanished, however, when Maximilian elected to leave the country of his own volition. Publicly Wilson applauded the wisdom of the archduke's decision, though he privately felt a twinge of regret at missing another opportunity to display the prowess of his command.[4]

Late in May 1865 it was decided that Wilson would remain in Georgia with 2,000 of his own troops plus a contingent of infantry. The balance of the Cavalry Corps returned to Tennessee where those whose terms of enlistment were due to expire by October 31 would be mustered out. The remainder of the corps would be reorganized and put to use as occupation troops in Kentucky and Alabama.[5]

On June 22, Wilson wrote to Brigadier General William D. Whipple, Thomas's chief of staff, recommending the withdrawal of all the cavalry from Georgia, pointing out that infantry was better suited to garrison work. A cavalryman could not take proper care of his horse and perform garrison duty at the same time. Still envisioning a future for his corps, he recommended that the cavalry be assembled at least on a brigade level and brought to a "high state of efficiency, ready to act anywhere with rapidity and force."[6]

In view of Wilson's recommendation that a force of mounted troops was not needed in the south, it was decided to muster out the corps. On June 26, 1865, through Special Order Number 3, Military Division of the Tennessee (newly created on June 7), General Thomas officially dissolved the Cavalry Corps, Military Division of the Mississippi, after 246 days of active service.[7]

Wilson was ordered to remain in Georgia as commander of the newly created District of Macon. He issued his farewell order to the corps on July 2, 1865. General Order Number 39 was a glowing tribute from a proud commander to his troops, recalling their many accomplishments of the past seven months:

> ORDERS. HDQRS. CAV.CORPS, MIL.
> DIV. OF THE MISSISSIPPI,
> Macon, Ga., July 2, 1865
>
> TO THE OFFICERS AND MEN OF THE CAVALRY CORPS,
> MILITARY DIVISION OF THE MISSISSIPPI:
>
> Your corps has ceased to exist. The rebellion has terminated in the establishment of your country upon the basis of nationality and perpetual unity. Your deeds have contributed a noble part to the glorious result. They have passed into history and need no recital from me. In the nine months during which I have commanded you, I have heard no word of reproach upon your conduct, have had no disaster to chronicle. The glowing memories of Franklin, Nashville, West Harpeth, Ebenezer Church, Selma, Montgomery, Columbus, West Point, and Macon may well fill your hearts and mine with pride. You have learned to believe yourselves invincible, and contemplating your honorable deeds may well justly cherish that belief. You may be proud of your splendid discipline no less than your courage, zeal, and endurance. The noble impulses which have inspired you in the

past will be a source of enduring honor in the future. Peace has her victories no less than war. Do not forget that clear heads, honest hearts, and stout arms, guided by pure patriotism, are the surest defense of our country in every peril. Upon them depend the substantial progress of your race and order of civilization, as well as the liberty of all mankind. Let your example in civil life be an incitement to industry, good order, and enlightenment, while your deeds in war shall live in the grateful remembrance of your countrymen. Having discharged every military duty honestly and faithfully, return to your homes with the noble sentiments of your martyr President deeply impressed upon every heart, "With malice against none, and charity for all, strive to do the right as God gives you to see the right."

J. H. WILSON
Brevet Major-General[8]

At one point Sherman had suggested that the bulk of the cavalry be marched back to Tennessee. Wilson considered this alternative wholly impractical as the country had long ago been picked clean and many areas were experiencing severe food shortages. Wilson believed the only practical solution was to rebuild the railroad from Atlanta to Chattanooga. General Steedman was already working south from Chattanooga and Wilson finally received permission to have Winslow, an experienced railroad builder, begin working north from Atlanta. Progress was swift; within three weeks the road was in operation, transferring regiments north to their mustering stations.[9]

A few regiments were mustered out prior to the June 26 order. Others were sent north to be processed at various points over the following five months. Six regiments were mustered in June, seven in July, eleven in August, six in September, four in October, one in November, and finally, the Twelfth Missouri nearly a year later on April 9, 1866.[10]

Thus Wilson's Cavalry Corps was dissolved. "The entire force," wrote Wilson, "disappeared from the service and dropped into the bosom of the people with no other commotion than that which naturally followed the return of war-worn soldiers to their homes and friends."[11]

For James Harrison Wilson, the organization and employment of Sherman's cavalry would prove to be the capstone of a long and distinguished career. From 1865 until the time of his death, 60 years later in 1925, Wilson added a number of significant accomplishments to his record, including service in the Spanish-American War and the Boxer Rebellion (in 1900). Not surprisingly, none of these ever quite equaled the sense of pride and fulfillment he experienced as commander of the Cavalry Corps, Military Division of the Mississippi. The challenge and excitement of an independent campaign such as Wilson had known during the Selma campaign is heady wine indeed, when one is 28 and filled with the rush of life's promise—a tough act to follow.

Wilson had not been particularly pleased at the prospect of leaving

Sheridan's Third Division to take over Sherman's cavalry. The responsibility of the western command was greater, but the action was where Grant was and so was the opportunity for glory and promotion. Nevertheless, he met his new assignment with gusto and enthusiasm. He very quickly came to appreciate the soldierly qualities of Thomas and soon recognized that Middle Tennessee in that autumn of 1864 was going to provide all the action that any young officer could possibly desire. The challenge was there and he met it head on. Wilson had a superb penchant for organization, as evidenced by what he accomplished in the face of Hood's invasion and later in preparing the corps for the Selma campaign.

He was frustrated and outmaneuvered by Forrest during the pull-back from Pulaski to Franklin, but it should be remembered that Wilson had only been in the field with his new command for nine days—scarcely enough time to develop the kind of rapport a commander needs. Add to this the fact that Schofield's army was backpedaling and Middle Tennessee was in a state of chaos. Given such conditions, it is a wonder that Wilson was able to accomplish as much as he did.

It has been suggested that Forrest's absence made it possible for the Federal horsemen to achieve the kind of success they enjoyed. Wilson himself admitted that they would have had a far tougher chore if Forrest had been present.[12] Unquestionably, Forrest would have added considerable authority to the Confederate resistance and Wilson's task would have been far more difficult if he had had to deal with the full weight of Forrest's cavalry, rather than just that of Chalmers's division. Forrest's great capacity as a combat leader notwithstanding, it seems unlikely that he would have been able to seriously affect the ultimate outcome of the battle.

The role of the Federal cavalry during the Battle of Nashville has seldom been fully appreciated. For the first time in the Civil War, cavalry was employed as part of the primary striking force, not in a supportive or cooperative role, but as an integral part of the main effort. If Wilson's horsemen were not the deciding factor in the battle, they were not far from it. Wilson and Thomas proved that the cavalryman was as good a fighter as a foot soldier. Cavalry could fight alongside infantry, then resume its traditional role as a mounted force in pursuit of a beaten foe.

Ironically, the pursuit of Hood's army was perhaps not as effective as it might have been because of the time lost in bringing the horses forward to the troopers who had been fighting on foot all day. It is interesting to speculate whether this weakness would have been corrected had the Civil War continued and cavalry been employed elsewhere as it was at Nashville. Yet despite this flaw, the pursuit of Hood's army was surely characterized by vigor and determination. Hood's army did finally manage to escape, not due to ineptness on the part of Wilson and his horsemen, but to the tenacity of the Confederate resistance.

Grant was critical of the Selma campaign because he felt that it got started too late to influence the outcome of the war and as such resulted in the unnecessary destruction of much valuable property and many lives.[13] Perhaps, but even if Wilson had been able to get under way early in March, or even sooner, it still would not have affected the end result. In truth, the Confederacy had lost the war long before Wilson struck south from the Tennessee River; so Grant made a moot point.

Wilson, not surprisingly, could not and would not accept such a conclusion, insisting that the campaign ensured, beyond a doubt, the futility of further resistance by the South. Once under way, Wilson could hardly have halted his campaign simply because he suspected the end might be at hand. Moreover, as was demonstrated, the surrender of Lee at Appomattox did not automatically and instantly cause Confederate resistance to cease. Until the various forces in the field received official notification of the war's end, they had no choice but to continue.

The Selma campaign was proof positive that a properly trained and organized cavalry force was indeed capable of conducting much more than a simple raid; it was fully able to carry out a large-scale, independent operation, including the attack and seizure of strongly defended works. In reviewing the Selma campaign some years later, Colonel George Denison, in his *History of Cavalry*, wrote:

> This was one of the most remarkable cavalry operations of the war, for, as we have said, it was not a mere raid or dash, but an invading army determined to fight its way through.... It is certainly one of the most extraordinary affairs in the history of the cavalry service, and recalls the romantic episodes of the Crusades, where the armies consisted almost solely of knights who dismounted to attack fortified places. It is a striking illustration of what can be done by the judicious use of a force of mounted riflemen if bravely led and skillfully commanded.[14]

Wilson's Cavalry Corps demonstrated the value and effectiveness of a highly mobile force, capable of rapid movement and quick deployment, yet with the firepower and strength of numbers to conduct totally independent operations. It is more than a little interesting to speculate on what the Cavalry Corps might have been able to accomplish had it been created a year earlier and been able to function at its full potential, i.e., with six divisions rather than three. Although that opportunity never presented itself during the Civil War, the legacy bequeathed by the Cavalry Corps may be seen in the armored tactics employed by General George Patton during World War II and, more recently, in Operation Desert Storm.

Notes

Introduction

1. Lewis, *Sherman, Fighting Prophet*, p. 490.
2. *Ibid.*, p. 338.
3. Sherman, *The Memoirs of William T. Sherman*, p. 104.
4. Lewis, *Sherman, Fighting Prophet*, p. 370.
5. Wilson, *Under the Old Flag*, vol. 2, p. 2.
6. *Ibid.*
7. *Ibid.*, p. 3.
8. *Ibid.*
9. *Ibid.*, pp. 3–4.
10. *Ibid.*
11. Longacre, *From Union Stars to Top Hat*, p. 23; Boatner, *The Civil War Dictionary*, p. 931.
12. Wilson, *Under the Old Flag*, vol. 1, p. 400.
13. Longacre, *From Union Stars to Top Hat*, pp. 25–94, 243–245.
14. *Ibid.*, pp. 95–106.
15. *Ibid.*, pp. 106, 110, 243–244.
16. *Ibid.*, pp. 118–128.
17. Wilson, *Under the Old Flag*, vol. 2, p. 4.
18. *Ibid.*, p. 4.
19. *Ibid.*, p. 5.

One: The Foal Is Sired

1. Wilson, *Under the Old Flag*, vol. 2, p. 4.
2. *Ibid.*, p. 6.
3. *Ibid.*
4. War Department, *War of the Rebellion: Official Records* (hereafter cited as *O.R.*), Serial 79, p. 87. Apparently the experience of leading a cavalry division in the field had altered some of Wilson's views regarding the use of cavalry. See also, *O.R.*, Serial 59, pp. 256–257.
5. Longacre, *From Union Stars to Top Hat*, p. 160.
6. Wilson, *Under the Old Flag*, vol. 2, pp. 11–14.
7. *Ibid.*, p. 14.

8. Marszalek, *Sherman: A Soldier's Passion for Order*, pp. 294–96; Grant, *Personal Memoirs of U.S. Grant*, vol. 2, pp. 356–358; Sherman, *Memoirs of General William T. Sherman*, pp. 167–168.

9. *O.R.*, Serial 79, p. 365.

10. Sherman, *The Memoirs of William T. Sherman*, p. 160.

11. *O.R.*, Serial 79, p. 358.

12. *O.R.*, Serial 59, p. 257.

13. Johnson and Buel, *Battles and Leaders of the Civil War*, vol. 4, p. 465.

14. Wilson, *Under the Old Flag*, vol. 2, p. 13.

15. *Ibid.*, p. 12.

16. *O.R.*, Serial 79, pp. 414–415.

Two: The Reins of Command

1. Wilson, *Under the Old Flag*, vol. 2, p. 5.

2. *O.R.*, Serial 76, p. 608; Wilson, *Under the Old Flag*, vol. 2, p. 10.

3. Wilson, *Under the Old Flag*, vol. 2, p. 20.

4. *Ibid.*, pp. 20–21.

5. *Ibid.*, p. 5.

6. *O.R.*, Serial 79, p. 443.

7. Wilson, *Under the Old Flag*, vol. 2, pp. 19–20.

8. *O.R.*, Serial 79, p. 443. Wilson's estimate, based on Sherman's report that Forrest had 26,000 men, says much about Forrest's ability to make the Federals believe he had more men than he actually did. At no time during the war did Forrest ever command a force of this size. Forrest seldom, if ever, had more than 10,000 men under his command. Since he was relatively new to the area, Wilson may have believed that the figure was genuine, or he may have used the figure as a bargaining point to gain the resources he was after.

9. *O.R.*, Serial 79, pp. 443–444.

10. *Ibid.*

11. *Ibid.*, p. 531.

12. *Ibid.*, p. 582.

Three: Prelude

1. *O.R.*, Serial 79, p. 365.

2. McKinney, *Education in Violence*, pp. 3–21, 399–403.

3. *Ibid.*, pp. 264–266.

4. *Ibid.*, pp. 372–373.

5. *Ibid.*, p. 376; *O.R.*, Serial 79, pp. 423, 442, 477, 511.

6. McKinney, *Education in Violence*, pp. 367, 376; *O.R.*, Serial, 79, p. 442.

7. McKinney, *Education in Violence*, p. 379; *O.R.*, Serial 93, p. 56.

8. McKinney, *Education in Violence*, pp. 378–379.

9. *Ibid.*, p. 378.

10. *O.R.*, Serial 39, p. 202, 449, 746; *O.R.*, Serial 45, pp. 920, 923, 933; Sword, *Embrace an Angry Wind*, p. 79.

11. *O.R.*, Serial 79, pp. 539, 584.

12. *Ibid.*, pp. 538, 655, 674, 691; *O.R.*, Serial 93, p. 340.

13. *O.R.*, Serial 79, p. 638; *O.R.*, Serial 93, p. 340.

14. McKinney, *Education in Violence*, pp. 386–387; Wilson, *Under the Old Flag*, vol. 2, p. 26; *O.R.*, Serial 93, p. 895; *O.R.*, Serial 94, pp. 55, 71.

15. *O.R.*, Serial 93, pp. 568, 1118.

16. *Ibid.*, p. 908.

17. Wilson, *Under The Old Flag*, vol. 2, p. 33.

18. *O.R.*, Serial 93, p. 568.

19. *Ibid.*, pp. 554–555.

20. *O.R.*, Serial 79, p. 714; *O.R.*, Serial 93, p. 555.

21. Wilson's decision to assign the Sixth Division to Johnson may have been based on the belief that Upton was not yet sufficiently recovered from his wound to assume a field command at this time. Also, both Garrard and Spalding lacked the necessary rank to hold a division command. *O.R.*, Serial 79, p. 444; *O.R.*, Serial 93, pp. 908–1026; Dyer, *A Compendium of the War of the Rebellion*, vol. 1, p. 464 (hereafter cited as Dyer, *Compendium*). During this period, some command assignments were changed so frequently as to make it all but impossible to know the official status of a given individual on a given day. Richard W. Johnson is a good illustration of this. In August 1864 he was made chief of cavalry for the Military Division of the Mississippi. On November 2, he was given command of the First Division, XIV Corps. One week later he was reassigned to command all the cavalry in the Department of Tennessee. On November 19, he was in charge of the Post of Pulaski, and, finally, on the twenty-fourth, assumed command of Wilson's Sixth Cavalry Division, the assignment having actually been made on the seventeenth. See *O.R.*, Serial 79, pp. 613–705; *O.R.*, Serial 93, pp. 926–927. The selection of Knipe was apparently a second choice for Wilson, who believed that Knipe was better suited to an infantry command. He was selected on the basis of Thomas's suggestion, or perhaps insistence. See *O.R.*, Serial 79, p. 444; *O.R.*, Serial 93, p. 908; Warner, *Generals in Blue*, p. 273.

22. *O.R.*, Serial 93, pp. 556–557.

23. Wilson, *Under the Old Flag*, vol. 2, p. 34; *O.R.*, Serial 93, p. 973.

Four: Florence to Columbia

1. *O.R.*, Serial 79, p. 523.

2. Wilson, *Under the Old Flag*, vol. 2, p. 169.

3. *Ibid.*, p. 366; Warner, *Generals in Blue*, p. 104; Boatner, *The Civil War Dictionary*, p. 211.

4. Boatner, *The Civil War Dictionary*, p. 211; *O.R.*, Serial 93, pp. 572–574, 1204.

5. *O.R.*, Serial 77, p. 586; *Battles and Leaders of the Civil War*, vol. 4, p. 465.

6. Thatcher, *A Hundred Battles in the West*, p. 191.

7. *O.R.*, Serial 93, p. 572.

8. *Ibid.*

9. *Ibid.*

10. Thatcher, *A Hundred Battles in the West*, p. 192.

11. *O.R.*, Serial 93, pp. 572–573.

12. *Ibid.*

13. *O.R.*, Serial 93, p. 575; Wilson, *Under the Old Flag*, vol. 2, pp. 172–173.

14. *O.R.*, Serial 93, p. 575.

15. *Ibid.*

16. One such episode involved an unsuccessful effort on the part of half a dozen troopers from the Second Michigan who set out in homemade canoes to cut the

Confederate pontoon bridge near Florence. See Thatcher, *A Hundred Battles in the West*, pp. 350–357.

17. *O.R.*, Serial 93, p. 928.

18. *Ibid.*, pp. 685, 687, 694, 933.

19. *Ibid.*, p. 887.

20. *Ibid.*

21. *Ibid.*, p. 888.

22. *Ibid.*, p. 897.

23. *Ibid.*, p. 575.

24. *O.R.*, Serial 79, pp. 525, 706–707.

25. McKinney, *Education in Violence*, pp. 379–380; *O.R.*, Serial 93, p. 885.

26. Boatner, *The Civil War Dictionary*, pp. 122, 801–802; McKinney, *Education in Violence*, p. 389.

27. *Battles and Leaders*, vol. 4, p. 443; *O.R.*, Serial 79, p. 573.

28. *O.R.*, Serial 93, p. 909; Wyeth, *That Devil Forrest*, pp. 468–469; Wills, *A Battle from the Start*, pp. 276–277.

29. *O.R.*, Serial 93, pp. 965–966.

30. *Ibid.*, pp. 910–911, 928; Scratches or grease heel is a mange-like inflammation of the surfaces of the fetlock. See Ensminger, *Horses and Horsemanship*, p. 409.

31. *O.R.*, Serial 93, p. 912.

32. *O.R.*, Serial 93, p. 582.

33. *O.R.*, Serial 93, pp. 760–762; Wills, *A Battle from the Start*, pp. 277–278; Wyeth, *That Devil Forrest*, p. 472.

34. *O.R.*, Serial 93, pp. 575, 587; Wyeth, *That Devil Forrest*, p. 471.

35. *O.R.*, Serial 93, p. 1236.

36. *O.R.*, Serial 93, p. 572.

37. *O.R.*, Serial 93, p. 963.

38. *Ibid.*

39. *O.R.*, Serial 93, p. 575; *Battles and Leaders*, vol. 4, p. 465.

40. Connelly, *Autumn of Glory*, pp. 490–491.

41. *O.R.*, Serial 93, pp. 955–956, 972.

42. *O.R.*, Serial 93, p. 956.

43. McKinney, *Education in Violence*, pp. 379–380.

44. *O.R.*, Serial 93, p. 964.

45. *Ibid.*, pp. 964–965.

46. *Ibid.*, p. 970.

47. *Ibid.*, p. 972.

48. *Ibid.*, p. 987.

49. *Ibid.*, p. 1025.

50. *Ibid.*, p. 997.

51. *Ibid.*, pp. 1001–1002.

52. *Ibid.*, p. 1005.

53. *Ibid.*, pp. 575–576; Thatcher, *A Hundred Battles in the West*, p. 198.

54. *O.R.*, Serial 93, pp. 575–576, 752.

55. *O.R.*, Serial 93, pp. 557, 576; Davenport, *History of the 9th Regiment*, p. 155.

56. *O.R.*, Serial 93, p. 1014.

57. Wyeth, *That Devil Forrest*, pp. 473–474.

58. *Battles and Leaders*, vol. 4, p. 443.

59. *O.R.*, Serial 93, pp. 341, 1085, 1105.

60. *Ibid.*, p. 1243.

Five: Columbia to Franklin

1. *O.R.*, Serial 93, p. 1169.
2. *Ibid.*, pp. 557–558, 588, 597, 1025–1027.
3. *Ibid.*, p. 1026.
4. Wilson, *Under the Old Flag*, vol. 2, pp. 35–36. Wilson was mistaken about the identity of the Michigan regiment. The Second Michigan was a part of Croxton's brigade and commanded by Colonel Benjamin Smith. The Eighth Michigan was attached to R. W. Johnson's division. See *O.R.*, Serial 93, p. 1205. As far as I am aware, this story only appears in Wilson's autobiography. It seems odd that such an event would not have been included in the regimental history, but Thatcher (*A Hundred Battles in the West*) makes no mention of the incident.
5. *O.R.*, Serial 93, p. 1040.
6. *Ibid.*, p. 1041.
7. *Ibid.*, p. 1050.
8. *Ibid.*, p. 1056.
9. *Ibid.*, pp. 1056–1057. The difficulties encountered in trying to get Winslow's cavalry to Nashville is typical of the administrative red tape experienced by Wilson and his staff. Winslow's horsemen were being used in Missouri and Arkansas and the Federal authorities in the region were not anxious to part with them. The fact that the division's units were scattered over a wide area added to the problem. The whole affair became such a confused mess that it is something of a minor miracle that they ever reached Nashville at all. See *O.R.*, Serial 93, pp. 955, 961, 1003, 1024, 1179–1180.
10. *Ibid.*, p. 1058.
11. *Ibid.*, pp. 1064–1065, 1107.
12. Wilson, *Under the Old Flag*, vol. 1, p. 252.
13. *Ibid.*, p. 174.
14. *Ibid.*, p. 176.
15. Warner, *Generals in Blue*, pp. 253–254; *O.R.*, Serial 93, p. 1118.
16. *O.R.*, Serial 93, p. 1085.
17. *O.R.*, Serial 93, pp. 341, 1036; Stanley, *Personal Memoirs*, p. 194.
18. *O.R.*, Serial 93, p. 652; Connelly, *Autumn of Glory*, vol. 2, p. 492; McDonough and Connelly, *Five Tragic Hours*, p. 35.
19. *O.R.*, Serial 93, p. 752.
20. *Ibid.*, pp. 558, 1110.
21. *Ibid.*, pp. 1111–1112.
22. *Ibid.*, p. 1112.
23. *Ibid.*, pp. 598, 604.
24. Wilson, *Under the Old Flag*, vol. 2, pp. 38–39.
25. *O.R.*, Serial 93, p. 1107.
26. *Ibid.*
27. *Ibid.*, pp. 1107–1108
28. *Ibid.*, p. 1108. In the *O.R.*, only a few communiqués are identified as to the hour sent or received. In this case, for example, I have assumed that Thomas's 8 P.M. response was in answer to Schofield's 6 P.M. report because it seems to fit contextually.
29. *Ibid.*
30. Connelly, *Autumn of Glory*, vol. 2, pp. 491–492; Horn, *The Army of Tennessee*, pp. 385–386; Losson, *Tennessee's Forgotten Warriors*, pp. 203–204; Sword, *Embrace an Angry Wind*, pp. 140–141.
31. *O.R.*, Serial 93, p. 1143.
32. *Ibid.*, p. 1137. In his memoirs, Wilson later claimed that, as a precaution, he

sent this dispatch by "several different couriers on different routes." See Wilson, *Under the Old Flag*, vol. 2, p. 42.

33. *Ibid.*, pp. 113–114, 122.

34. *Ibid.*, pp. 113, 148; Stanley, *Personal Memoirs*, p. 200.

35. *O.R.*, Serial 93, pp. 113, 148.

36. Schofield, *Forty-six Years in the Army*, pp. 213–216.

37. *O.R.*, Serial 93, p. 1112.

38. Wilson, *Under the Old Flag*, vol. 2, p. 46.

39. *O.R.*, Serial 93, p. 588.

40. *Ibid.*, p. 559.

41. *Ibid.*, p. 1146. This almost suggests a moment of panic on Wilson's part. His fear that Forrest was going to slip around his flank and reach Nashville was unrealistic. In the first place, there would have been little that Forrest alone could have accomplished at Nashville, except perhaps to cause Thomas some annoyance. Secondly, Forrest's job was to support Hood (even as Wilson's was to support Schofield), a responsibility he would have evaded by striking out toward Nashville on his own. One suspects that Wilson feared the embarrassment of being outflanked by his opponent more than he feared for the safety of Nashville.

42. *Ibid.*, p. 559.

43. There are several excellent studies of Hood's Tennessee campaign, all of which provide detailed coverage of the Spring Hill episode. The best of the recent studies is Sword, *Embrace an Angry Wind*. Others include Groom, *Shrouds of Glory*; McDonough and Connelly, *Five Tragic Hours*; Connelly, *Autumn of Glory*; Horn, *The Army of Tennessee*; and Losson, *Tennessee's Forgotten Warriors*.

44. Stanley, *Memoirs*, p. 201; *O.R.*, Serial 93, p. 113; McDonough and Connelly, *Five Tragic Hours*, p. 45.

45. Sword, *Embrace an Angry Wind*, pp. 118–120.

46. *O.R.*, Serial 93, p. 753.

47. *Ibid.*; Sword, *Embrace an Angry Wind*, pp. 118–120; McDonough and Connelly, *Five Tragic Hours*, p. 45.

48. *O.R.*, Serial 93, pp. 653, 763; Sword, *Embrace an Angry Wind*, pp. 124–127; McDonough and Connelly, *Five Tragic Hours*, pp. 45–46.

49. Sword, *Embrace an Angry Wind*, pp. 124–127, 136; McDonough and Connelly, *Five Tragic Hours*, pp. 37–59.

50. Sword, *Embrace an Angry Wind*, p. 131.

51. *Ibid.*, pp. 126–127, 133–139; Losson, *Tennessee's Forgotten Warriors*, pp. 203–207.

52. *Ibid.*, pp. 143–144, 147–148; McDonough and Connelly, *Five Tragic Hours*, p. 50.

53. *O.R.*, Serial 93, pp. 148–149; Sword, *Embrace an Angry Wind*, pp. 143–145.

54. *O.R.*, Serial 93, pp. 148–149, 769–770.

55. *O.R.*, Serial 93, p. 403.

56. *O.R.*, Serial 93, p. 342; McDonough and Connelly, *Five Tragic Hours*, p. 52.

57. *O.R.*, Serial 93, pp. 339, 753.

58. *Ibid.*, pp. 112, 339.

59. Perhaps this might have happened. But what of the huge Federal wagon train? It was night; much of Schofield's command (especially Cox's troops) was exhausted; and moving cross-country to the next north-south turnpike with a huge wagon train in tow would not have been as feasible as it might seem. See McDonough and Connelly, *Five Tragic Hours*, pp. 55–56.

60. *O.R.*, Serial 93, p. 1169.

Six: Franklin

1. *O.R.*, Serial 93, p. 343.
2. *Ibid.*, p. 1177.
3. *Ibid.*, p. 1169.
4. *Ibid.*, p. 1170.
5. *Ibid.*
6. Wilson, *Under the Old Flag*, vol. 2, pp. 36, 49; *O.R.*, Serial 93, p. 752; Wills, *A Battle from the Start*, p. 278.
7. *O.R.*, Serial 93, p. 589.
8. *Ibid.*, pp. 559, 1151.
9. *Ibid.*, pp. 559, 1145.
10. *Ibid.*, pp. 559, 1146.
11. *Ibid.*, pp. 1182–1183.
12. *Ibid.*, p. 1177.
13. *Ibid.*, pp. 559, 1146.
14. *Ibid.*, pp. 559, 598.
15. *Ibid.*, pp. 753–754; *O.R.*, Atlas, Plate CV.
16. *O.R.*, Serial 93, pp. 557, 752.
17. *Ibid.*, pp. 557, 573.
18. Reconciling the differences in opposing forces during the Civil War is always a chancy undertaking. However, with that in mind, the effective strengths of Hatch, Croxton, and Harrison (Capron's old brigade) as reported by Wilson was 2,500, 1,000, and 800, respectively, or a total of 4,300. Hammond's arrival increased this figure by approximately 1,000, so that Wilson's overall effective strength at Franklin would have been in the neighborhood of 5,500. However, on November 30, both Hammond and Stewart were absent, leaving Wilson with about 4,000, or actually some 800 fewer if one considers that Harrison's brigade was not engaged. Forrest, even without the services of Chalmers would have had 2,500–3,000. See *O.R.*, Serial 93, pp. 557–560, 752; Wyeth, *That Devil Forrest*, pp. 471–72; *Civil War Times Illustrated*, December 1964, pp. 22–23; McDonough and Connelly, *Five Tragic Hours*, p. 153.
19. *Battles and Leaders*, vol. 4, p. 466.
20. *O.R.*, Serial 93, p. 572.
21. The reporter is in error here, as there were no Louisiana units in either Jackson or Buford's division. These were probably the Texans of Ross's brigade.
22. This is an exaggeration. Forrest had no more than half that number in action at that point.
23. Thatcher, *A Hundred Battles in the West*, pp. 305–307.
24. *Ibid.*, pp. 589, 754, 770.
25. *Ibid.*, pp. 1184–1185. Actually, Hammond had sent a communiqué providing Wilson with an update at 6:25 P.M., but it had obviously not arrived by the time Wilson sent off his message to Hammond. See also, *Ibid.*, p. 1184.
26. *Battles and Leaders*, vol. 4, p. 466.
27. *Ibid.*, p. 435.
28. *Ibid.*, p. 439.
29. *O.R.*, Serial 93, p. 241.
30. Livermore, *Numbers and Losses in the Civil War*, pp. 131–132; McDonough and Connelly, *Five Tragic Hours*, pp. 157–58.
31. Livermore, *Numbers and Losses in the Civil War*, pp. 131–132.
32. *O.R.*, Serial 93, p. 1171.
33. Wilson, *Under the Old Flag*, vol. 2, pp. 53–54.

34. *Battles and Leaders*, vol. 4, p. 435.

35. *O.R.*, Serial 93, p. 560.

36. *Ibid.*

37. *Ibid.*, pp. 671, 688, 731.

Seven: Hood's Dilemma

1. Hood, *Advance and Retreat*, p. 299.

2. *O.R.*, Serial 93, pp. 664, 754; Horn, *Decisive Battle of Nashville*, p. 37.

3. *O.R.*, Serial 93, p. 754.

4. Horn, *Decisive Battle of Nashville*, p. 34; *O.R.*, Serial 93, p. 754; Fisher, *They Rode with Forrest and Wheeler*; Wills, *A Battle from the Start*, p. 286; Sword, *Embrace an Angry Wind*, p. 275; Connelly, *Autumn of Glory*, p. 508.

5. Connelly, *Autumn of Glory*, p. 506.

6. *Ibid.*, pp. 470–514.

7. Hood, *Advance and Retreat*, pp. 299–300.

8. *O.R.*, Serial 94, pp. 639–640, 765–766.

9. For recent studies that address Hood's generalship, see Sword, *Embrace an Angry Wind*, pp. 278–285; Connelly, *Autumn of Glory*, pp. 492–493; McMurry, *John Bell Hood and the War for Southern Independence*, pp. 176–178; McDonough and Connelly, *Five Tragic Hours*, pp. 168–178.

10. *O.R.*, Serial 93, p. 654.

11. *Ibid.*, p. 744. In fact, Rousseau's garrison strength was about 8,000. See *O.R.*, Serial 93, p. 36.

12. Hood, *Advance and Retreat*, p. 298; *O.R.*, Serial 93, pp. 654, 754–755; *O.R.*, Serial 94, p. 652.

13. *O.R.*, Serial 93, p. 754; Wills, *A Battle from the Start*, p. 286.

14. *O.R.*, Serial 93, p. 754.

15. *Ibid.*, p. 755.

16. *O.R.*, Serial 93, pp. 617, 618, 755.

17. *Ibid.*, p. 755; Horn, *Decisive Battle of Nashville*, p. 38.

18. *O.R.*, Serial 93, pp. 613, 756.

19. *Ibid.*, pp. 654–655, 740–741; Wills, *A Battle from the Start*, pp. 288–289.

20. *O.R.*, Serial 93, p. 756.

21. *Ibid.*

22. *Ibid.*, pp. 763–764.

23. *Ibid.*

24. The official records state that the brigade numbered fewer than 600. Stanley Horn says it had about 700. See *O.R.*, Serial 93, pp. 677, 680, 765; Horn, *Decisive Battle of Nashville*, p. 81.

25. *O.R.*, Serial 93, p. 756.

26. Thomas's troop strength actually exceeded 70,000. However, of this number, Rousseau's command at Murfreesboro and Wilson's First and Second divisions under McCook and Long were not available for the Battle of Nashville. When these units are subtracted from the available total, Thomas had some 50,000 men. See *O.R.*, Serial 93, p. 55; Livermore, *Numbers and Losses in the Civil War*, pp. 132–133; Connelly, *Autumn of Glory*, p. 507.

27. Sword, *Embrace an Angry Wind*, p. 305.

Eight: Interlude

1. *O.R.*, Serial 94, p. 114.
2. Wilson, *Under the Old Flag*, vol. 2, p. 63; *O.R.*, Serial 94, p. 3; McKinney, *Education in Violence*, pp. 399–400.
3. Wilson, *Under the Old Flag*, vol. 2, p. 99.
4. *Ibid.*, p. 61.
5. *Ibid.*
6. *Ibid.*, pp. 58–59.
7. *O.R.*, Serial 94, p. 20. Ideally, cavalry horses were fed a diet consisting primarily of hay or "long forage," and supplemented by grain, with the amount of grain being dependent on a horse's daily routine. Since grain is a high-energy food, an animal undergoing the rigors of campaigning would require more grain than one that was not. General Allen's point here was that a horse could subsist exclusively on grain for a short time, providing its owner made certain the animal had sufficient exercise.
8. Starr, *The Union Cavalry in the Civil War*, vol. 3, p. 590. For a contrasting view of this, see Scott, *The Story of a Cavalry Regiment*, p. 29.
9. *O.R.*, Serial 94, p. 55. One wonders how Halleck could have accused the western cavalry of losing all those horses *without having been involved in a campaign*, unless somehow he had failed to read the daily reports concerning Hood's advance.
10. *Ibid.* Glanders, or "farcy," is a very old disease, dating back to ancient Greek days. It can be acute or chronic and is thought to originate in the lungs, producing ulcers either on the skin or in nasal passages. Symptoms are loss in condition and lack of endurance. There is no known cure. See Ensminger, *Horses and Horsemanship*, p. 409.
11. Lewis, *Sherman, Fighting Prophet*, p. 336.
12. Davenport, *History of the Ninth Illinois Cavalry*, p. 40.
13. Starr, *The Union Cavalry in the Civil War*, vol. 1, pp. 265–287; Wilson, *Under the Old Flag*, vol. 2, p. 28.
14. *O.R.*, Serial 94, p. 18.
15. Wilson, *Under the Old Flag*, vol. 2, p. 58.
16. *Ibid.*; *O.R.*, Serial 94, pp. 18, 106.
17. Wilson, *Under the Old Flag*, vol. 2, pp. 33–34.
18. *O.R.*, Serial 94, p. 139.
19. *Ibid.*, p. 135.
20. Wilson, *Under the Old Flag*, vol. 2, p. 58; Davenport, *History of the Ninth Illinois Cavalry*, p. 31.
21. *O.R.*, Serial 93, p. 598; Horn, *Decisive Battle of Nashville*, p. 77.
22. Wilson, *Under the Old Flag*, vol. 1, pp. 332–333.
23. *Ibid.*, p. 334.
24. Wilson, *Under the Old Flag*, vol. 1, pp. 336–337; Longacre, *From Union Stars to Top Hat*, pp. 101, 102, 231.
25. Wilson, *Under the Old Flag*, vol. 1, p. 335.
26. *O.R.*, Serial 79, pp. 428, 528.
27. *Ibid.*, pp. 661–662.
28. *Ibid.*, pp. 919, 954–955.
29. *Ibid.*, p. 1003.
30. *Ibid.*, pp. 919, 952, 954–955.
31. *O.R.*, Serial 93, pp. 953–955.
32. *O.R.*, Serial 94, p. 61.
33. *O.R.*, Serial 79, pp. 661–662.
34. *O.R.*, Serial 41, pp. 427–429, 464, 469, 470, 799.

35. Wilson, *Under the Old Flag*, vol. 2, p. 61.
36. *Ibid.*, pp. 9–10; *O.R.*, Serial 93, pp. 954–955, 1179–80.
37. Although he served with distinction in the Civil War, Frederick W. Benteen is best known for his part in the disaster at the Battle of Little Bighorn on June 25, 1876.
38. Scott, *The Story of a Cavalry Regiment*, pp. 324, 328, 336.
39. *Ibid.*, p. 357; *O.R.*, Serial 94, pp. 144, 204, 210.
40. *O.R.*, Serial 94, pp. 82, 106–107.
41. *Ibid.*, p. 204; Scott, *Story of a Cavalry Regiment*, p. 359.
42. *O.R.*, Serial 94, p. 173.
43. Ambrose, *Upton and the Army*, pp. 40–43; Coffman, *The Old Army*, pp. 271–74.
44. Wilson, *Under the Old Flag*, vol. 1, p. 554.
45. Ambrose, *Upton and the Army*, pp. 40–43; Warner, *Generals in Blue*, pp. 519–520.
46. *O.R.*, Serial 93, pp. 844–873; Scott, *The Story of a Cavalry Regiment*, p. 357.
47. Scott, *Story of a Cavalry Regiment*, p. 357.
48. Wilson, *Under the Old Flag*, vol. 2, p. 65.
49. *Ibid.*, p. 73.
50. Horn, *Decisive Battle of Nashville*, pp. 24, 43, 44.
51. Wilson, *Under the Old Flag*, vol. 2, pp. 64, 98, 99.
52. *Battles and Leaders of the Civil War*, vol. 4, p. 454.
53. Wilson, *Under the Old Flag*, vol. 2, pp. 66–67.
54. *O.R.*, Serial 94, p. 15.
55. *Ibid.*, p. 17.
56. Wilson, *Under the Old Flag*, vol. 2, p. 59.
57. *O.R.*, Serial 94, pp. 17–18. Although Thomas's point is well taken, it hardly seems fair to say that Hood was taking advantage of the Federal handicap.
58. *Ibid.*, pp. 70–71. Federal commanders were always exaggerating the size of Forrest's command, probably because it helped to make his battlefield record a little more explainable. However, at no time during the Nashville campaign did Forrest have more than 5,000 men. See Wyeth, *That Devil Forrest*, p. 471; Wills, *A Battle from the Start*, p. 278.
59. Wilson, *Under the Old Flag*, vol. 2, pp. 80–81.
60. *O.R.*, Serial 94, p. 97.
61. *Ibid.*, p. 114.
62. *Ibid.*, pp. 114–115.
63. *Ibid.*, pp. 96, 114.
64. *Ibid.*, p. 96.
65. *Ibid.*, p. 116.
66. Wilson, *Under the Old Flag*, vol. 2, p. 99; Boynton, *Was General Thomas Slow at Nashville?*, p. 33.
67. Wilson, *Under the Old Flag*, vol. 2, p. 100.
68. *Ibid.* There is rather compelling evidence to suggest that Schofield was attempting to gain control of the Nashville command by undermining Thomas's position. See Horn, *Decisive Battle of Nashville*, pp. 53–57; Wilson, *Under the Old Flag*, vol. 2, pp. 100–102; McKinney, *Education in Violence*, p. 403.
69. Wilson, *Under the Old Flag*, vol. 2, p. 102.
70. *O.R.*, Serial 94, p. 143.
71. *Ibid.*
72. Wilson, *Under the Old Flag*, vol. 2, p. 99.
73. *O.R.*, Serial 94, p. 149.
74. Abbott, *Military Order of the Loyal Legion of the United States* (hereafter cited as *MOLLUS*), Nebraska Commandery, vol. 6, p. 238.

75. *O.R.*, Serial 94, p. 155.

76. *Ibid.*, p. 180.

77. *Ibid.*

78. *Ibid.*, p. 171.

79. *Ibid.*, p. 195; Horn, *Decisive Battle of Nashville*, pp. 60–61; Wilson, *Under the Old Flag*, vol. 2, pp. 60–61.

80. *O.R.*, Serial 93, pp. 37–38.

81. Wilson, *Under the Old Flag*, vol. 2, pp. 107–108.

82. *Ibid.*, p. 109. Wilson does not identify the friend to whom he was writing, but a fair guess would be Rawlins or Badeau, although the fact that he failed to reveal the name is curious. In other letters to both men he was not reluctant to identify them, so the possibility exists that the person was someone else on Grant's staff.

83. Davenport, *History of the Ninth Illinois Cavalry*, p. 155.

Nine: Nashville

1. Wilson, *Under the Old Flag*, vol. 2, p. 126.

2. Horn, *Decisive Battle of Nashville*, p. 73.

3. Davenport, *History of the Ninth Illinois Cavalry*, p. 157.

4. Horn, *Decisive Battle of Nashville*, p. 73.

5. *Battles and Leaders of the Civil War*, vol. 4, p. 457.

6. *O.R.*, Serial 93, p. 128; Horn, *Decisive Battle of Nashville*, p. 87.

7. Horn, *Decisive Battle of Nashville*, pp. 87–88; Catton, *The Coming Fury*, p. 460.

8. Horn, *Decisive Battle of Nashville*, p. 74.

9. *Ibid.*, pp. 75–77.

10. *Ibid.*, *O.R.*, Serial 93, pp. 504–505, 526, 528, 536–539.

11. *O.R.*, Serial 93, p. 536; Horn, *Decisive Battle of Nashville*, p. 76.

12. *O.R.*, Serial 93, p. 437; Wilson, *Under the Old Flag*, vol. 2, p. 109; Horn, *Decisive Battle of Nashville*, pp. 78–79.

13. *O.R.*, Serial 93, p. 344–345; *O.R.*, Serial 94, pp. 183–184; Horn, *Decisive Battle of Nashville*, pp. 62–65.

14. *O.R.*, Serial 93, p. 562; Wilson, *Under the Old Flag*, vol. 2, pp. 107–108.

15. *O.R.*, Serial 93, pp. 576–577; Wilson, *Under the Old Flag*, vol. 2, p. 108.

16. *O.R.*, Serial 93, pp. 55, 128, 434.

17. *Ibid.*, p. 129.

18. *Ibid.*, pp. 433–434.

19. *Ibid.*

20. *O.R.*, Serial 93, pp. 764–765; Horn, *Decisive Battle of Nashville*, p. 40.

21. *O.R.*, Serial 93, p. 709; Horn, *Decisive Battle of Nashville*, p. 91; Warner, *Generals in Gray*, p. 94.

22. *O.R.*, Serial 93, p. 722.

23. Wilson, *Under the Old Flag*, vol. 2, p. 110; Horn, *Decisive Battle of Nashville*, pp. 80–81.

24. *O.R.*, Serial 93, p. 577; Wilson, *Under the Old Flag*, vol. 2, p. 110.

25. *O.R.*, Serial 93, pp. 576–577.

26. *Ibid.*, pp. 437, 589; *MOLLUS*, vol. 6, p. 238.

27. *O.R.*, Serial 93, pp. 589–590.

28. *Ibid.*

29. *Ibid.*, pp. 434, 577; Horn, *Decisive Battle of Nashville*, p. 94.

30. *O.R.*, Serial 93, p. 438; *MOLLUS*, vol. 6, p. 239.

31. *O.R.*, Serial 93, p. 590.
32. *Ibid.*
33. Davenport, *History of the Ninth Illinois Cavalry*, p. 157.
34. *O.R.*, Serial 93, p. 590.
35. *Ibid.*, pp. 590–591.
36. *Ibid.*, p. 591.
37. Wilson, *Under the Old Flag*, vol. 2, p. 112.
38. *O.R.*, Serial 93, pp. 345, 434.
39. *Ibid.*, p. 722.
40. *Ibid.*, pp. 722–723.
41. *Ibid.*
42. *Ibid.*, p. 765.
43. *Ibid.*, p. 562.
44. Wilson, *Under the Old Flag*, vol. 2, p. 112; *O.R.*, Serial 93, p. 562.
45. *O.R.*, Serial 93, p. 765; Horn, *Decisive Battle of Nashville*, pp. 80–82.
46. *O.R.*, Serial 93, p. 599.
47. *Ibid.*, pp. 599–600.
48. *Ibid.*, p. 600.
49. *Ibid.*, pp. 600, 765.
50. *Ibid.*, p. 600.
51. *Ibid.*, pp. 600–601, 765.
52. *Ibid.*, p. 573.
53. Wilson, *Under the Old Flag*, vol. 2, p. 112.
54. *Ibid.*, pp. 112–113.
55. McKinney, *Education in Violence*, p. 137.
56. Wilson, *Under the Old Flag*, vol. 2, p. 114.
57. *O.R.*, Serial 94, pp. 194–195.
58. Horn, *Decisive Battle of Nashville*, p. 113; Wilson, *Under the Old Flag*, vol. 2, pp. 113–114; *O.R.*, Serial 94, p. 202; Cox, *Campaigns of the Civil War*, p. 116.
59. *O.R.*, Serial 93, p. 434; Horn, *Decisive Battle of Nashville*, p. 115.
60. *O.R.*, Serial 93, p. 130.
61. *Ibid.*, pp. 39, 505.
62. *Ibid.*, p. 505.
63. *Ibid.*, pp. 131, 505.
64. Horn, *Decisive Battle of Nashville*, p. 118.
65. *Ibid.*; *O.R.*, Serial 93, p. 749.
66. *O.R.*, Serial 93, p. 578.
67. *Ibid.*; Wilson, *Under the Old Flag*, vol. 2, p. 114.
68. *O.R.*, Serial 94, pp. 215–216.
69. Wilson, *Under the Old Flag*, vol. 2, p. 115. Wilson cites *O.R.*, Serial 94, p. 693, as the source for this statement, but no such dispatch appears at that location in *O.R.*, nor can it be found on any of the preceding or succeeding pages. Wilson claimed the dispatch was sent directly to Thomas without a copy being made, which supports the idea of its having been lost. On the other hand, the fact that there is a volume and page number in Wilson's citation would seem to rule out the possibility of the dispatch either having been inadvertently omitted or lost.
70. *Ibid.*, p. 125.
71. *Ibid.*, pp. 115–116.
72. *Ibid.*, pp. 116–117.
73. *O.R.*, Serial 93, pp. 435, 438, 439.
74. *Ibid.*, p. 438.

75. *Ibid.*, p.442.
76. *Ibid.*, p. 443.
77. *Ibid.*, pp. 577–578.
78. *Ibid.*, p. 591.
79. *Ibid.*, pp. 578–579; Wilson, *Under the Old Flag*, vol. 2, p. 117.
80. *O.R.*, Serial 93, p. 689; Horn, *Decisive Battle of Nashville*, pp. 144–147.
81. Horn, *Decisive Battle of Nashville*, pp. 145–146.
82. *O.R.*, Serial 93, p. 601.
83. *Ibid.*, pp. 133–134; Horn, *Decisive Battle of Nashville*, p. 149.
84. *Battles and Leaders of the Civil War*, vol. 4, p. 437.
85. *Ibid.*; *O.R.*, Serial 93, pp. 765–766.
86. Wilson, *Under the Old Flag*, vol. 2, p. 117–118.
87. *O.R.*, Serial 93, pp. 591–592.
88. Wilson, *Under the Old Flag*, vol. 2, pp. 124.
89. *Ibid.*, pp. 122–123. Twenty-five years after the war, Spalding returned Rucker's sword in what must have been an emotional moment for both men. See Sword, *Embrace an Angry Wind*, p. 389.
90. Wilson, *Under the Old Flag*, vol. 2, p. 124.
91. *Ibid.*, pp. 124–125.
92. *Ibid.*, pp. 124–126.
93. Sword, *Embrace an Angry Wind*, p. 391.

Ten: Pursuit

1. *O.R.*, Serial 94, p. 238.
2. Wilson, *Under the Old Flag*, vol. 2, p. 127.
3. *O.R.*, Serial 94, pp. 214–215, 218–219. Thomas's dispatch was dated 9:10 P.M., but it was probably close to midnight by the time it reached Wilson.
4. *Ibid.*, pp. 218–219, 237.
5. *O.R.*, Serial 93, p. 134; *O.R.*, Serial 94, pp. 234–236, 239–240.
6. *O.R.*, Serial 93, p. 689.
7. *Ibid.*, pp. 606, 607, 689.
8. *Ibid.*, pp. 565, 601, 690.
9. *Ibid.*, pp. 565, 601, 606, 607.
10. *Ibid.*, p. 690; Hattaway, *General Stephen D. Lee*, p. 146; Wilson, *Under the Old Flag*, vol. 2, p. 130.
11. *O.R.*, Serial 93, pp. 573–574.
12. *Ibid.*, p. 565.
13. *Ibid.*, p. 565; Wilson, *Under the Old Flag*, vol. 2, pp. 131–132.
14. *O.R.*, Serial 93, p. 696.
15. *Ibid.*, pp. 566, 696
16. *Ibid.*, pp. 696, 699.
17. Wilson, *Under the Old Flag*, vol. 2, p. 132.
18. *O.R.*, Serial 94, p. 238.
19. Wilson, *Under the Old Flag*, vol. 2, p. 173.
20. Sword, *Embrace an Angry Wind*, p. 400.
21. *O.R.*, Serial 93, p. 690.
22. *Ibid.*, pp. 592, 602, 607.
23. *O.R.*, Serial 94, pp. 257–258.
24. Wilson, *Under the Old Flag*, vol. 2, p. 137.

25. *O.R.*, Serial 94, p. 263.

26. *O.R.*, Serial 93, pp. 756–757; Horn, *Decisive Battle of Nashville*, p. 160.

27. *O.R.*, Serial 93, pp. 135, 566.

28. *Ibid.*, pp. 135, 566, 578.

29. *Ibid.*

30. *Ibid.*

31. *Ibid.*, pp. 578, 592–593.

32. *O.R.*, Serial 94, pp. 276–277.

33. *O.R.*, Serial 93, pp. 136, 593.

34. *Ibid.*, p. 757.

35. Horn, *Decisive Battle of Nashville*, p. 162; *O.R.*, Serial 93, p. 757.

36. *O.R.*, Serial 93, pp. 593, 757.

37. *Ibid.*, pp. 42, 136–137.

38. *Ibid.*, p. 574.

39. Comstock, *Indiana Volunteers (Ninth Cavalry)*, p. 40.

40. *O.R.*, Serial 93, pp. 593, 757–758.

41. *Ibid.*, pp. 567, 603; Wilson, *Under the Old Flag*, vol. 2, p. 140; Dyer, *Compendium*, vol. 2, p. 877.

42. *O.R.*, Serial 93, pp. 567, 603, 757; Wilson, *Under the Old Flag*, vol. 2, pp. 140–141.

43. *O.R.*, Serial 93, p. 608.

44. *Ibid.*, p. 758.

45. Wilson, *Under the Old Flag*, vol. 2, p. 141.

46. *O.R.*, Serial 93, p. 567.

47. Wilson, *Under the Old Flag*, vol. 2, p. 142; *O.R.*, Serial 94, pp. 231, 263, 389, 403.

48. *O.R.*, Serial 94, pp. 398, 408.

49. *Ibid.*, pp. 402–403.

50. *Ibid.*

51. *Ibid.*, p. 430.

52. *Ibid.*, pp. 446–447, 477.

53. *Ibid.*, pp. 540–542; *O.R.*, Serial 93, pp. 45, 641, 644.

54. *O.R.*, Serial 93, pp. 568, 571.

55. Wilson, *Under the Old Flag*, vol. 2, pp. 142–143.

56. *O.R.*, Serial 93, p. 568.

Eleven: "Lyon Was an Illusive Cuss"

1. *O.R.*, Serial 94, p. 149.

2. Wilson, *Under the Old Flag*, vol. 2, p. 144; Warner, *Generals in Gray*, p. 197.

3. *O.R.*, Serial 93, pp. 803, 1221.

4. *Ibid.*, p. 804.

5. *Ibid.*

6. *Ibid.*; *O.R.*, Serial 94, p. 153.

7. *O.R.*, Serial 94, pp. 79, 92, 128, 136.

8. *Official Atlas of the Civil War*, plate 150.

9. *O.R.*, Serial 94, pp. 136, 154, 166–167.

10. *Ibid.*, pp. 149–150.

11. *O.R.*, Serial 93, p. 556; *O.R.*, Serial 94, pp. 8, 47–48.

12. *O.R.*, Serial 93, pp. 795–796; *O.R.*, Serial 94, pp. 150, 175; Dyer, *Compendium*, pp. 462–463.

13. *O.R.*, Serial 93, p. 804.

14. *O.R.*, Serial 94, pp. 161–162, 174.
15. *O.R.*, Serial 93, pp. 792–796.
16. *Ibid.*, pp. 792, 796.
17. *Ibid.*, p. 804.
18. *Ibid.*, pp. 804, 1221.
19. *Ibid.*, p. 796.
20. *Ibid.*, p. 792.
21. *Ibid.*
22. *Ibid.*, pp. 797–798.
23. *Ibid.*, p. 792.
24. *Ibid.*, p. 796.
25. *Ibid.*, pp. 796, 804.
26. *Ibid.*, p. 792.
27. *Ibid.*
28. Wilson, *Under the Old Flag*, vol. 2, p. 170.
29. Wilson stated that McCook's two brigades numbered about 3,000, although the returns for the period suggest a higher figure. LaGrange's brigade, being understrength, would almost certainly have accounted for less than half the division's total strength, so at the outside, LaGrange's command almost certainly did not exceed 1,200. See Wilson, *Under the Old Flag*, vol. 2, pp. 143–144; *O.R.*, Serial 93, pp. 53–56.
30. *O.R.*, Serial 93, p. 794.
31. *Ibid.*
32. *Ibid.*, pp. 794, 465.
33. *Ibid.*, pp. 804–805. It is interesting to note that in his official report, LaGrange stated that even though his senior subordinates all approved of his strategy, he was not fully certain that his superiors would not censure him for his decision; he felt it might have been a mistake to wait for the main column. Back in May 1864, early in the Atlanta campaign, LaGrange had come up against a similar situation at Dalton, Georgia, and it had cost him heavily. It may well have been that the Dalton incident influenced his decision at Green River. See *O.R.*, Serial 73, p. 766.
34. *O.R.*, Serial 93, pp. 794–795.
35. *Ibid.*, p. 805.
36. *Ibid.*, pp. 793, 805.
37. *Ibid.*, p. 795.
38. *Ibid.*
39. *Ibid.*, p. 805.
40. *Ibid.*, pp. 795, 805.
41. *Ibid.*, p. 795.
42. *Ibid.*, p. 805.
43. *Ibid.*, pp. 799, 805.
44. *Ibid.*; Wilson, Column South, p. 254.
45. *O.R.*, Serial 93, p. 793; Wilson, *Under the Old Flag*, vol. 2, pp. 144–145.
46. *O.R.*, Serial 93, pp. 84–86.
47. *Ibid.*, p. 805.
48. *Ibid.*, p. 793.
49. *Ibid.*

Twelve: Winter Quarters

1. *O.R.*, Serial 103, p. 586.
2. *Ibid.*, p. 355; Wilson, *Under the Old Flag*, vol. 2, p. 164.

3. Wilson, *Under the Old Flag*, vol. 2, p. 164.

4. *O.R.*, Serial 94, p. 90; Scott, *The Story of a Cavalry Regiment*, p. 409. See also Chapter Seven of this volume.

5. McGee, *A History of the 72nd Indiana Volunteer Infantry*, p. 513. A froe is a wedge-shaped tool, which, among other things, was used to split shingles from a block of wood. See *O.R.*, Serial 93, p. 355.

6. *O.R.*, Serial 93, p. 704; *O.R.*, Serial 94, p. 627.

7. *O.R.*, Serial 93, p. 355.

8. *Ibid.*, pp. 586–587.

9. *O.R.*, Serial 94, p. 441.

10. *Ibid.*, pp. 441–442.

11. *Ibid.*, p. 609.

12. *Ibid.*, pp. 614, 620–621, 627, 628.

13. *Ibid.*, p. 621–622.

14. *O.R.*, Serial 103, pp. 638–639.

15. *Ibid.*, pp. 509–510, 522, 525.

16. Wilson, *Civil War Journals*, January 13, 1865.

17. *O.R.*, Serial 94, pp. 518–519.

18. *Ibid.*, p. 547.

19. *Ibid.*, p. 489.

20. *Ibid.*, p. 500.

21. *Ibid.*, pp. 516–518. The main reason for keeping Johnson's Sixth Division in Tennessee was to have a mounted force capable of dealing with guerrilla bands. Knowing this, one wonders why Wilson suggested dismounting Johnson's command.

22. *Ibid.*, p. 582.

23. *O.R.*, Serial 103, p. 585.

24. *O.R.*, Serial 94, p. 489; *O.R.*, Serial 103, p. 712.

25. *O.R.*, Serial 103, p. 597; *O.R.*, Serial 94, p. 610. It is interesting that the Federal government had no reservations about impressing horses in Tennessee and Kentucky during Hood's invasion. One can only assume that despite their political importance both Tennessee and Kentucky were not considered quite "northern" enough to exempt them from horse impressment.

26. *O.R.*, Serial 94, pp. 488–489; *O.R.*, Serial 103, p. 773; *O.R.*, Serial 93, pp. 1092–1093.

27. *O.R.*, Serial 103, pp. 596–597.

28. McGee, *A History of the 72nd Indiana Volunteer Infantry*, p. 505.

29. Dornblaser, *Saber Strokes*, pp. 204–205.

30. McGee, *A History of the 72nd Indiana Volunteer Infantry*, pp. 522–523.

31. Crofts, *History of the Service of 3rd Ohio Veteran Volunteer Cavalry*, p. 187.

32. Dornblaser, *Saber Strokes*, pp. 204–205.

33. Goddard and Goddard, *Tom Goddard's War*, p. 23.

34. Gilpin, *The Last Campaign*, p. 621.

35. McGee, *A History of the 72nd Indiana Volunteer Infantry*, pp. 511–512.

36. *Ibid.*, p. 499; Gilpin, *The Last Campaign*, p. 618; Scott, *Story of a Cavalry Regiment*, pp. 369, 426.

37. McGee, *A History of the 72nd Indiana Volunteer Infantry*, p. 512.

38. Scott, *Story of a Cavalry Regiment*, p. 426.

39. *Ibid.*

40. *Ibid.*, p. 428; Gilpin, *The Last Campaign*, p. 622.

41. Gilpin, *The Last Campaign*, pp. 656, 691, 696.

42. *O.R.*, Serial 103, pp. 679–680, 695–696, 722, 725.

43. *Ibid.*, pp. 689–690.
44. *Ibid.*, pp. 710–711.
45. Jones, *Yankee Blitzkrieg*, pp. 22–24; Wilson, *Under the Old Flag*, vol. 2, pp. 184–185; Hosea, "The Campaign of Selma," p. 81. Jones (*Yankee Blitzkrieg*) and Longacre (*From Union Stars to Top Hat*) identify Hosea as "Lewis." He is also so identified on the paper he read to the *Ohio Commandery of the Military Order of the Loyal Legion*. Jones also states that he was a West Point graduate. However, Heitman identifies him as "Louis," showing him serving as a private in the Sixth Ohio Infantry before being appointed an officer. See Heitman, *Historical Register*, volume 1, p. 543.
46. *O.R.*, Serial 103, pp. 725–726; McPherson, *Battle Cry of Freedom*, p. 622.
47. *O.R.*, Serial 103, pp. 708–709.
48. *Ibid.*
49. *Ibid.*, pp. 716–717.
50. *Ibid.*, pp. 789–790.
51. *Ibid.*, p. 355.
52. *Ibid.*; Wilson, *Under the Old Flag*, vol. 2, pp. 180–181.
53. *O.R.*, Serial 103, p. 355.
54. *Ibid.*, pp. 850–851; McKinney, *Education in Violence*, pp. 434–435.
55. *O.R.*, Serial 103, p. 356.
56. *Ibid.*, pp. 402–404.
57. *Ibid.*, pp. 402–403.
58. *Ibid.*, p. 356.
59. *Ibid.*
60. *Ibid.*, p. 404.
61. Wilson, *Under the Old Flag*, vol. 2, pp. 178–179.
62. *O.R.*, Serial 103, p. 777.
63. *Ibid.*, pp. 355–356.
64. *Ibid.*, pp. 356, 773–774; McGee, *A History of the 72nd Indiana Volunteer Infantry*, p. 521.
65. Wilson, *Under the Old Flag*, vol. 2, p. 180.
66. *O.R.*, Serial 103, p. 812.
67. *Ibid.*, p. 807.
68. *Ibid.*, p. 825.
69. *Ibid.*, p. 855.
70. *Ibid.*, pp. 908–909.
71. *O.R.*, Serial 104, pp. 29, 38.

Thirteen: In the Confederate Camp

1. Wills, *A Battle from the Start*, pp. 301–302.
2. *Battles and Leaders of the Civil War*, vol. 4, p. 437.
3. *O.R.*, Serial 103, pp. 929, 939, 949.
4. Wyeth, *That Devil Forrest*, p. 512.
5. Henry, *First with the Most*, p. 418.
6. Wyeth, *That Devil Forrest*, p. 511.
7. *Ibid.* Hood claimed that 9,000 men deserted between Tupelo and North Carolina. See *Battles and Leaders of the Civil War*, vol. 4, p. 471.
8. Wyeth, *That Devil Forrest*, p. 521.
9. *Ibid.*, pp. 512–513; Wills, *A Battle from the Start*, pp. 300.
10. Wyeth, *That Devil Forrest*, p. 513.

11. *Ibid.*
12. Henry, *First with the Most*, pp. 425–426.
13. Wyeth, *That Devil Forrest*, p. 513.
14. Boatner, *The Civil War Dictionary*, p. 477.
15. Wills, *A Battle from the Start*, p. 217.
16. Wyeth, *That Devil Forrest*, p. 516.
17. Henry, *First with the Most*, p. 427. This was a column under the command of General Fred Steele. See Jones, *Yankee Blitzkrieg*, p. 51.
18. Henry, *First with the Most*, p. 428.
19. Wyeth, *That Devil Forrest*, p. 520.

Fourteen: South to Selma

1. *O.R.,* Serial 104, p. 247.
2. Curry, *Four Years in the Saddle*, p. 99.
3. Scott, *Story of a Cavalry Regiment*, p. 431.
4. *O.R.,* Serial 103, p. 356; *O.R.,* Serial 104, p. 28.
5. *O.R.,* Serial 103, p. 356.
6. McGee, *A History of the 72nd Indiana Volunteer Infantry*, p. 528.
7. Wilson, *Under the Old Flag*, vol. 2, pp. 202–203.
8. *O.R.,* Serial 103, pp. 356–357.
9. *Ibid.,* p. 403.
10. *Ibid.,* p. 437.
11. *Ibid.,* p. 416.
12. *Ibid.,* p. 419.
13. Wilson, *Under the Old Flag*, vol. 2, p. 193.
14. Gilpin, *The Last Campaign*, p. 629.
15. *O.R.,* Serial 103, pp. 410–411.
16. *Ibid.,* p. 357.
17. Gilpin, *The Last Campaign*, p. 631.
18. *Ibid.*
19. Wilson, *Under the Old Flag*, vol. 2, p. 203. One account states that the Fourth Michigan lost one man and 40 horses. See Vale, *Minty and the Cavalry*, p. 428.
20. *O.R.,* Serial 104, p. 111.
21. *O.R.,* Serial 103, p. 503.
22. Gilpin, *The Last Campaign*, p. 632.
23. *O.R.,* Serial 104, p. 125.
24. *Ibid.*
25. Scott, *Story of a Cavalry Regiment*, p. 432; Gilpin, *The Last Campaign*, p. 632; *O.R.,* Serial 103, p. 472.
26. McGee, *A History of the 72nd Indiana Volunteer Infantry*, p. 534.
27. Jones, *Yankee Blitzkrieg*, p. 57.
28. Scott, *Story of a Cavalry Regiment*, p. 433.
29. McGee, *A History of the 72nd Indiana Volunteer Infantry*, pp. 535–536.
30. *O.R.,* Serial 103, pp. 357, 708–709.
31. *Ibid.,* p. 419. I have chosen to use the spellings "Cahaba" and "Centreville" since they appear this way on maps and in most sources. Wilson, however, uses "Centerville" and "Cahawba."
32. *O.R.,* Serial 103, pp. 359, 500.
33. *Ibid.,* pp. 357–358, 472, 479, 500, 503.

34. *Ibid.*, p. 358.

35. *Ibid.*

36. *Ibid.*, p. 359.

37. *Ibid.*; Wyeth, *That Devil Forrest*, pp. 530–531.

38. Wyeth, *That Devil Forrest*, p. 530.

39. *O.R.*, Serial 103, p. 437; Wilson, *Under the Old Flag*, vol. 2, p. 217.

40. Wilson, *Under the Old Flag*, vol. 2, p. 244.

41. *O.R.*, Serial 103, p. 359.

42. Wilson, *Under the Old Flag*, vol. 2, pp. 219–220.

43. *O.R.*, Serial 103, p. 359; Wilson, *Under the Old Flag*, vol. 2, p. 221.

44. Wilson, *Under the Old Flag*, vol. 2, pp. 222–225; *O.R.*, Serial 103, pp. 359–360.

45. *O.R.*, Serial 103, pp. 359–360. Long felt that his division alone was not strong enough to assault the Selma works and supposedly told Wilson that Upton's division should follow behind in support. Long claimed that Wilson initially agreed to this, then later changed his mind. See *O.R.*, Serial 103, p. 438.

46. *Ibid.*, p. 359.

47. *Ibid.*, pp. 360, 361, 438; Wilson, *Under the Old Flag*, vol. 2, pp. 221–222.

48. Wilson estimated 5,000 (*O.R.*, Serial 103, p. 359), but others thought 6,000–8,000. Assuming that Forrest had 2,000 men at Ebenezer Church, it does not seem likely he could have mustered an additional 4,000–6,000 men from the city itself. See Wyeth, *That Devil Forrest*, p. 534; Scott, *Story of a Cavalry Regiment*, p. 448.

49. *O.R.*, Serial 103, pp. 248, 416–417, 427.

50. Wyeth, *That Devil Forrest*, p. 535; *O.R.*, Serial 103, pp. 438, 447.

51. *O.R.*, Serial 103, pp. 438–439.

52. *Ibid.*, p. 454.

53. *Ibid.*, p. 361; Wilson, *Under the Old Flag*, vol. 2, p. 228.

54. *O.R.*, Serial 103, pp. 438–439, 447–448, 452, 454; Evans, *Sherman's Horsemen*, pp. 21, 408.

55. *O.R.*, Serial 103, p. 480; Scott, *Story of a Cavalry Regiment*, pp. 449–450.

56. Scott, *Story of a Cavalry Regiment*, pp. 449–450.

57. Wilson, *Under the Old Flag*, vol. 2, p. 230.

58. *Ibid. O.R.*, Serial 103, p. 470.

59. Scott, *Story of a Cavalry Regiment*, p. 456; Vale, *Minty and the Cavalry*, p. 431; *O.R.*, Serial 103, p. 480.

60. *O.R.*, Serial 103, p. 360.

61. Wyeth, *That Devil Forrest*, p. 536.

62. Dornblaser, *Saber Strokes*, p. 212.

63. Wilson, *Under the Old Flag*, vol. 2, pp. 232–234.

64. Cunningham, *The Confederate Veteran*, vol. 19, p. 67.

65. Curry, *Four Years in the Saddle*, p. 24; Gilpin, *The Last Campaign*, p. 640.

66. Gilpin, *The Last Campaign*, p. 640.

67. *O.R.*, Serial 103, p. 360.

68. Wilson, *Under the Old Flag*, vol. 2, p. 234.

Fifteen: Selma to Montgomery

1. *O.R.*, Serial 104, p. 347.

2. McGee, *A History of the 72nd Indiana Volunteer Infantry*, p. 561; Gilpin, *The Last Campaign*, p. 641.

3. *O.R.*, Serial 103, p. 347.

4. Gilpin, *The Last Campaign*, pp. 641–642.

5. *Confederate Veteran*, vol. 19, p. 67; Wilson, *Under the Old Flag*, vol. 2, pp. 237–238.

6. *Historical Sketch of the Chicago Board of Trade Battery*, p. 31.

7. Rogers, "A Wisconsin Raider," p. 27.

8. Phillips, *Reminiscences*, p. 5.

9. Wilson, *Under the Old Flag*, vol. 2, p. 236.

10. Gilpin, *The Last Campaign*, p. 645.

11. *Ibid.*, pp. 645–646, 672.

12. *O.R.*, Serial 103, p. 361; *O.R.*, Serial 104, p. 347; Wilson, *Under the Old Flag*, vol. 2, pp. 238–239. In his autobiography, Wilson states that he deemed it wiser to send one courier to Canby, a man who knew the country and would be able to get through. Accordingly, a black man, Charles Marven was reportedly given a dispatch written on tissue paper and concealed in his clothing. After making certain that Marven understood the contents perfectly, Wilson sent him on his way. Marven started on April 4, floated down the Alabama River, and delivered the message to Canby several days later. Marven supposedly received $200 for his services.

13. *O.R.*, Serial 103, p. 361.

14. *O.R.*, Serial 104, pp. 201–202, 217.

15. *Ibid.*, pp. 218–219.

16. *Ibid.*, p. 218.

17. *Ibid.*, p. 239.

18. *O.R.*, Serial 103, pp. 386, 391

19. Wilson, *Under the Old Flag*, vol. 2, pp. 241–242.

20. *Ibid.*, pp. 244–245.

21. *O.R.*, Serial 103, pp. 362, 412.

22. *Ibid.*, pp. 412, 442.

23. *Ibid.*, pp. 362, 412, 442, 473; Wilson, *Under the Old Flag*, vol. 2, pp. 245–246.

24. Scott, *Story of a Cavalry Regiment*, pp. 468–469.

25. *Ibid.*, p. 469.

26. *O.R.*, Serial 103, p. 412.

27. *Ibid.*, p. 407.

28. Wilson, *Under the Old Flag*, vol. 2, pp. 247–248.

29. *O.R.*, Serial 103, p. 362.

30. Wilson, *Under the Old Flag*, vol. 2, p. 248.

31. *O.R.*, Serial 103, pp. 362, 442.

32. *Ibid.*, pp. 362, 436, 442.

33. Scott, *Story of a Cavalry Regiment*, pp. 472–473.

34. *O.R.*, Serial 103, p. 433.

35. Wilson, *Under the Old Flag*, vol. 2, p. 250.

36. *Ibid.*, p. 251.

37. *Ibid.*, pp. 251–252. As a man firmly opposed to drinking, Wilson probably applauded this action. See also Longacre, *From Union Stars to Top Hat*, pp. 38–39.

38. *O.R.*, Serial 103, p. 363; Scott, *Story of a Cavalry Regiment*, p. 475; Wilson, *Under the Old Flag*, vol. 2, p. 250; Jones, *Yankee Blitzkrieg*, pp. 112–114.

39. *O.R.*, Serial 103, pp. 362–363, 407.

40. *Ibid.*, p. 434; Wilson, *Under the Old Flag*, vol. 2, p. 253; Scott, *Story of a Cavalry Regiment*, pp. 475–476.

41. *O.R.*, Serial 103, p. 434.

42. *O.R.*, Serial 104, p. 344.

43. *Ibid.*, pp. 344, 376.

44. *Ibid.*, p. 347.

45. Wilson, *Under the Old Flag*, vol. 2, p. 254; Jones, *Yankee Blitzkrieg*, p. 105.

46. Wilson, *Under the Old Flag*, vol. 2, p. 254. Wilson must have attached some credence to the rumors because in his April 13 letter to Thomas he referred to the fall of Richmond and the defeat of Lee. Also, Montgomery newspapers carried stories describing how Lee had suffered a disastrous setback in Virginia. The important point here is that without official orders to the contrary, Wilson had no choice but to press ahead. See also Wilson, "How Jefferson Davis Was Overtaken," pp. 564–567.

Sixteen: Montgomery to Columbus

1. *O.R.*, Serial 104, p. 383.

2. *O.R.*, Serial 103, p. 363.

3. *Ibid.*, pp. 428, 434. Of his three division commanders, Wilson was unquestionably partial to Upton. They were kindred spirits and alike in many ways. He also seems to have had much respect for Eli Long. McCook, on the other hand, usually a competent commander, had been known to lose his poise at times, as during the Atlanta campaign the previous summer. Wilson certainly knew of this, but it seems not to have enjoined him from dispatching McCook on independent missions, this being the second of the campaign. See Evans, *Sherman's Horsemen*, pp. 264–265.

4. *O.R.*, Serial 103, p. 401; Wilson, *Under the Old Flag*, vol. 2, p. 255.

5. Wilson, *Under the Old Flag*, vol. 2, pp. 256–257.

6. *O.R.*, Serial 103, p. 363; Wilson, *Under the Old Flag*, vol. 2, p. 258.

7. *O.R.*, Serial 103, p. 501; Scott, *Story of a Cavalry Regiment*, pp. 487–488.

8. *O.R.*, Serial 103, pp. 474, 480; Scott, *Story of a Cavalry Regiment*, pp. 482–484; Jones, *Yankee Blitzkrieg*, pp. 127–128.

9. Warner, *Generals in Gray*, p. 55; Scott, *Story of a Cavalry Regiment*, p. 484.

10. *O.R.*, Serial 103, p. 364; Scott, *Story of a Cavalry Regiment*, p. 486. *The Columbus Enquirer* stated that the defenders consisted of detachments of Buford's and Wofford's cavalry units, some reserves of the Georgia line and a few militia, all together some 2,000 men. See *The Columbus Enquirer*, June 27, 1865.

11. Worsley, *Columbus on the Chattahoochee*, p. 294.

12. *O.R.*, Serial 103, p. 484.

13. *Ibid.*; Scott, *Story of a Cavalry Regiment*, p. 490.

14. *O.R.*, Serial 103, pp. 363, 474; Scott, *Story of a Cavalry Regiment*, p. 490.

15. *O.R.*, Serial 103, pp. 474, 478; Scott, *Story of a Cavalry Regiment*, p. 490; Ambrose, *Upton and the Army*, pp. 48–49.

16. *O.R.*, Serial 103, p. 363; Wilson, *Under the Old Flag*, vol. 2, p. 259.

17. Wilson, *Under the Old Flag*, vol. 2, p. 259.

18. *Ibid.*, p. 260. A slightly different version appears in the Official Records. Wilson's report states that Upton proposed a night assault and that Wilson concurred in that judgment. Upton's report, however, makes no mention of this. Scott's version is essentially the same as that found in Wilson's memoirs. See *O.R.*, Serial 103, pp. 363, 474; Scott, *Story of a Cavalry Regiment*, p. 492.

19. *O.R.*, Serial 103, p. 363; Scott, *Story of a Cavalry Regiment*, p. 494.

20. Scott, *Story of a Cavalry Regiment*, p. 494.

21. Eleven years later, Fred Benteen played a key role in the controversial Battle of Little Bighorn. Emory Upton once described Benteen as the "most gallant man he'd ever seen under fire." Gilpin, *The Last Campaign*, p. 671.

22. Scott, *Story of a Cavalry Regiment*, p. 495.

23. *Ibid.*, pp. 496–498.

24. *Ibid.*, pp. 498–499.
25. *Ibid.*; Wilson, *Under the Old Flag*, vol. 2, p. 265.
26. Worsley, *Columbus on the Chattahoochee*, p. 294; Scott, *Story of a Cavalry Regiment*, p. 500.
27. Gilpin, *The Last Campaign*, p. 654.
28. *O.R.*, Serial 103, p. 428.
29. *Ibid.*, pp. 428, 432.
30. *Ibid.*, pp. 428–429.
31. *Ibid.*; Warner, *Generals in Gray*, p. 313.
32. *O.R.*, Serial 103, p. 429.
33. *Ibid.*, pp. 429–435; Waterman, "The Rosendale Squad," p. 30.
34. *O.R.*, Serial 103, p. 429.
35. Waterman, "The Rosendale Squad," p. 30.
36. Love, *Wisconsin in the War*, pp. 884–885.
37. *O.R.*, Serial 103, p. 429.
38. *Ibid.*
39. *O.R.*, Serial 104, pp. 367, 379.
40. *O.R.*, Serial 103, pp. 387, 429.
41. Wilson, *Under the Old Flag*, vol. 2, p. 265.

Seventeen: Columbus to Macon

1. *O.R.*, Serial 104, p. 416.
2. *O.R.*, Serial 103, pp. 486–487; Wilson, *Under the Old Flag*, vol. 2, p. 265; Scott, *Story of a Cavalry Regiment*, pp. 501–502.
3. Wilson, *Under the Old Flag*, vol. 2, p. 268.
4. *Ibid.*
5. *O.R.*, Serial 104, p. 383.
6. *O.R.*, Serial 103, pp. 365, 442.
7. *Ibid.*, p. 465.
8. *Ibid.*
9. *Ibid.*, pp. 465–466.
10. *Ibid.*, pp. 442, 466.
11. McGee, *A History of the 72nd Indiana Volunteer Infantry*, pp. 583–585; Jones, *Yankee Blitzkrieg*, pp. 161–163.
12. *O.R.*, Serial 103, pp. 442–443, 457.
13. *Ibid.*, p. 457; Jones, *Yankee Blitzkrieg*, pp. 162–163.
14. *O.R.*, Serial 103, pp. 457–458; Jones, *Yankee Blitzkrieg*, pp. 162–163.
15. *O.R.*, Serial 103, pp. 365, 443, 458.
16. *Ibid.*, p. 366; Wilson, *Under the Old Flag*, vol. 2, p. 278.
17. *O.R.*, Serial, 103, pp. 443, 458.
18. *Ibid.*, p. 458.
19. *Ibid.*
20. *Ibid.*, p. 459.
21. *Ibid.*
22. *Ibid.*, p. 366.
23. *Ibid.*; Wilson, *Under the Old Flag*, vol. 2, p. 281.
24. *O.R.*, Serial 103, p. 367.
25. *Ibid.*; Wilson, *Under the Old Flag*, vol. 2, pp. 283–284.
26. *O.R.*, Serial 104, p. 426.

27. *Ibid.*
28. Harwell, *The Journal of a Confederate War Nurse*, p. 275.
29. Gilpin, *The Last Campaign*, p. 657.
30. Scott, *Story of a Cavalry Regiment*, p. 521.

Eighteen: Croxton's Odyssey

1. *O.R.*, Serial 103, p. 368.
2. *Ibid.*, p. 419.
3. *Ibid.*, pp. 357, 419.
4. *Ibid.*, pp. 357, 419–420; Wilson, *Under the Old Flag*, vol. 2, p. 144.
5. *O.R.*, Serial 103, pp. 419–420; Miller, *Croxton's Raid*, p. 29.
6. *O.R.*, Serial 103, pp. 419–420.
7. *Ibid.*, p. 357; Wilson, *Under the Old Flag*, vol. 2, p. 205.
8. *O.R.*, Serial 103, p. 420.
9. *Ibid.*
10. *Ibid.*
11. *Ibid.*; Wyeth, *That Devil Forrest*, p. 523.
12. *O.R.*, Serial 103, p. 420.
13. *Ibid.*, p. 421; Miller, *Croxton's Raid*, pp. 30–31.
14. *Ibid.*, pp. 416–417; Wyeth, *That Devil Forrest*, pp. 523–527.
15. Wyeth, *That Devil Forrest*, pp. 526–528; *O.R.*, Serial 103, p. 421.
16. *O.R.*, Serial 103, p. 421; Jones, *Yankee Blitzkrieg*, pp. 146–147.
17. Jones, *Yankee Blitzkrieg*, pp. 146–147.
18. *Ibid.*
19. *Ibid.*
20. *Ibid.*, pp. 421, 426; Miller, *Croxton's Raid*, pp. 36–38; Jones, *Yankee Blitzkrieg*, pp. 146–149.
21. Miller, *Croxton's Raid*, pp. 40–44; Jones, *Yankee Blitzkrieg*, p. 150. It is interesting to note that Croxton himself died of consumption (tuberculosis) nine years later. See Warner, *Generals in Blue*, p. 104.
22. *O.R.*, Serial 103, pp. 421, 426; Jones, *Yankee Blitzkrieg*, pp. 150–152.
23. *O.R.*, Serial 103, p. 422; Wilson, *Under the Old Flag*, vol. 2, p. 206; Miller, *Croxton's Raid*, p. 54.
24. *O.R.*, Serial 103, p. 422; Miller, *Croxton's Raid*, pp. 53–56.
25. *O.R.*, Serial 103, pp. 422, 425–426; Miller, *Croxton's Raid*, pp. 56–57.
26. *O.R.*, Serial 103, p. 422.
27. *Ibid.*
28. *Ibid.*, p. 422; Miller, *Croxton's Raid*, pp. 59–60; Jones, *Yankee Blitzkrieg*, pp. 154–155.
29. *O.R.*, Serial 103, pp. 422–423; Miller, *Croxton's Raid*, pp. 65–66.
30. *O.R.*, Serial 103, p. 423.
31. *Ibid.*
32. Wyeth, *That Devil Forrest*, p. 524.
33. *O.R.*, Serial 103, p. 423.
34. *Ibid.*
35. *Ibid.*
36. *Ibid.*
37. *Ibid.*

38. *Ibid.*

39. *Ibid.*

40. *Ibid.*, p. 424.

Nineteen: The Pursuit and Capture of Jefferson Davis

1. *O.R.*, Serial 104, p. 732.

2. Long, *The Civil War Day by Day*, pp. 663–664; Vandiver, *Their Tattered Flags*, p. 299; Davis, *Jefferson Davis*, pp. 604–605.

3. Long, *The Civil War Day by Day*, p. 664; Davis, *Jefferson Davis*, pp. 606–607.

4. Vandiver, *Their Tattered Flags*, p. 306; Davis, *Jefferson Davis*, pp. 629–630. One rumor circulating among the Federals at that time was to the effect that Davis was bound for Mexico and had promised every man who accompanied him a bonus of $400 in gold. See *O.R.*, Serial 103, p. 608.

5. Long, *The Civil War Day by Day*, pp. 677, 683; Davis, *Jefferson Davis*, pp. 625–626.

6. Duke, *History of Morgan's Cavalry*, pp. 575–576; Wilson, "How Jefferson Davis Was Overtaken," pp. 554–555; Davis, *Jefferson Davis*, p. 633; Long, *The Civil War Day by Day*, pp. 685–687. Speculation as to the size of the Confederate treasury ranged as high as $8 million. See *O.R.*, Serial 104, p. 593.

7. Wilson, "How Jefferson Davis Was Overtaken," p. 564.

8. *Ibid.*, pp. 567–568.

9. *O.R.*, Serial 103, p. 372.

10. *Ibid.*

11. *Ibid.*, pp. 372, 546–548; Wilson, "How Jefferson Davis Was Overtaken," p. 571.

12. Wilson, "How Jefferson Davis Was Overtaken," pp. 568–569; *O.R.*, Serial 103, p. 373.

13. *O.R.*, Serial 103, pp. 374, 517.

14. *Ibid.*, p. 374.

15. *Ibid.*

16. *Ibid.*, pp. 517–518.

17. *Ibid.*

18. *Ibid.*, p. 518.

19. *Ibid.*

20. *Ibid.*, pp. 518, 535.

21. *Ibid.*, pp. 518–519.

22. *Ibid.*, p. 519.

23. *Ibid.*

24. *Ibid.*, pp. 534–535.

25. *Ibid.*, p. 535. Pritchard does not elaborate on what these additional facts were. Wilson tried to defend the zeal and aggressiveness of both officers, pointing out that the dissolution of the Cavalry Corps occurred so quickly after the apprehension of Davis that there was no time to conduct a serious inquiry. See Wilson, "How Jefferson Davis Was Overtaken," p. 576. It is difficult to imagine that Pritchard, being so close, was willing to pass up an opportunity for Michigan to share in the glory of Davis's capture. Despite his official response that the train might elude Harnden, Pritchard must have known that Harnden would soon make contact. Yet he made no effort to apprise Harnden of his plan.

26. *Ibid.*, p. 535. Given the speech patterns and mode of dress, some of which must

still have looked like Union uniforms, one wonders how the local citizenry could have been persuaded to believe that these Michigan men were Confederates.

27. *Ibid.*, pp. 535–536; Wilson, "How Jefferson Davis Was Overtaken," p. 576.

28. *Ibid.*, p. 536.

29. *Ibid.*

30. *Ibid.*

31. *Ibid.*, pp. 519–520, 527–528.

32. *Ibid.*, p. 537.

33. Wilson, "How Jefferson Davis Was Overtaken," pp. 554–589; *O.R.*, Serial 103, p. 537; Wilson, *Under the Old Flag*, vol. 2, pp. 331–334; Longacre, *Union Stars to Top Hat*, p. 224.

34. *O.R.*, Serial 103, p. 537.

35. *Ibid.* As far as the reward is concerned, one account states that Wilson, Pritchard, Harnden, and Yoeman each received $3,000, with the balance of the $100,000 being equally divided among the members of the First Wisconsin and Fourth Michigan. See Robertson, *Michigan in the War*, p. 684.

36. Longacre, *From Union Stars to Top Hat*, pp. 223–224; Wilson, *Under the Old Flag*, vol. 2, pp. 335–342; Davis, *Jefferson Davis*, pp. 641–644.

Twenty: Epilogue

1. Wilson, *Under the Old Flag*, vol. 2, p. 371.

2. *O.R.*, Serial 104, pp. 321, 427–428, 504, 909.

3. *Ibid.*, pp. 552, 568–569.

4. Wilson, *Under the Old Flag*, vol. 2, p. 364; *O.R.*, Serial 104, p. 903.

5. *O.R.*, Serial 104, pp. 902, 909–910.

6. *Ibid.*, p. 1023.

7. *Ibid.*, pp. 1035–1036.

8. *Ibid.*, p. 1059.

9. Wilson, *Under the Old Flag*, vol. 2, pp. 346, 364.

10. Dyer, *Compendium*, vol. 3, pp. 1021–1666.

11. Wilson, *Under the Old Flag*, vol. 2, p. 365.

12. *Ibid.*, p. 120.

13. Longacre, *From Union Stars to Top Hat*, pp. 215–216.

14. Denison, *History of Cavalry*, p. 478.

Bibliography

Abbott, Othman. "The Last Battle of Nashville." *Military Order of the Loyal Legion of the United States*, Nebraska Commandery, vol. 6.

Ambrose, Stephen. *Upton and the Army*. Baton Rouge: Louisiana State University Press, 1964.

Angle, Paul M., ed. *Three Years in the Army of the Cumberland: The Letters and Diaries of Major James A. Connolly*. Bloomington: Indiana University Press, 1959.

Battles and Leaders of the Civil War, 4 vols. Edison, N.J.: Castle Reprint.

Boatner, Mark M. *The Civil War Dictionary*. New York: Vintage Civil War Library, 1991.

Boynton, Henry V. *Was General Thomas Slow at Nashville?* New York: Francis P. Harper, 1896.

Brown, Charles O. "The Battle of Selma." Copy of original manuscript furnished by Illinois State Historical Society.

Cate, Wirt A. *Two Soldiers: The Campaign Diaries of Thomas J. Key and Robert J. Campbell*. Chapel Hill: University of North Carolina Press, 1938.

Catton, Bruce. *The Coming Fury*. New York: Doubleday, 1961.

Coffman, Edward M. *The Old Army: A Portrait of the American Army in Peacetime, 1784–1898*. New York: Oxford University Press, 1986.

Comstock, Daniel. *One Hundred and Twenty-First Regiment of Indiana Volunteers (Ninth Cavalry)*. Richmond, Ind.: J. M. Coe, 1890.

Connelly, Thomas L. *Autumn of Glory: The Army of Tennessee, 1862–1865*. Baton Rouge: Louisiana State University Press, 1971.

Cox, Jacob D. *Campaigns of the Civil War: The March to the Sea—Franklin and Nashville*. New York: Charles Scribner's Sons, 1882.

Crofts, Thomas. *History of the Service of the 3rd Ohio Veteran Volunteer Cavalry*. Columbus, Ohio: Stoneman Press, 1910.

Cunningham, S. A., and Edith D. Pope, eds. *Confederate Veteran*, 40 vols. Nashville, Tenn.: S.A. Cunningham, 1893–1932.

Curry, William L. *Four Years in the Saddle: History of the First Regiment, Ohio Volunteer Cavalry*. Columbus, Ohio: Champlin, 1898.

Davenport, E. A. *History of the Ninth Regiment of Illinois Cavalry Volunteers*. Chicago: n.p., 1888.

Davis, William C. *Jefferson Davis: The Man and His Hour*. New York: HarperCollins, 1991.

Denison, Colonel George. *A History of Cavalry*, 2d ed. London: Macmillan, 1878.

Dornblaser, Thomas Franklin. *Saber Strokes of the Pennsylvania Dragoons in the War of 1861–1865*. Philadelphia, Pa.: Lutheran Publication Society, 1884.

Duke, Basil W. *A History of Morgan's Cavalry*. Bloomington: Indiana University Press, 1960.

Dyer, Frederick H. *A Compendium of the War of the Rebellion*. New York: Thomas Yoseloff, 1959.

Ensminger, M. E. *Horses and Horsemanship*. Danville, Ill.: Interstate Printers and Publishers, 1963.

Evans, David. *Sherman's Horsemen: Union Cavalry Operations in the Atlanta Campaign*. Bloomington: Indiana University Press, 1996.

Fisher, John E. *They Rode with Forrest and Wheeler: A Chronicle of Five Tennessee Brothers' Service in the Confederate Western Cavalry*. Jefferson, N.C.: McFarland, 1995.

The *Georgia Enquirer* (Columbus), June 27, 1865.

Gilpin, E. N. *The Last Campaign: A Cavalryman's Journal*. Leavenworth, Kans.: The Press of Ketcheson Printing Company, n.d. Reprint from the *Journal of the U.S. Cavalry Association*.

Goddard, Mary, and Guy Goddard. *Tom Goddard's War: Being an Account of the Union Army Service of Thomas Miller Goddard, Company E Third Iowa Veteran Volunteer Cavalry*. Manuscript copy in author's possession.

Grant, Ulysses S. *Personal Memoirs of U.S. Grant*. Cleveland, Ohio: World, 1952.

Groom, Winston. *Shrouds of Glory: From Atlanta to Nashville: The Last Great Campaign of the Civil War*. New York: Pocket, 1995.

Harwell, Richard B., ed. *Kate: The Journal of a Confederate War Nurse*. Baton Rouge: Louisiana State University Press, 1959.

Hattaway, Herman. *General Stephen D. Lee*. Jackson: University Press of Mississippi, 1976.

Heitman, Francis B. *Historical Register and Dictionary of the United States Army, from Its Organization, September 29, 1789 to March 2, 1903*. Urbana: University of Illinois Press, 1965.

Henry, Robert Selph. *First with the Most: Forrest*. Indianapolis, Ind.: Bobbs-Merrill, 1944.

Historical Sketch of the Chicago Board of Trade Battery, Horse Artillery, Illinois Volunteers. Chicago: n.p., 1902.

Hood, John Bell. *Advance and Retreat*. Secaucus, N.J.: Blue and Grey, 1985.

Horn, Stanley. *The Army of Tennessee*. Norman: University of Oklahoma Press, 1952.

_____. *The Decisive Battle of Nashville*. Baton Rouge: Louisiana State University Press, 1957.

Hosea, Lewis M. "The Campaign of Selma." *Sketches of War History, 1861–1865, Papers Read Before the Ohio Commandery of the Military Order of the Loyal Region of the United States*, vol. 1. Cincinnati, Ohio: 1888.

_____. "Some Side Lights on the War for the Union." *Papers Read Before the Ohio Commandery of the Military Order of the Loyal Legion of the United States*. Cleveland, Ohio, 1912.

Johnson, Robert Underwood, and Clarence Buel, eds. *Battles and Leaders of the Civil War, Being for the Most Part Contributions by Union and Confederate Officers. Based Upon "The Century War Series."* 4 vols. Edison N.J.: Castle. (reprint), n.d.

Jones, James Pickett. *Yankee Blitzkrieg: Wilson's Raid Through Alabama and Georgia*. Athens: University of Georgia Press, 1976.

_____, ed. "Your Left Arm: James H. Wilson's Letters to Adam Badeau." *Civil War History*, vol. 12, no. 3, September 1966.

Keenan, Jerry. "Wilson's Selma Raid." *Civil War Times Illustrated*, vol. I, no. 9, January 1963, pp. 37–44.

King, Spencer B. "April in Macon." *The Georgia Review*, vol. 14, no. 2, summer 1960.

Lewis, Lloyd. *Sherman, Fighting Prophet*. New York: Harcourt, Brace, 1958

Livermore, Thomas L. *Numbers and Losses in the Civil War*. Bloomington: Indiana University Press, 1957.

Long, E. B. *The Civil War Day by Day: An Almanac—1861–1865*. New York: Doubleday, 1971.

Longacre, Edward G. *From Union Stars to Top Hat: A Biography of the Extraordinary General James Harrison Wilson*. Harrisburg, Pa.: Stackpole, 1972.

Losson, Christopher. *Tennessee's Forgotten Warriors: Frank Cheatham and His Confederate Division*. Knoxville, Tenn.: University of Tennessee Press, 1989.

Love, William DeLoss. *Wisconsin in the War*. Milwaukee, Wis.: Church and Goodman, 1866.

McDonough, James Lee, and Thomas L. Connelly. *Five Tragic Hours: The Battle of Franklin*. Knoxville: University of Tennessee Press, 1983.

McGee, Benjamin F. *A History of the 72nd Indiana Volunteer Infantry of the Lightning Brigade*. LaFayette, Ind.: S. Vater, 1882.

McKinney, Francis F. *Education in Violence: The Life of George H. Thomas and the History of the Army of the Cumberland*. Detroit: Wayne State University Press, 1961.

McMurry, Richard M. *John Bell Hood and the War for Southern Independence*. Lexington: University Press of Kentucky, 1982.

McPherson, James M. *Battle Cry of Freedom: The Civil War Era*. New York: Oxford University Press, 1988.

Marszalek, John F. *Sherman: A Soldier's Passion for Order*. New York: Vintage Civil War Library, 1994.

Maxwell, Lieutenant James R. Personal correspondence describing experiences while serving as an officer in the Ninety-Eighth Illinois Mounted Infantry. Copies furnished through the courtesy of Charles E. Maxwell.

Miller, Francis Trevelyan, ed. *The Photographic History of the Civil War*. New York: Thomas Yoseloff, 1957.

Miller, Rex. *Croxton's Raid*. Fort Collins, Col.: Old Army Press, 1979.

The Official Atlas of the Civil War. New York: Thomas Yoseloff (reprint), 1958.

Peterson, Harold. "The Repeater Lincoln Tested." *The American Gun*, vol. I, no. 1.

Phillips, Sarah Ellen. *Reminiscences Written by Sarah Ellen Phillips of Her Experience in April 1865, During Wilson's Raid Near Selma, Alabama*. Typed manuscript copy.

Reagan, John H. "Flight and Capture of Jefferson Davis." *Annals of the War*. Philadelphia: The Times Publishing Company.

Robertson, John. *Michigan in the War*. Lansing, Mich.: W. S. George, 1882.

Rogers, F. A. "A Wisconsin Raider: With Wilson from Chickasaw Landing to Montgomery, Company G, 1st Wisconsin Cavalry." Washington, D.C.: *The National Tribune*, November 1, 1900.

Schofield, John McAllister. *Forty-six Years in the Army*. New York: Century, 1897.

Scott, William Forse. *The Story of a Cavalry Regiment: The Career of the Fourth Iowa Veteran Volunteers*. New York: G.P. Putnam's Sons, 1893.

Seavey, Webber S. "Personal Recollections of the 5th Iowa Cavalry." Washington, D.C.: *The National Tribune*, Scrapbook 3.

Sherman, William T. *The Memoirs of William T. Sherman*. Bloomington: Indiana University Press, 1957.

Stanley, David S. *Personal Memoirs of Major-General D. S. Stanley, U.S.A.* Cambridge, Mass.: Harvard University Press, 1917.

Starr, Stephen Z. *The Union Cavalry in the Civil War*, 3 vols. Baton Rouge: Louisiana State University Press, 1979–1985.

Sword, Wiley. *Embrace an Angry Wind: The Confederacy's Last Hurrah: Spring Hill, Franklin, and Nashville*. New York: HarperCollins, 1992.

Thatcher, Marshall P. *A Hundred Battles in the West: St. Louis to Atlanta 1861–1865*. Detroit, Mich.: Detroit Book Press, 1884.

Vale, Joseph G. *Minty and the Cavalry*. Harrisburg, Pa.: Edwin K. Meyers, 1886.

Vandiver, Frank E. *Their Tattered Flags*. New York: Harper's Magazine Press, 1970.

War Department, U.S. *War of the Rebellion: Official Records of the Union and Confederate Armies*. Washington, D.C.: U.S. Government Printing Office, 1880–1901.

Warner, Ezra. *Generals in Blue: Lives of the Union Commanders*. Baton Rouge: Louisiana State University Press, 1964.

_____. *Generals in Gray: Lives of the Confederate Commanders*. Baton Rouge: Louisiana State University Press, 1959.

Waterman, J. M. "The Rosendale Squad: A Narrative of Varied Service with the 1st Wisconsin Cavalry, 1862–1865." Washington, D.C.: *The National Tribune*, April 5–December 11, 1902.

Wigginton, Thomas A. "Cavalry Operations." *Civil War Times Illustrated*, vol. 3, no. 8, December 1964.

Williamson Peter J. "The Rosendale Squad: With the 1st Wisconsin Cavalry, 1862–1865." Madison: *Wisconsin Magazine of History*, Vol. 26, 1943.

Wills, Brian Steel. *A Battle from the Start: The Life of Nathan Bedford Forrest*. New York: HarperCollins, 1992.

Wilson, James Harrison. *Civil War Journals, 1861–1865*. Microfilm copy furnished by Department of History, Southern Illinois University, Carbondale, Illinois.

_____. "How Jefferson Davis Was Overtaken." *Annals of the War*. Philadelphia, Pa.: The Times Publishing Company, 1879.

_____. *Personal Papers*. Microfilm collection. The State Historical Society of Colorado.

_____. *Under the Old Flag: Recollections of Military Operations in the War for the Union, the Spanish War, the Boxer Rebellion, etc.* 2 vols. New York: D. Appleton, 1912.

Wilson, Suzanne C. *Column South: With the 15th Pennsylvania Cavalry*. Flagstaff, Ariz.: J. F. Colton, 1960.

Worsley, Etta B. *Columbus on the Chattahoochee*. Columbus, Ga.: n.p., 1915.

Wyeth, John A. *That Devil Forrest*. New York: Harper and Brothers, 1959.

Index

Numbers in **boldface** refer to pages with photographs.